Praise for Nasrin Parvaz's
The Secret Letters from X to A

Stories are the frailest and most ephemeral of weapons, and yet they may be all we have to fight the multiple forms of power that oppress us. In a story about story-telling, resistance and love set in Tehran in 2002, *The Secret Letters from X to A* offers us a nail-biting account of a young historian who finds a secret cache of letters hidden in an interrogation centre that put him at great risk.

Faraz' uncle offers him a devil's bargain: help the regime turn a notorious torture centre into a museum about oppression under the Shah, thereby erasing the true history of the centre's use by the Islamic Regime. He goes to uncover truth and finds himself whitewashing it. Then he discovers a series of notebooks written by a young woman prisoner to her lover years before. Two love stories weave together, and the past threatens the present. A book with the grip of a thriller, it is also an exploration of what it means to live and resist, in a world where everyone becomes "just another prisoner who [hasn't] been arrested yet."

Catherine Davidson, author of *The Priest Fainted*
(New York Times Notable Book of the Year)

A deeply affecting work. Nasrin Parvaz succeeds in conveying the intense fear and claustrophobia of what it must be like to live under any intolerant, fundamentalist regime. Even reading the story felt like a subversive act in itself.

It raises challenging issues, especially for those of us who are lucky enough to live in more broad-minded societies. There is a warning too, not to take our own freedoms lightly. I came away thinking that no truly humane society can be built on a foundation of extremism, whether that be right-wing or left-wing. We should be genuinely fearful when any kind of politics is more concerned with adherence to strict ideologies than having empathy for individual human rights.

Rhiannon Lewis, acclaimed author of
My Beautiful Imperial (Victorina Press, 2018)

Inside story of Tehran's museum of atrocities

'Museums are generally regarded as institutions dedicated to the conservation and display of valued objects and histories, but, in some cases, they are the sites of erasure of national memory, where the past is obliterated for political ends.

That's the focus of this novel, in which young history teacher Faraz accepts his uncle Rohulah's offer of a summer job to helping convert the Joint Committee Interrogation Centre, one of Tehran's most notorious prisons, into a museum, the Ebrat, commemorating repression under the Shah.

solitary confinement. She was denied medical treatment and kept under the threat of execution. Throughout, she refused to recant and confess to charges against her as an infidel.

In order to drive through Iran, a revolutionary guard travelled on board the lead bus and directed the driver to pass through Tehran. Here people were friendly and waved to us through the windows. In country areas whenever our bus parked it was ambushed by angry mobs. They thought we were Americans. They pounded and rocked the bus until we moved on. It was only possible to go outside safely in unpopulated areas. This included climbing the desert lighthouse near Bam in Southern Iran.

Although travelling through Iran was dangerous and scary, many of the places on our journey were remote and beautiful. These experiences contrast drastically with those of Nasrin, who was forced to wear a blindfold and chador in captivity. She suffered numerous interrogations and episodes of torture but never gave away information relating to her comrades. In one of the most chilling descriptions of intimidation, the women were forced to sit in constructions that represented their own graves and not allowed to move. From Nasrin's memoir, it seems that friendships developed in prison enabled her to survive and glimpses of sky and other small gifts of nature brought joy.

Nasrin gives a frank account of her time in Iran's prison system which has opened my eyes to the extremes that can be endured and overcome. It is a testament to her resilience and that of others who remained resolute and refused to recant their beliefs. Nasrin survived and I celebrate her ability to share these experiences from which we can all learn. I recommend this memoir to you.'

Gail Aldwin, acclaimed author of *Paisley Shirt*
(Chapeltown Books, 2018)

Against the wishes of his own family, who despised Rohulah and his work for the Islamic regime, Faraz accepts the job, but he soon realises that by replastering and repainting the cells once filled with prisoners' graffiti and messages, he will be destroying all evidence of atrocities committed by the present regime. While examining the wall of one of the cells, Faraz makes a remarkable discovery. Behind a waste pipe he finds hidden notebooks of a former woman prisoner Xavar, who movingly describes her daily interrogations and the appalling conditions she was held in while pregnant.

Xavar writes in detail about all manner of physical and psychological torture. Her letters are addressed to her activist partner Azad, who opposed the regime of Ali Khamenei, the present Supreme Leader of Iran.

During the summer, Faraz finds more hidden notebooks and letters, which allow him at long last to comprehend the enormity of the horrors and barbarity perpetrated by the regime. But it is through Xavar's letters that he, and the reader, come face-to-face with the realities of unlawful imprisonment, daily interrogations, torture, rape and giving birth in prison. Xavar is forced to give her baby girl to her parents in one of their last visits before her own execution.

With the help of a close friend, Faraz decides to publish all the notebooks on the internet, with dangerous consequences for him and his girlfriend. *The Secret Letters From X To A* is a remarkable and courageous book, written by civil rights activist Nasrin Parvaz, who was herself arrested, tortured and sentenced to death in 1982.

Her sentence was commuted to 10 years imprisonment and she was actually released after eight years in 1990.

She managed to escape to Britain, where she was granted refugee status in 1994.

Having spent six months of her sentence at the Interrogation Centre, her narrative is based on actual facts and her book examines a country torn by violence and decades of human rights abuses where entire families are divided between supporters and opponents of the regime. Her novel is a warning of how museums can so easily be used to selectively rewrite history.'

Leo Boix, poet and journalist. (This review
appeared first on 'The Morning Star'
September 8-9, 2018)

One Woman's Struggle in Iran

A Prison Memoir

One Woman's Struggle in Iran

A Prison Memoir

Nasrin Parvaz

Victorina Press
www.victorinapress.com

Typesetting and Layout: Heidi Hurst
Inside illustrations © Nasrin Parvaz
Cover design © Fiona Zechmeister
British Library Cataloguing in Publication Data
A catalogue record for this book is available from the
British Library.

ISBN: 978-1-9996195-0-3 (Paperback)

Typeset in 11pt Adobe Garamond Pro
Printed and bound in Great Britain by Biddles

PROLOGUE
London, 2002

I was in Tesco when I saw an outline of a woman, familiar but shadowy as if I had seen her in another world. I could not see her face. It was hidden behind a copy of Hello! magazine, but her clothing stirred my memories. She was dressed in the shoulder-to-toe gown we call manto in Farsi and her hair was completely covered. Near her stood a boy aged about five.

I moved closer and stood right in front of her, only a few inches between us. I caught a glimpse of her face and recognised her. It was Hasani. But she wouldn't look at me. At that moment, the years since I'd last seen her felt like glaciers melting in the gap between us.

I saw beads of sweat emerging on her forehead. She was visibly shaking. The little boy had caught his mother's fear and he looked up at me wide-eyed, clutching at her long skirts.

Hasani was terrified. Terrified of me.

CHAPTER 1

Arrest

Tehran, 13 November 1982

I was twenty-three and I'd just started to feel I had a purpose in life. Like so many of my generation, just after the Shah was toppled I'd joined one of the groups opposed to the new Islamic regime. These groups had been sprouting up in the void of power: this was the time when the Shah was on its knees and the new regime was not yet strong enough to force people to abandon their demands. We all thought we would be able to overthrow Khomeini's government just as easily as it seemed the Shah's had been turned to dust.

War came when Iraq invaded Iran on September 22, 1980. It changed everything for the worse.

Khomeini used to say the war was a blessing, a divine gift. I only understood what he meant later on; because we were at war, no one could make demands, not even for food, and the Islamic regime could get rid of all the people and groups who wanted a secular government, freedom, justice and equality.

I was living at home and my parents knew I was attending political meetings and demonstrations. They saw my copy of Towards Socialism and all my other socialist books and pamphlets. They became increasingly worried.

'Be careful!' they always used to say. Yet I don't think they really believed I was putting myself in any real danger. At first I didn't either. On TV, the Islamic regime's newscasters talked constantly of the arrest and execution of armed fighters, terrorists and traitors. I wasn't armed, and I didn't see myself as a traitor. All I was doing was talking to workers about the need to organise and struggle for employment rights.

Yet in 1981, I was shocked out of my complacency when Ali and some other friends of mine were arrested and executed as traitors and infidels. All they had been doing was printing Peykar, a socialist newspaper. After Ali was hanged, his father came to Tehran and visited us. He told us that before he was hanged, Ali had been beaten to such a total pulp that when they showed his father the swollen, purple, faceless corpse of his son, he had not recognised him.

It was really only when we heard Ali's father that my parents and I fully realised the danger I was in. They decided it would be safer for me if I left Tehran, even though it meant I would have to give up my job as a dental nurse.

It was not easy to move. When the war began, the Islamic regime introduced a new emergency law which meant that all landlords had to inform the authorities when a tenant moved in or out. Yet my father managed to rent an apartment from someone he knew and could trust in the town of Karaj, an hour's bus ride from Tehran. I went to live there with my mother and one of my younger sisters, while my father continued to live and work in Tehran. We only got to see him on the weekends.

Although I had moved to Karaj to escape danger, I did not give up my political work, and I often went to Tehran. One Saturday, I had to take a letter from an activist to Hooshy, my handler. This involved a long walk from the coach stop, and I passed a parade of young conscripts, no more than thirteen or fourteen years old. Just boys, children dressed as soldiers. They were cannon fodder, and melancholy gripped me.

They each wore a bandana decorated with the slogan 'In the name of god' and they were shouting out, 'War, war until victory!', 'The road to Jerusalem goes through Baghdad!', 'Down with Saddam!', 'Down with America!', 'Down with Russia!'

The TV news regularly used to show these boy-conscripts parading before they left for the front. They were given a Koran and a key that was supposed to unlock Paradise for them if they were killed. Most of them were blown to pieces. It was rumoured that when they first reached the front, they were used to clear minefields. Later on, when young boys were no longer sent to the front, donkeys were used to clear minefields: tears filled their eyes as they were pushed to run for their death.

As I moved past the boy-conscript parade, I began to feel uneasy for myself. I now know it was a premonition, or a sixth sense, yet I ignored it and just carried on. Then, suddenly, a car stopped just ahead of me. I saw Hooshy in the back seat. He was pointing me out to the man sitting beside him. I knew at once that he had been caught and had betrayed me, and that I was trapped.

Shocked, my brain still remembered the letter I was carrying. I'd folded it several times and hidden it in a

5

cigarette packet, but the Islamic guards would surely find it when they searched me. Still, I tried to stay calm, to act the innocent and deny everything. No matter what Hooshy had said, I would deny!

The driver of the car, a plain-clothes Islamic guard, stepped out. He was good-looking and clean-shaven. No one would imagine he was an Islamic guard, but coming close to me, he gripped my wrist and it was obvious to me.

'Come with me,' he ordered.

I was defiant. 'Show me your identity card.'

With a mocking expression, he took a card out of his pocket and held it up. The people passing by were oblivious and continued strolling along. It seemed I was alone in the street, yet it was full of people going about their business.

'Look everyone!' I wanted to shout out to them. *'They're arresting me! Here before your very eyes!'* But my throat dried up and no words came out. I heard the guard, who was tightening his hold on my arm.

'Get in the car.'

As he pushed me into the front passenger seat, I smelt cologne on him. He got in the car, took the wheel and switched on the engine.

'Put your head on your knees,' he ordered.

The position was awkward. When I moved my head to try to make myself more comfortable, he grabbed my hair from under my compulsory headscarf. He toyed with it for a moment, unpleasantly sexual and aggressive, and then pushed my head further down past my knees, hurting my neck and back.

We drove for about twenty minutes, so we must still have been in Tehran. When the car stopped, the driver sounded the horn and I heard large metal gates opening; the car moved on again, but stopped after less than a minute.

'Blindfold,' the driver shouted out to someone. He got out of the car and came round to open the door on my side. 'Get out but keep your eyes shut. Here's a blindfold. Put it on. And follow me.'

How could I follow him if I was blindfolded and couldn't see where I was going? I put the blindfold on. It was elasticated, and when I opened my eyes I realised that if I looked down, I could see just a little bit of the ground in front of me, so I was able to stumble after him.

We went inside a building, down a long corridor until he opened a door and told me to go in.

'Stand still. Don't touch your blindfold.'

Somehow I knew I was alone in the room. I pulled the blindfold up. The small room was empty. I had been left alone before being searched. I wasted no time – very quickly, with my hands shaking, I took the cigarette packet out of my handbag, took out the secret letter, tore it into shreds and stuffed the pieces behind the radiator. I put my blindfold back on with a small sense of triumph.

It was difficult to believe they had left me alone to destroy evidence. Surely the Shah's Savak would never have left a prisoner alone before a thorough search. Were the Islamic guards amateurs?

I was not left alone for long; the door soon opened and the same plain-clothes Islamic guard who had driven me here came back in and told me to follow him to another room. When we got there, he ordered me to take my blindfold off, I pulled it down off my face and let it hang there like a necklace.

7

There was a large man with a camera seated behind a desk full of papers and files. He called the guard by his first name, Ibrahim. In one corner of the room, there was a group of young men, little more than boys, standing and staring at me.

'Name, age, address?' the large man asked. I told him and then he took pictures of my face from three angles. He asked me for my watch and then emptied my handbag on the table to pick through its contents.

The large man kept my handbag, but gave me back my purse with my money still in it. 'Alright, put your blindfold back on,' he ordered.

As I put it back on, my headscarf slid down onto my shoulders, revealing my long hair, and all the boy-men in the corner burst out laughing crudely. Ibrahim snapped at me. 'Put your headscarf on properly!'

Even the accidental sight of a woman's hair was offensive to the morality of the Islamic regime. Abolhassan Banisadr, the very first president of the Islamic regime, had publicly declared that women's hair had always to be covered as it emitted a special radiation inducing lust in men.

Ibrahim ushered me out of the room and started asking me questions in the corridor.

'What were you doing in the street?'

'I was going shopping. Look, I have to call my family.'

'You can't,' he said bluntly.

'They'll be worried.'

Ignoring me, he called out 'Sister!'. Although I was blindfolded and couldn't see, I knew a woman had appeared. 'Go with her,' he told me, 'and consider your situation. I'll be back for you tomorrow and you will co-operate.'

Still blindfolded, though able to see a bit of light if I looked down or if I threw my head back, I stumbled after the woman up a long flight of stairs. She took me to a room and gave me a body search. As she bent down to examine me, the position of the blindfold allowed me to catch a glimpse of her head – she was wearing a burqa, not the usual hajib or chador. I was taken aback. Even the most religious Islamic women seldom wore burqas in Iran.

It seemed odd and paradoxical. Here she was encased in a walking prison, yet she was the jailor. I wondered whether all the women jailors working in the prison wore burqas or if it was her own choice – or the choice of whatever male relative was in charge of her life.

'You have your period,' she told me, and pressed a small plastic bag and a fresh sanitary napkin into my hand. 'Put the dirty one in here.' She pushed a bin towards me.

'You want me to change it here in front of you?'

'Yes.'

I found it degrading, but I did what she said.

She instructed me to remove my shoes and gave me some plastic slippers to put on and asked me to follow her.

As we entered another corridor, I could just make out that it was lined on both sides with blindfolded women. They were all lying or sitting down on the floor just a short distance from each other, I could also see some of them had big bandaged feet with blood seeping through the bandages. After a while, my guard told me to sit as she pointed to a blanket on the floor. It was obvious she knew I could see from under the blindfold. All the guards knew. It must have made their work, moving us about, easier or they would have given us bigger blindfolds.

I didn't sit down. 'I need the toilet,' I said.

Without speaking, she led me down the corridor to a small room with three toilet cubicles. 'Hurry up!'

Afterwards, she took me back and again told me to sit down on the blanket, not to talk and not to touch the blindfold. 'Raise your hand if you need to speak to me.'

I was so tired and disorientated that I barely took in what she said. I was now just thinking of how worried my family must be. It even took me some time to take in the horrors around me. The blindfolded women lining the walls were all silent, but every so often I could hear whispers coming from the cells.

As the lights dimmed, I felt an exhaustion I had never felt before, and I lay down to sleep. My mind went to my family, I was always at home by this time, and I knew my parents must have realised I'd been arrested; they would surely be destroying anything incriminating: socialist books and papers and the bottles of wine my sisters and I shared with my father when my mother wasn't around.

I was thinking my thoughts when the woman lying next to me whispered, 'When were you arrested?'

'This evening.'

'Why did they arrest you?'

'I don't know.' I said and asked, 'Where are we?'

'The Joint Committee Interrogation Centre. It's in Firdausi Street.'

A guard shouted 'Shut up' so we stopped talking.

I knew the building, it was a circular complex built for the government of Reza Shah by the Germans in 1932, and I now wondered how many prisoners it had housed and how many of them had come out alive.

I longed to fall asleep but couldn't, and then I heard the faint sad voice of a prisoner in one of the cells singing Nouri's song. It made me long for freedom and the outside world – the world that seemed impossible to ever reach again.

Dear Maryam, open your eyes …

call my name …

I'm still awake,

I wish I could sleep and see you in my dreams…

CHAPTER 2
Interrogation
The Joint Committee Interrogation Centre, 1982

In the morning, a female guard dished out lukewarm tea to everyone in the corridor. She was wearing a chador, and I realised that my suspicion from last night was right: the guard from the night before had worn the burqa by 'choice'.

Another female guard came into the corridor and opened one of the cell doors. She called out 'toilet'. Blindfolded women came out of the cell and made their way down the corridor. With horror, from under my blindfold I saw a little girl about six years old among them. She wasn't wearing a blindfold, yet she was obviously used to this daily routine. I wondered if I was hallucinating. I couldn't quite believe children were also locked up in this nightmare.

Later, I learnt the little girl was Golaleh. She was Kurdish and had been imprisoned with her aunt. They were hostages because the Islamic regime wanted her father, the great Kurdish leader Sedigh Kamangar, to surrender to them.

That very first day, Golaleh noticed me and, realising I was new, came over and sized me up, more like an adult than a small child. I smiled at her and she smiled back.

After all the women in the cells had used the toilets, it was the turn of the women in the corridor. We were to use the toilet three times a day. I told a guard that I needed a toothbrush and toothpaste.

'Do you have any money?'

'Yes.'

'Then you can have them.'

The guard told me how much they would cost and fetched the items, took the money and then led me to the washing facilities and toilet.

Afterwards, when I was sitting down among the other silent corridor prisoners and worrying about my family again, a guard came up and stood in front of me. I looked up at her from under my blindfold. She was impassive. 'Put on your headscarf and follow me,' she said.

I stood up and followed her. Finally, she opened a door and told me to go in. Once I entered I recognised the voice of Ibrahim, the Islamic guard who had arrested me and driven me here.

'Are you ready to answer my questions now?' he asked.

From under my blindfold I could just see his hands, and I noticed for the first time that he was wearing a gold wedding ring. Did his wife know what kind of job he had, or did she think he worked for a bank? I wondered. For what kind of woman could live with an interrogator?

I said nothing to him; he suddenly went to the door and started banging on it. The same woman guard put her head in the door. 'Yes, brother?'

'Give this prisoner a chador. I can't take her downstairs naked.'

I was fully dressed – he was referring to my headscarf,

which did not cover me enough for his high Islamic standards.

'Brother, I'm sorry, we don't have any chadors to spare.'

'Then get one from another prisoner.'

After a few minutes, the guard returned with a chador. I put it on and Ibrahim led me out across an open yard. I could just see there was a small round pond in the centre. No sooner had I seen it than we were gone and inside another part of the complex. I was taken into a room with only one chair with a wooden writing tablet on it.

'Sit on that chair,' Ibrahim demanded, 'and tell me how many years you've been collaborating with the enemies of the Islamic regime.'

'I don't know what you're talking about.'

He left, but returned quickly with Hooshy. He too was blindfolded.

'Tell her to talk!' Ibrahim demanded.

'Everyone's been arrested,' Hooshy said.

I could feel he was shattered and could hardly speak for terror. His words came out very slowly.

'I was arrested two nights ago. I told them everything I know. Best that you tell them everything you know. They want Bahar and Kokab.'

'And the others,' Ibrahim said. 'And their addresses too.'

'Give them all your contacts,' Hooshy said. I could not believe my ears. This man had been my handler. I had trusted him. Now I did not recognise him as the same man. His manner was so abject and defeated. What had they done to him? What kind of torture had he endured before he had given me up?

My brain was still lost, but as Hooshy was taken out of

the room, I managed to work out that there was a message in what he had said. He had told me they already knew about Bahar and Kokab, but by implication nothing about other comrades.

My thoughts were interrupted as Ibrahim, the interrogator, returned and demanded, 'How long has Hooshy been your contact?'

I did not answer.

'Where do Kokab and Bahar live?'

I kept silent.

'You won't talk, you spoilt brat? It's easy enough for us to make you. We made Hooshy.'

He slapped a pen and some paper down on the desk in front of me. 'Write down everything about yourself and everyone you know. I'll be back in an hour.'

Ibrahim left but instead of writing anything, I thought of Ali and my other executed friends. I wondered whether they had been here and what they had suffered. I was deep in those bitter thoughts when Ibrahim came back to see what I had written. The paper remained blank.

'Fine,' he said. 'Come with me.'

With me still blindfolded, he led the way out of the building, across the courtyard with the pond, back into another building. We were in a lobby with a queue of men and women. I could make out that the women were blindfolded like me, but some of the men had hoods on. There were several guards milling about as well. No one spoke.

There were whimpers, like some animal with a trapped legs coming from behind a door, but we all knew the sounds were human.

I realised I was in a queue for torture just as, like everyone else, I had been in queues for bread, oil, meat, chicken ever since the war with Iraq.

The animal whimpers stopped after a while and Ibrahim took me out of the queue and into the very room where the noises had come from. As we went in, another interrogator dragged the tortured man out of the room. From under my blindfold I could see he had two great swollen and bloody feet. They must have been agony to walk on.

The room I was now in had an unmistakeable purpose: torture. There was a gurney with straps for the prisoner's hands and feet. Blood, new and old, stained the floor. And there was a smell in the room I had never come across anywhere else. A smell of screaming and agony mixed with blood and sweat.

'Lie face down on the gurney.'

I didn't move, so Ibrahim pushed me onto it. I sat on it, and as he pulled off my socks, the sight of my small bare feet seemed to make him angry.

'Look at what I have to hit,' he shouted to the other guard as if only some big men's feet were worthy of receiving the bastinado from him.

Then Ibrahim grabbed my hands and wrists while the guard grabbed my feet and strapped them into the metal cuffs. My hands were pulled before he strapped them above my head. My feet were strapped with the soles pointed upwards. The position was awkward, and I felt pain throughout my joints as if my bones were being dislocated. Then I heard a whip crack and a searing pain shot through the soles of my feet and went up through my body like electricity. The whip cracked again and again, and each time

17

agony entered into my bones. My feet were soon burning as if I were walking on fire. I was engulfed by pain; with every crack of the whip my body convulsed.

With each stroke Ibrahim cried out, 'In the name of God!', 'Ya Ali!', 'Ya Hussein!'

I wanted to die. Yet I did not cry out. Some strange strength came to me in my desolation.

The bastinado finally stopped – after how long I have no idea. Ibrahim was completely out of breath. He sat down heavily on the gurney. Incredibly, he used the curve of my waist as a backrest and propped his arm on my back as he lit a cigarette. The thought came to me that he might stub his cigarette out on my skin.

'You're very young,' he said after a while. 'Too young to be beaten to death. Just tell me where Bahar and Kokab live and all this can be over. It's up to you.'

I said nothing. He finished his cigarette and just got up and started beating my feet again. He had just had a rest, a break, that's all, this was his job. He got up in the morning and went to work to torture people. What a world it is where people earn a living for beating people to death.

Ibrahim finally ran out of steam, but instead of the torture ending, he switched places with the guard, who had been waiting to take over.

Though every stroke still seared me to the quick, to escape the torture I began to think of my family and friends.

The bastinado finally stopped completely. My hands and legs were untied.

'Stand up and get out of here,' Ibrahim told me.

I stared down under the blindfold at my feet in disbelief. Were these swollen, purple things really mine? Just standing on them was agony, and yet I managed to stumble out of that room.

Outside in the lobby, the queue for torture was still there. It was as long as before, and a guard pulled a male prisoner into the room to take my place on the gurney. Ibrahim made no move to take me away; instead, in front of the queuing prisoners, he ordered me to jump up and down on the spot. I could hardly lift my feet, but even the small jumps I could do sent shoots of agony to my feet. While this was going on, the male prisoner who had gone in to be tortured after me began screaming.

I don't know how long I was kept there, but after a while the screaming male prisoner was dragged out of the room and I was dragged back in.

I went back face down on the gurney, my hands went back in the cuffs, my feet were bound again, my soles in the air. My blindfold was looser and I could just make out a collection of whips hanging on the wall. They had different thicknesses, and later on I learnt that the levels of pain they inflicted would vary. Ibrahim chose one and started whipping my swollen feet. I tried to ignore the sound of that whip and his cries to the prophets. Through the agony, I heard Ibrahim passing the whip to the guard and saying, 'Harder this time!'

Ibrahim came over and stooped close to my ear. 'If you don't talk, we'll carry on beating you until you die. But if you tell us what we want to know, the pain will stop.'

I said nothing. I thought he was telling the truth, but I knew that I preferred to die rather than betray my comrades and drag them here into this hell.

'Are you deaf, slut? No one holds out against us forever.'

I said nothing so Ibrahim went back to beating me. This time he shouted out, 'O Mohammad!' He was using a different whip. Thicker or thinner? Who knows. My body now began to shake violently. My mind was consumed with pain. I felt I would need an ocean to cool my feet, to extinguish the fire. It was beyond bearing, and I couldn't keep silent any longer. I began screaming. It made no difference to Ibrahim. He just kept on whipping my feet and I kept on screaming.

Eventually he stopped; he put his whip down and just walked out, leaving me alone in the room. Still manacled, the pain I felt was intense beyond all belief or reason, but lying alone I began to think of Sorkh, the man I loved. I knew he had not been arrested or they would have interrogated me about him. I had been very discreet about Sorkh, and I was sure that even Hooshy didn't know I was even seeing him, let alone that I loved him. Sorkh must know I had been arrested by now. Had he flown? I hoped so; I hoped against hope that he would not get arrested but would live a long and happy life in the struggle and taste victory.

My mind went to the first time I saw him. I was at my party stall at the Democratic Crossing in Narmak selling socialist pamphlets, talking to some workers as normal, when Sorkh just appeared and backed up what I was saying about the need to organise. I liked him instantly. It was coming up for dinnertime and the crowd around my stall thinned, but Sorkh stayed and told me he belonged to my group but was in a different branch. We talked for a long time about politics, but he managed to make it clear that he was single and I realised he was attracted to me. I went home happy.

I don't know how long I lay there on the gurney, but my thoughts stopped when Ibrahim and the guard came back. They selected a whip and Ibrahim was about to start again when I called out that I had to go to the toilet. They stopped in their tracks – not with solicitude; they just didn't want me to lose control of myself because they would have to endure the smell too. They untied my hands and feet and gave me some massive men's slippers which, amazingly, fitted my normally tiny feet. Ibrahim told me to follow him.

I don't know how I got up off the gurney and put my full weight on my feet, but I did, and I stumbled and shuffled behind Ibrahim. Once we passed the torture queue we went into a corridor lined with men on both sides. From underneath my blindfold I saw some of the men were blindfolded too, but others were wearing hoods covering their faces and heads. All of them had great swollen feet. They were bandaged, so perhaps their own tortures were over for now. Still, they were close enough to the torture rooms to hear the whiplashes, screams and whimpers.

When I got to the toilet, I discovered my period had stopped, but my urine came out red. I was puzzled by that. I also saw that below my knees, my legs were black, my knees were purple and my thighs were bright red. They were swollen too and were hot and painful to the slightest touch. Ibrahim was waiting. Without saying anything, he took me back past the corridor of blindfolded and hooded men, back to the lobby with the torture queue of men and women. In front of these prisoners waiting their turn to be tortured, Ibrahim told me to start jumping on the spot again. Another person was under torture in the room.

After a while, I was taken back to the torture room. As

I went in, a blindfolded man with black and swollen feet was led out. At first, Ibrahim followed his previous routine and I tried not to hear the whip-lashes or his voice calling out to Mohammed, Ali or Hussein, but then he started asking me questions about my comrades. I kept silent. My silence infuriated him, and he hit me ever more fiercely. He handed the whip to the guard and told him to hit 'the whore' really hard.

Ibrahim went out, but the guard kept whipping me. He asked no questions, though, and with my brain free, a thought came to me that perhaps I could get them to stop by giving them some false information. Ibrahim came back after a while and sat down beside my head.

'Who is Mojtaba Ahmadzadeh?' he asked.

'He was my handler until last year.'

'Where is he now?'

'You executed him.'

The thought of Mojtaba gave me new courage. His strong and handsome face came into my mind. He had known where I lived and my work phone number, and I was sure he knew the personal details of many other comrades, but we all knew that under torture he had not betrayed any of us. He might have been allowed to live if he had, but he had stood silent, and because he had stayed firm, I had kept my freedom for another year. And if Mojtaba could keep silent under torture, surely I could too.

'I know you also visit Zoë. Where does she live?'

'I don't know. She always took me to her home and I never noticed her address.'

'Where did she meet you then?'

'Revolution Square.'

'Which factory does she work in?'

'I don't know. She never told me.'

I was lying. I knew where Zoë lived. I often went straight to her place after work. I'd arrive before her, but she kept her key on top of her door so I could go inside and make myself a cup of tea while I waited for her. When she came back we used to eat and afterwards we'd read Marx's Capital together. She worked at the national shoe factory and was trying to organise the workers there. I wasn't going to tell Ibrahim and have Zoë in here to be tortured too.

'Where do Bahar and Kokab live?'

'I don't know. We always met in the street.'

That was not true either. I always went to their houses.

'When's your next meeting?'

'4 p.m. tomorrow.'

The words just popped out. If I had thought more clearly I would have said 4 p.m. sometime next week as it was a lie. I had no meeting arranged; I just wanted the torture to stop.

It did stop. Ibrahim told the guard to stop beating me and asked, 'Where?'

I had to invent a meeting place, and I gave the name of a street I knew none of us ever went. Ibrahim believed me.

Then I wondered what he would do to me when he found out I had lied. Still, I had gained twenty-four hours respite from this torture.

Ibrahim took me to another room and brought me some food. He left me to eat by myself, but, like a dying person, I had no appetite, and though I told myself I needed to eat, I couldn't force down a mouthful. Instead, I pushed my blindfold up to look around and see if there was anything I could use to kill myself. I saw an electric socket. Using the spoon, I tried to lever it from the wall so I could electrocute myself. I was able to grip the naked wires but the electricity was weak and the shock only went up to my elbows. I was furious to find myself still alive. The wires were still in my hands when the door opened and Ibrahim came back in. He shoved me away from the wires.

'What are you doing? Are you mad? Sit in that chair.' He had brought in some letters. 'Do you recognise these?'

I saw one of them was a letter I'd written to a friend who had joined the Komalah in the Kurdistan Mountains.

'No,' I said.

He stood up in front of me and stepped down hard on my swollen feet. A horrific pain surged through me. I was sitting, and without thinking, I just pushed him hard with both hands. He jumped back sharply, but he was surprised more than outraged and just went back to questioning me.

'Who else did you meet apart from Zoë, Kokab and Bahar?'

'No one. I've only been back in Iran for a couple of years, I don't know anybody.'

'Where were you before that?'

'I was in England.'

'Why did you go there?'

'To study.'

Ibrahim decided to usher me back along the corridor. I stumbled; my feet had blisters and as I put weight on them, it was as if they screamed in agony. The distance I had to struggle may have been just a couple of hundred metres, but it seemed a couple of hundred years before we reached the women's wing, where I'd slept the night before.

I was exhausted, but the pain made it impossible to sleep. Yet I was able to think in a disjointed way. I knew my family must have known I had been arrested and would also know I would be tortured. I felt for them. I also thought fleetingly how it was that the Islamic regime insisted on women's inferiority in everything, but in torture and execution, women were equal. I knew I could be hanged, as well as tortured, as easily as Mojtaba.

The next day towards 4 p.m, I was taken out to a waiting car. My feet were still on fire and I don't know how I walked, but soon I was squeezed into the backseat of the car between two male guards holding Kalashnikovs.

Ibrahim did not come, but as well as the male driver, there were two further male guards, also with Kalashnikovs.

'Put your head down between your knees.'

I was driven down Firdausi Street to where I'd told Ibrahim, Bahar and Kokab had arranged to meet me. When we got there, I was told to remove my blindfold and sit up normally. The car didn't stop but crawled slowly up the street and then back again. It gave me time to look at the guards properly. They were all young about twenty years old at most.

'This Kokab or Bahar. Where exactly are you supposed to meet them?'

'It's always vague. They usually walk down from that end of the street. I come from over there. We usually catch sight of each other about halfway.'

As I spoke, a youngish woman came walking along the pavement. She had a headscarf.

'Is that her?'

'No.'

Another headscarfed young woman walked past the slowly moving car.

'Is that her?'

'No.'

'Are you sure?'

'Yes.'

After we had driven up and down the street a few times, the driver said, 'This is useless. We'd better go back. Put the blindfold back on. Head on your knees.'

We went back to the prison, and almost as soon as the car pulled to a stop, I recognised Ibrahim's voice telling me to follow him.

'You slut,' he said. 'You didn't point them out.'

'They didn't come.'

'Liar.'

He pushed me towards the landing and then into the torture room. He was angry as he tied my hands and feet really tight. He shouted, 'I know what to do to you, liar. I will whip you until you give me the names and addresses of each and every one of your infidel contacts.'

Using all his brute and angry strength, he cracked the whip in the air and lashed my already agonised feet. He didn't stop with my feet this time, but whipped me up and down my legs up to my thighs and then back down.

I don't know how long it went on. Time no longer existed, yet eventually the lashes stopped. From beneath my blindfold, I could see Ibrahim studying my feet. He had something in his hand, pen-shaped. I saw him using it to prod my feet, but I couldn't feel anything. It was as if my feet no longer existed.

He left the room. I tried to comfort myself with the thought that everything eventually comes to an end and that they would execute me and my sufferings would be over; and if I continued to stay firm, at least my friends would escape my fate.

Ibrahim came back in with a guard, and again he used the pen-shaped thing to prod my feet. Yet I couldn't feel it. After some more prodding they untied my hands and legs and told me to get up and follow them. I struggled up with real difficulty, and when I went to move my legs I just couldn't. I had to take my legs in my hands to move them and put my feet to the ground. Using the wall to lever myself, I placed my legs so I could stand up on them, but they still wouldn't move on their own. Leaning on the wall, I could balance on them but I couldn't take a step, and just to avoid falling down on the floor I had to sit back again on the gurney.

'Do you want a walking stick?'

'No,' I said.

Ibrahim left me sitting on the gurney unable to move. He came back with an old man pushing a sort of cart. I don't know how I got on it, but somehow, resting my weight against the wall, I was able to sidle from the gurney to the cart.

The old man pushed me out into the corridor and took me to the bottom of a staircase. There, the burqa'd guard from the first evening was waiting for me.

She picked me up and carried me up the stairs. I am slight, but I would have still been a heavy weight to carry. She was big and strong, but she was still breathless long before we reached the top. She managed to get me up to the right landing and laid me down in the same place I had slept the previous night.

'I need the toilet.'

She took a deep breath and picked me up again and carried me to the toilet at the end of the corridor.

'Do you want any help?'

'No.'

She waited outside. As I was now alone, I lifted up my blindfold properly and saw that my legs were swollen and black right up to my buttocks and my urine was deep red. The burqa'd guard took me and settled me down onto a blanket in the corridor. She fetched a bowl of water and a cloth. Silently, she washed my feet and then wiped them with some stinging antiseptic, before using a pair of scissors to open the blisters. Blood gushed. She wiped my feet again with the same stinging antiseptic and then bandaged them. When she had finished, she left me without saying anything.

Despite my blindfold, I slowly became aware of the other women in the corridor. I knew they were also blindfolded and that we were all forbidden to speak, but still the woman closest to me whispered, 'Did you give anything away?'

'No.'

'Then you have been loyal to your friends.'

Her simple words sent a wave of intense emotional joy over me: a feeling I'd never had before, and one I did not know existed. It was euphoria, a calm but triumphant euphoria. It was cosmic; I felt I was not a lone individual, but part of a great struggle for freedom and equality, which would in the end prevail.

I thought of my friends who were still free and how

perhaps they would escape capture and suffering and continue the fight. If they did, even if I was long dead, I would be part of their victory to create a world where no one would sleep hungry or drink filthy water.

Although I was imprisoned and in the hands of my enemies, who had arrested and tortured me, they could not arrest my resistance, and neither could torture vanquish my struggle. In resisting the Islamic regime, I was not alone – all the other men and women, imprisoned in here like me, blindfolded, hooded, beaten to a pulp, and in torment, we were all part of the ultimate victory of humanity.

CHAPTER 3
Paralysed
The Joint Committee Interrogation Centre, 1982

For the next few days, I slept most of the time. It surprised me that I was so exhausted. Between bouts of sleep, I thought of my family and how they must be feeling not knowing where I was. Sometimes I registered the whispering of the other prisoners in the corridor. They seemed to be talking about new arrests – who had endured torture and who had betrayed their friends – but I didn't recognise any names, and I was too tired to try to pick up the details of what they were saying. I did once hear them telling each other that two prisoners had died under torture.

I was woken one day by a prisoner kicking my feet. The pain from her kick was incredible, but I did not cry out. She silenced me with a gesture. She was blindfolded like me, just as I could see her from under the bottom of my blindfold. She was not looking at me, but towards the end of the corridor, where I had already known that the guards sat.

'We have to talk quickly,' she whispered. 'The guard has just left me here for a minute. I am waiting for the toilet. If the guard comes back, I'll hiss. When I do, say nothing back to me. My name is Mahnaz. I have a message for you

31

from Raz. She told me to say hello to you.'

I was horrified; I had no idea my comrade Raz had been arrested. 'Raz is here? When was she arrested?'

'A few days ago. She was arrested at home with her husband. Her blanket is next to mine. We are right at the other side of the corridor. We want to know who betrayed you?'

I did not hesitate. 'Hooshy.'

Mahnaz clearly recognised the name, but said, 'Listen, you know the guard who wears a burqa? There is only one. That's Mehri. She's not a normal guard. She was a prisoner who betrayed her comrades and was made a guard. She wears the burqa because she doesn't want anyone to recognise her, but we all know her. She was one of the leaders of Peykar. She and her husband were arrested last year. She and her rotten husband live together in one of the cells. Be careful of her.'

Mahnaz's flow was stopped when we heard a warning cough. She hissed as she had said she would and I said nothing else to her. A guard was returning: it was Mehri.

I heard a rattle as she unlocked a door, and I worked out that one woman was being let out of the toilet as Mahnaz was being let in.

With so many of us, and so few toilets, they were in permanent use from morning to night.

As I remained paralysed, one of the guards had to take me to the toilet. And once I was there, I had difficulty managing my body and staying clean.

Mehri used to change the dressing on my feet. I wondered how she lived with herself after having betrayed her comrades and being both a prisoner and a guard. Was life bearable for her because she still had her husband, or had their shared betrayal poisoned their love?

It was beyond logic, but it turned out that after two years as a trusty, Mehri's husband was hanged, but after another two years, Mehri herself was released.

About a week after my arrest, I began to sleep less, and even while wearing the blindfold, I began to focus on my surroundings, and I realised that the child I had seen on my first night was not the only child in the prison. I could hear them and, looking beneath my blindfold, I saw them clinging to their mother as they went to one of their only three daily trips to the toilet. The cruelty of it for a child made me gasp.

They sometimes came and looked at my bandaged feet with innocent curiosity. I used to smile at them. Sometimes they smiled back, but the smiles didn't erase the deep sadness from their faces. Sometimes one of the children could be heard crying. The guards would bang on the cell door, shouting at the prisoner-mother to make her child quiet.

I thought of my own childhood and of music. When I was little, I had gone to bed with a small radio. My mother used to turn it off when she got up to do her morning prayers. My mother and I were often in conflict, and I was judged to be naughty as a child. I had dark skin and the neighbours and shop-keepers called me Blackie. I took it as a compliment, yet I was very aware that my mother preferred white skin and how whiteness was generally seen as better and more beautiful. The manufacturers of skin creams claimed their lotion made women's skin whiter. I was too young to understand racist language and that there was – and still is – a large industry behind this racist notion of white supremacy and how it was interwoven into our language and culture.

As I began to sleep less and less, I also began to long for books to read and to have some paper and pens to draw or write. Doing nothing day after day was mental torture. My thoughts were mostly of my family and their suffering. I knew they must fear that I would be executed, as my friend Ali and so many others had been.

Occasionally the guard sitting at the end of the corridor was called away and we prisoners had whispered conversations. The woman next to me quickly warned me that there was a trusty in the cell nearest us and that we had to be careful as she might hear us through the cell door.

Our short snippets of conversation were welcome in the long days we spent sitting blindfolded on blankets in the corridors, not knowing what was coming next.

Although I was convinced I would be executed, I was also worried that I would stay paralysed. In one way it didn't matter, yet I hated being carried to the toilet and having to struggle to make my unresponsive body keep itself clean.

Lying on the blanket with nothing to do, I began to remember other things: how I was nearly arrested once and, just by luck, had got away. When the war began in 1980, the Mujahidin, an Islamic organisation, began its campaign of bombings and the killing of government officials. The Islamic regime set up checkpoints around Tehran (and other towns) to help monitor people's movement and make it more difficult for dissidents to operate. Once after I had moved to Karaj, when I was on my way back there with some messages, I'd folded one up very small and put it in a cigarette packet in my bag, I took a public taxi. I was in the front seat. There were three male passengers as well as the driver, so the taxi was full. At the Tehran-Karaj checkpoint, we were hailed by Islamic guards and told to stop. It took the taxi driver a few seconds to park, which gave me just enough time to take the cigarette packet and push it into the space under the dashboard. No one seemed to notice. The Islamic guards told us to get out. They questioned us. Where we were coming from? Where we were going? They told the driver and the three male passengers that they could all get back in the taxi and be on their way, but they took me about five hundred metres further up the road to be questioned by a senior Islamic guard.

After about half an hour I was released. But it was now dark and no public taxis were passing that motorway. It was a long way from a bus stop. I was standing there, wondering how I could get home, when I saw the same public taxi I had been in parked about two hundred metres further up the road. The driver and his passengers were waiting for me. I was elated by this unexpected act of kindness. They all told me that they could not leave me there alone in the middle of nowhere. None of them knew me and none of them wanted anything from me; they simply acted out of humanity. As we drove on I took the cigarette packet from where I'd hidden it and put it in my bag. None of the men appeared to notice, but perhaps they had and they knew. Anyway, that time I had arrived home safely.

One day, we had whispered news. A male prisoner had hanged himself, but guards had saved him so they could continue torturing him.

I remained paralysed for about three weeks. There were no wheelchairs in the prison. Either Mehri or another guard had to carry me to the toilet, but slowly I realised I was regaining movement. I felt extraordinarily happy; soon I'd be able to go to the toilet unaided, and I would also be able to walk to the scaffold.

We prisoners were allowed to have a shower once a week. I still hadn't had one. As my paralysis receded, I told the guard I wanted to have a shower. Once she knew I had money, she brought me a bar of soap and shampoo. I wondered what I'd do when my money ran out.

To prevent infection, the guard gave me two plastic bags with strong elastic bands to wrap around my feet. She also gave me a fresh set of prison clothes and told me to wash my dirty things in the shower. Then she led me to the hall at the head of the corridor, where other prisoners were waiting. She instructed us all to follow her. We all went out of the building and passed through an open space where some construction was going on. My feet still hurt terribly and it was difficult to walk; so I was soon straggling behind and the guard shouted at me to hurry. I just couldn't. She told the others to wait until I caught up with them. Finally we got to the shower room. She said we had fifteen minutes to wash ourselves and our dirty clothes. I was exhausted and too slow, and when the time was up I was still under the shower with my washing. She drew the curtain back.

'This isn't a hotel. Come out now.'

I dressed as quickly as I could in my new set of clean prison clothes. The others were waiting for me. They began to walk, and I started to follow, slowly and painfully. We did not go straight back. The guard took us to a space within four walls with wire mesh instead of a ceiling. It was full of washing lines. Along with the others, I hung up my wet clothes. It seemed I was entering the normal life of the prison. Perhaps the torture was finished.

CHAPTER 4
A Different Sort of Abortion
The Joint Committee Interrogation Centre, 1982

After about a month, when I was still weak and walking with difficulty, a guard came and told me to follow her. Although I was still blindfolded, moving my head in the way I'd learnt meant I could make out that we had stopped in a small corridor lined with four doors. She went up to door nine, opened it and told me to go in. Without saying anything else, she left, locking the door behind her. I removed my blindfold. I saw I was alone in a small cell. I was disappointed. I knew by then that after spending my first weeks in the corridor, I would be moved to a cell, but I'd expected to be placed with other prisoners. In a way, I had been looking forwards to it, but this cell was so small I thought no one else could be placed in it with me. It was just too tiny, about one-and-a-half by two metres.

There was no toilet, so I knew I would still be brought out three times a day for that and would see other prisoners then, but otherwise I was alone.

The cell was dark. There was a small window up near the ceiling, but it had been covered to keep out the daylight and the sight of the sky. It took a while for me to adjust my eyes. When I did, I caught my breath in horror. The lower part of the cell walls were covered with bloody hand and fingerprints. They all seemed to be the same size and obviously belonged to the same woman. From the position of the prints, I worked out that she had put her hands on the wall for support as she had struggled to stand up. But why were they bloody? Had she been beaten or had she died here in the agony of her injuries? My mind whirled with a thousand thoughts. I decided to try to make contact with the prisoner in the next cell and ask her if she knew what had happened. I tapped on the wall a few times; finally I heard tapping coming from the other side. It may have meant something, but at that time, I knew nothing of the elaborate codes of prison life and it had no meaning to me, just as I suppose my tapping made no sense to the woman in the other cell either. Finally I just spoke in my normal voice close up to the wall.

'Do you know who was here before me?'

The woman ignored my question but asked me my name. Her voice was warm and friendly.

'Nasrin, and yours?'

'Pari.'

'Do you know what happened to the woman in here?'

'I know she was pregnant.'

'Is she alive or dead? The walls are all bloody.'

'Don't think about it. And listen. We mustn't talk. Mojgan is on the other side of me. She is a penitent and will report us.'

That silenced me at once. What a risk I had taken in just tapping on a wall, and Pari had equally endangered herself by replying to me.

Penitents was the word the Islamic regime used for

prisoners who had recanted and confessed their "crimes", supposedly of their own free will. In reality, penitents had been broken by torture. After betraying their friends and comrades, they "recanted and confessed" in exchange for the Islamic regime's promise that they would not be executed but released after a few years of prison. Some of them became trusties. Perhaps Mojgan was a trusty.

Later, I heard Pari talking in her cell. I couldn't make out what she said, and I realised there was another prisoner with her.

Thoughts of the pregnant woman who had been in my cell before me, needing help and receiving none, filled my mind. I wondered if the baby was her husband's or a lover's or the product of rape by the guards. I knew such rapes happened in prison. Long before I had been arrested, a friend of mine had introduced me to Yas, a young girl of fifteen, who had been arrested at a demonstration. She was not kept in prison, but before she was released, she was raped by several guards. She became pregnant, and I met her because she wanted an abortion. My friend thought I might know a willing doctor.

Abortion was illegal, and a safe abortion by a qualified doctor was expensive. We all had a whip-round, but we couldn't find anyone reliable who was willing to do it for the money we had raised. Yas was already five months pregnant when I went to meet her in a café. She was very beautiful, but there was no softness about her. I told her that I'd tried hard but I hadn't succeeded, and now it was too late anyway –she was too far gone and an abortion was now too dangerous.

'I'm sorry you'll have to have the baby, but a comrade

41

will marry you. You won't be punished and you can get divorced afterwards,' I told her.

'I know, but it would always remind me of that night. It would always be the child of those men. You know, the guards were playing games – laughing. I worked out they were playing for a prize, but I'd no idea the prize was me, not until they raped me one by one in the order of who had won most points in the game.' Yas paused and said, almost like a curse, 'I don't want it. I hate it as much as I hate them.'

I tried to argue. 'What wrong has the child done?'

'Every time I looked at it, I'd remember those bastards.'

'I'm sorry,' I said again, 'but it's just too late now!'

Yas looked at me with steel-hard eyes. She thanked me politely for my efforts and we parted. A few months later, I discovered that, close to the delivery date, Yas and her comrade-husband had gone to stay in another city. They came back to Tehran after the birth without the child. Yas had got hold of some drug and given it to the baby when it was just born, and when she was sure it was dead, she had thrown it in a rubbish bin.

After a few days alone in the blood-stained cell, a guard came and told me to come for interrogation. I put on my blindfold and chador and followed the silent guard. Eventually, I was led into a room. As I sat down on a chair, out of nowhere I was given such a blow to the head that my skull hit the wall with a force that seemed to split it open. I saw millions of stars. They were pouring out of my head and out of my eyes. In the midst of this mad disorientation, a brand-new male voice said, 'It's nothing for us to kill you or any other infidel. Killing infidels guarantees us a place in heaven. We could kill you for just talking to the prisoner in the next cell. Don't you know you're in prison? You're not allowed to talk without our permission. What we did to the last prisoner in your cell is none of your business, and you're not allowed to talk about her.'

I understood: the penitent, Mojgan, had heard me talking to Pari and had reported both of us.

Somehow I still managed to ask, 'Is the woman alive?'

The man said nothing for a moment. 'Yes, she's alive. She was pregnant and had a miscarriage. Such things happen.'

This new interrogator then began lecturing me about Islam. I didn't listen, and after a while I interrupted his flow about Allah the Merciful to ask if I could contact my parents.

'That's up to your interrogator, and he's not at all happy with you.'

CHAPTER 5

A Little Boy

The Joint Committee Interrogation Centre, 1982

The Joint Committee Interrogation Centre was in the middle of Tehran, and in the afternoons when the city was less crowded, I could make out the street cries of the pedlars shouting 'Vegetables!', 'Pomegranates!' It was some two months since my arrest, yet it felt like years. And it was as if the hawkers' voices came from another world. From my cell, it was difficult to believe I was near houses where ordinary people lived. When there were no cries from the streets, the very silence could be loud and overwhelming. And there were so many sounds I longed to hear: the bark of a dog or the purr of a cat, the crunching sounds of autumn leaves under my feet. I dreamt of the beauty of flowers, the aromas of coffee and the taste of chocolate.

Sometimes my mind went to the times just before the Islamic regime, when the Shah was still in power. I remembered October 1977. I was nineteen and had gone to a big literary festival held over ten days at the Goethe Institute in Tehran. It was a major event. There were more than fifty writers, poets, playwrights, critics and translators all speaking against censorship and the oppression suffered under the Shah. Tens of thousands of people were there, standing in the streets, listening to the loudspeakers broadcasting stories and poems. It was electric, and even when the sky became overcast, we all stayed, struggling to make out the words as the rain drummed on our umbrellas.

The event was surrounded by the Shah's security forces, but still we stayed. What was it that we never had such a freedom till then? Why only when the poor people had risen against the Shah, the international power organised ten days of luxurious 'freedom of thoughts' for us!

I was alone, as always, in my cell thinking my thoughts when a guard opened the door and pushed a woman in. I was overjoyed. A companion, another human soul to talk to. She took off her blindfold. She was younger than me, pretty with a heart-shaped face. She introduced herself as Neda. She told me she was from the north near the Caspian Sea and explained how she had been arrested.

'I was active politically and six months ago, I thought it was wiser to come to Tehran. I also thought I could trust the landlord, but he reported that I'd rented a room from him. He was only obeying the new emergency law and he was worried about what would happen to his family if he didn't comply. Anyway, it meant I was summoned to the Islamic Guards' Centre to explain why I had come to Tehran. I told them I had come for work, simply work. They let me go, but after a few days they came to the factory where I was working and arrested me.'

Neda's story of torture was like mine; they had flogged her feet, demanding information about the political activists where she worked, but she had revealed nothing. This gave us a bond. We liked each other and we also began to talk about our life outside. I told her that she looked like the first friend I had in school, called Afsaneh.

'Did you stay in touch?'

'No. You looking so much like her just reminded me of her, and of something that happened. I was nine years old and I went to Afsaneh's to study together. She was one of five children, but her family lived in just one room, with a small kitchen and toilet. At lunchtime her mother spread a tablecloth on the floor and gave us bread. I sat down beside Afsaneh, expecting other food to be served, but everyone just ate the cheap Barbari bread with nothing else. I realised they must be very poor, and I felt so sad that I wept when I got home.'

Neda became upset too and changed the subject.

'Whenever my brothers came to see me, they went straight to the Jameh mosque in Fereshteh Avenue in North Tehran.'

'Why? Are they religious?' I asked, surprised.

'No. No one of my family is religious. They only went to the mosque to get good shoes. They took off their poor worn-out ones at the door and picked up newer and better ones when they left.'

We both bent over with laughter.

I recalled when I was little and my mother dragged us all to the mosque. We had to leave our shoes by the door and go inside barefoot. Some women, in fear of poor people picking up their good shoes, put them in a carrier bag and took them in with them while they prayed, even though taking dirty shoes inside the mosque was sacrilegious in their own eyes.

To stop getting sinful thoughts at mosque, the men

47

always prayed on the ground floor while the women went upstairs to the first-floor gallery. There was a curtain all around, and if it was moved to one side, the women could see the men downstairs, but as only men were supposed to have sinful thoughts, nobody really bothered about the women being able to see them.

In the particular mosque where we went, the young women always used to move the curtain so they could see the young men below, and they would point out the ones they liked to each other. After prayers, the young men used to stand and wait in front of the mosque. The young women were all in chadors, yet the young men had no problem recognising the ones they loved or found attractive.

Time in the prison was marked by our weekly routines. Showers on Wednesdays gave an opportunity to see and maybe talk to other prisoners and hear about the new arrests. It was also wonderful to come back clean.

On Mondays, there was another weekly ritual. A man came by with a bag full of books and we could choose one. They were either Islamic texts or attacks on Marxist materialism and dialectics. One day, the man showed us a book by somebody called Mohsen Makhmalbaf. I didn't know him.

'Makhmalbaf was in this prison during the Shah's time,' the bookman said. I was interested and took the book. I also asked him if he had any pencils and paper.

'I'm not allowed to give you any, because you would only use them to write to each other.'

The bookman was back, talking about his books, when the door of the cell opened and the guard told him he was wanted on the phone. He left so quickly he didn't take his book-bag with him. Neda and I rummaged through it and found a small pencil at the bottom. We hid it in a corner, and by the time the bookman came back we were innocently reading.

I now had a pencil but no paper. How I longed for just a piece of paper. I decided I had to use the pencil anyway, and I drew on the wall beside the door. It was a blind spot that the guards looking through the peephole couldn't see. I drew a large tulip with a petal falling from it and next to it, a young tulip bud that had not yet opened out.

Neda and I read Makhmalbaf's book. It was propaganda for the Islamic regime. And it made us feel depressed and dispirited, but we both laughed and made jokes about the name Makhmalbaf, which meant weaving velvet, when he should have been called 'weaving bullshit.'

One day, unexpectedly, we were taken to a large hall divided by curtains. We couldn't see the prisoners on the other side of the curtain, but we were aware they were there. Neda and I sat beside each other. It turned out we had been brought to watch a play by Makhmalbaf. Some of the prisoners were acting in it, and Mehri's husband directed it. They had been given time to rehearse as the prison governor thought the play's message of repentance would do us good.

Makhmalbaf had been opposed to the Shah because he was an Islamist, but he totally supported the Islamic regime and was obviously highly regarded by it or his writings would not have been promoted in prison. Yet later I learnt that Makhmalbaf had won several international prizes for his films as well as honorary degrees and that Western governments praised him as a 'reformist'. He was no more of a reformist than Khomeini, and the West could not have been ignorant of this.

One day when it was our turn to go to the toilet and Neda and I were walking through the corridor, I saw from beneath my blindfold a woman sitting on a blanket with a little boy on her lap. She had just been tortured. The dressings on her feet were soaked with fresh blood. Neda saw the woman and the child too. When we returned to our cell and could talk, we both agreed the woman must have had held out or they wouldn't have beaten her so ferociously.

The woman was still there the next time we went to the toilet, and the next and the next, still with her little boy. Every time we passed her she threw her head back so she could see us from under her blindfold too. Seeing us smile at her, she smiled back. After four days, she was brought into our cell. The woman stumbled in on her terrible feet. She steadied herself on the wall with one arm and carried her little son in the other. She literally dragged herself into our cell and then sat down with the child on her lap. Her name was Soraya and she was twenty-five years old, a very attractive woman with commanding eyes. Her son, Arash, was also beautiful. She explained things to him, softly telling him that we were friends.

'They're your aunts. They're not like the guards,' she said. Even so, Arash was too scared to leave her arms.

When Arash was asleep, Soraya talked to us.

'When they took me to be tortured, he wouldn't leave me. They pulled him out of my arms by force. They just put him outside the room. While they were beating me, I could hear him screaming Madar, Madar. I'd been arrested in the evening, and they flogged me until the next morning. Then, with my feet cut and drenched in blood, they took me to him. That's why he's sticking to me.'

Soraya also talked about her husband. 'He was executed

a year and a half ago when we were in the north near the Caspian Sea. They gave me his body. They said he was an infidel and they wouldn't allow me to bury him in the city's graveyard, so we buried him in our garden at home.'

After a couple of days, Arash felt more at ease with us. I enjoyed playing with him and made him little figures of a fish and a duck from the dough of the bread we were given to eat. If he laughed, the guard banged on the door and shouted at him to be quiet, and he would jump with terror. Since Soraya had difficulty walking, I took Arash to the toilet, and once a week I took him to the shower and washed him.

Soraya's feet became infected. Every day, one of the guards came and changed the dressing, but without antibiotics the infection refused to be cured; she didn't complain, though she knew she might lose her legs. She was a strong woman.

About two weeks after Soraya and Arash entered our cell, the guards came and told us all to get out. They ran their hands over our bodies and told us to stay in the corridor. They searched the cell looking for forbidden items: a pencil or a note. They found nothing and we were allowed to go back into our cell. Half an hour later, a guard opened the door and asked, 'Who drew the drawings on the wall?'

We knew they would punish all of us unless I admitted it was me, so I said, 'I drew them.' The guard just smiled and said, 'You are good. Your interrogator has said you are to draw a picture of Khomeini.'

I said instantly, 'No, I won't.'

'It would be much better for you to do the drawing. Let me know, if you change your mind.'

I didn't.

CHAPTER 6
Confession
The Joint Committee Interrogation Centre, 1982

Soraya had a beautiful voice. One evening when she was whispering Arash to sleep in her lovely northern accent, I was taken away for interrogation. Neda and Soraya wished me luck.

I had another new interrogator. He told me to remove my blindfold. I didn't. I didn't want to see him, but he ripped it off my face. Then he started talking about Islam and said I'd soon be released if I just repented for all I had done against it and confessed. I continued to say nothing. He told me, 'Your family have searched everywhere for you. They don't know where you are or if you're alive.'

'I want to speak to them.'

'If you're a good girl and do as I say, I'll let you.'

He continued to speak, but I didn't listen. I had got the measure of the interrogation: they wanted me to become a penitent, but I knew I never would. The interrogator's voice went on and on. By the time it got to midnight, I felt very sleepy. I could sense somehow that everyone else in the whole building had left – there was just no sound. As he went on speaking, he moved his leg next to me. I pulled my leg away sharply. He didn't react. The thought came to me that he might rape me; I'd try to stop him. He was thin, and might not even be strong enough, but then I thought realistically that he would find the strength if he wanted and what could I really do against him?

Now and then he asked, 'What do you think?', but as I wasn't paying attention to what he was saying, I could not respond even if I had wanted to, so I remained silent. After endless hours, I was returned to the cell, where Soraya and Neda were wide awake and waiting for me. They were relieved I had not been tortured. The very next night I was taken for interrogation again. This happened for several nights and was always the same. The interrogator talked and talked, and I sat silently, deep in thought, reflecting on the outside world. I sometimes looked at the interrogator and saw his angry frustrated face with spit forming sickeningly around his mouth. Then, one night, I actually tried to listen to him, and I found he wasn't talking about penitence at all but all kinds of personal things, even his non-existent sexual relations with his pregnant wife. It was disgusting. Why was he talking like this? I tried to imagine what kind of woman could live with an interrogator, a torturer. Maybe she was a guard.

The interrogator took me back to my cell, always at about two o'clock in the morning. I found myself increasingly agitated and unable to sleep; I lost weight.

One night, the interrogator took me back to my cell by a different route and briefly left me on a balcony. I pulled my blindfold up a little so I could see. The balcony railings were covered with tarpaulin; when I drew it back, I saw the railings were decorated with Nazi symbols. It seemed appropriate. I enjoyed being out there on the balcony.

There were lights on in the building and looking beyond, I could make out the courtyard and a pond. Above all, I could feel the fresh air.

The interrogator finally returned, and he now took me to a 'clinic'. There was a 'doctor' who told me to sit on a chair. He attached a device to the back of my neck. A pain shot through my body and my heart wrenched. I couldn't breathe and felt as if my heart had stopped beating. I realised he had given me an electric shock. The interrogator took me back to my cell without saying anything. Yet I understood: if I didn't co-operate and agree to become a penitent, there was not only the bastinado, but electric shocks waiting for me.

The following night, I was taken for interrogation again. Just questions this time, and I found that most of the time I could focus on my own thoughts and tune everything out, but sometimes the questions got through and rattled me. These nightly interrogations seemed to have no end, and during the day the thought of them made me edgy. One night, out of the blue, the interrogator revealed why they had decided to work on me like this. They planned to broadcast a group confession on television, and they had selected several prisoners to participate. I was to be one of them. He told me that they wanted me to repent on air, to abjure my struggle against the Islamic Republic – and ask Imam Khomeini to forgive me. I felt I'd rather die a thousand deaths, but I just said, 'I shan't.'

'Then I'll be forced to flog you.'

'I'll become paralysed again if you torture me.'

I don't know why I said that as what would he care? He wouldn't have to lift me up and take me to the toilet. That was Mehri or some other guard's job.

'This time, we won't nurse you. Your legs will get infected and we'll amputate them from the knee down. You won't be the first. It's not torture. We don't torture. It's tazir. The Koran is clear – we can tazir infidels until they repent and accept Islam.'

Imagining my legs amputated sent me into a freezing cold sweat. It was as if I was naked outside in the coldest of winters. He threatened to call my first interrogator, Ibrahim. Not to torture me, he said, but to tazir me. But torture is no less torture because it is given a different name.

He said he couldn't tazir me himself; he didn't have the time as he was going to the front to be martyred. A little warmth returned to my body at the thought of him getting his wish.

In the end, I wasn't taken to be flogged. Instead, I was taken to the 'clinic' and given another searing electric shock before I was returned to my cell.

Whenever the guards left the wing – possibly to go to some meeting – and the trusties also disappeared, we could feel it, and we prisoners all in our different cells tried to speak to each other. We got down on our knees and spoke through the space at the bottom of the cell door. This way we exchanged the little news we had, and we came to know that a large number of prisoners were being interrogated and tortured just like me, because the Islamic regime wanted mass recantation and confession on television. Yet afterwards the new penitents would still be taken, along with all the other prisoners, to Evin Prison to stand trial.

Just at this time, Neda was taken away to Evin. We wished her freedom, which is what we all said when someone was moved or transferred. Soraya and I soon got a new cellmate. She introduced herself as Mojgan, and I thought immediately of my arrival in this very cell and how I had been horrified by the blood-stained hands on the walls and how Pari in the next cell had warned me about a penitent with this name. It could be a different Mojgan, but I doubted it, and soon I was sure that she was the same woman who'd reported my conversation with Pari. This Mojgan was just too obviously a trusty, as she started praising the Islamic regime and saying how wrong she had been to oppose it. She was really talkative and, ignoring our dislike of her, she insisted on telling us about her fiancé, Siamak, a member of Peykar, who had been executed a year earlier. Yet even this did not stop her heaping praise on the Islamic regime.

Life changed when Mojgan came into the cell. It was a new kind of daily hell as Soraya and I could say nothing to each other, since we realised Mojgan would report anything we said. She sized up everything, never missing a move. She was called for interrogation every few days, probably to report on us. She told us she had agreed to take part in the televised group recantation and confession they had been trying to get me to join.

Mojgan left after about ten days. We surmised that she was moved from cell to cell so she could report on as many prisoners as possible. Soraya and I 'celebrated' when she left.

It was now winter and the cold was absolutely ferocious. I felt it had taken hold of my very being. I had no warm clothes; neither did poor little Arash. My heart bled for him spending his childhood here, badly clothed, badly fed, without any toys or entertainment. One evening, something different in the light made me feel it was snowing. In the scullery where we washed our own dishes, there was an uncovered window. It was still high up, but I managed to clamber up onto the draining board so I could see a corner of the sky. It was dusk, but I could just make out a tree bent under the weight of the snow. It was beautiful, and the sight somehow warmed me.

Not long after this, a guard came to the cell and told us to put on our blindfolds and chadors and go and sit in the corridor so we could hear the loudspeakers. We were to listen to recantations and confessions. One by one, through the loudspeakers, we heard some thirty prisoners introducing themselves; as expected, Mojgan was among them, but so was Hooshy and the sound of his abject voice was heart-breaking. All the prisoners said their names, and then five of them, acting as spokesmen, said they had all been wrong to oppose and try to fight the Islamic regime and they all begged Khomeini for forgiveness.

I grabbed Soraya's hand, and she squeezed it back. These recantations and confessions were also being televised, and I imagined my family and friends, sitting in front of their television sets, waiting to see if I was one of them. Through my sorrow, I was also happy, almost exultant, that they wouldn't see me debase myself.

Through all these extreme emotions, I also wondered if the people outside knew that the prisoners had been coerced by torture and given promises of freedom? Or did they believe the Islamic regime's claim that all the recantations were voluntarily?

CHAPTER 7
My Parents
The Joint Committee Interrogation Centre, 1982

Soon after this, Soraya and I received two new cellmates, Malek and Zari. With Arash, that now made five of us in our cramped little cell. Most of us were in our twenties, but Malek was well into her forties, tall, with straight black hair with just a few grey strands. She explained that she hadn't been a political activist, but some of her family were and she had been arrested as a hostage to put pressure on them to hand themselves in.

Zari was our age and a mother. She told us how she'd been arrested with her two-month-old baby. When Zari had been buckled into the gurney, her baby had been taken outside and Zari said that all throughout her ordeal she could hear her crying. Each day after the torture, the baby was brought to Zari to be breastfed.

She went on to tell her story. 'They wanted to trap an activist called Nasser. They suspected that I had arranged a meeting with him, but I revealed nothing. After the fifth day of torture, they just left me alone with my poor baby in one of these cells. She was sick. My milk had gone peculiar and was upsetting her. I begged the guards to give her to my family, but they refused. I had a second meeting arranged with Nasser, in case one of us had not been able to make the first. I decided to give them the details after the date was passed. Even though they would not catch Nasser, I thought just telling them would demonstrate that I was no longer interested in politics. My baby needed me and I wanted to stay alive for her. On the day of the meeting, I told the guard I wanted to see the interrogator. I told him that I had this second meeting with Nasser set for ten that morning. It was too late for them to catch him, and he was furious. "You kept this to yourself all this time?" He took me back to be tortured and gave me twenty lashes on my feet, which were still in agony from being flogged before.'

Soraya asked her, 'What happened to your child?'

'The very next day they gave her to my family, so what I did saved her this horror. Yet I can still hear her cries.'

What could we say?

In the short time we shared a cell, Malek struck me as an ordinary type of person, yet she believed strongly in justice. Zari was more complicated. Despite what had happened to her, she was supremely self-confident, even self-righteous, and she saw things totally in black and white.

Malek and Zari were soon transferred to Evin Prison. They were happy because though they would stand trial, their torture sessions were over – for now, at least. But Evin was not their final destination, only a staging post. At their trial they would either be sentenced to several years in prison or be condemned to death. Executions were carried out at Evin, while sentences of imprisonment were usually served elsewhere.

It was around then, some five months after I had been

arrested, that I was told by an interrogator that I was to be allowed to phone my family as a preliminary to them being allowed to visit me. I could barely take it in. The interrogator told me that he would listen in to what we said and if we said anything subversive, our phone call would be disconnected and I'd be punished.

He also said that I was not allowed to tell my parents I was in the Joint Committee Interrogation Centre; instead I had to tell them I was in Wing 3000 at Evin Prison.

The interrogator dialled my parents' number. My father answered. I was so emotional all I could say was, 'Hello.'

My father just said hello back and I realised he hadn't recognised my voice. So I said, 'It's me, Nasrin.'

My father was astonished. 'Nasrin?'

He became speechless and I knew he was crying. My mother took the phone and said briskly, 'Are you OK?'

'I'm OK. Don't worry. Is everyone all right?'

'Yes, where are you?'

'Evin Prison in Wing 3000.'

She continued, 'Can we visit? Can we bring you money and clothes?'

Listening in, the interrogator nodded and I said, 'Yes.'

My father took the phone. He was still tearful as he said, 'I went to Evin and other prisons looking for you, but they all said you hadn't been arrested. I went to hospitals and even cemeteries. I filed a complaint with the Judiciary Office, and now, after five months, they've finally allowed you to call us. Why did they arrest you? You were always good. You never bothered anyone. Did they arrest you by mistake? You haven't killed anyone.'

Again, my father broke down. I didn't know what to

say. I wanted to cry too, but managed to control myself in front of the interrogator. 'Don't be upset,' I said, but my father just kept crying.

The interrogator took the phone and started talking to my father; I couldn't hear what he was saying. I was too distressed. My thoughts had stayed with my family, their misery and at the pressure they were under. Yet though I was sad for their grief, I felt relief that I had spoken to them and that they finally knew I was alive.

There were always fewer guards on Fridays and national holidays. One Friday, there were no guards or trusties around, so we talked from cell to cell and told each other about the phone calls, and we learnt that some prisoners had visits. Then, unexpectedly, Soraya started to sing a northern folk song in beautiful voice. When she'd finished, another prisoner with a good voice sang another song, but soon sounds told us the guards were coming back into the wing and we returned to silence. A guard came to our cell door and moved the peephole shutter to look at us. It was as if she was taking a picture of us, fixing us in time.

The day of the family visits came. Soraya, Arash and I were taken out together, and male guards put us in a car and took us to Evin Prison.

Each prisoner was placed standing in a glass cubicle facing another glass cubicle where our families would be brought in to stand opposite us. We could see each other, but we could only talk by phone. I was told that if we said anything subversive, the phone would be disconnected and I'd be punished, so a guard would be listening in to our conversations. I stood in my cubicle, waiting along with all the other prisoners in their individual cubicles. Suddenly, some doors were flung open in the hall opposite to ours and there were voices. The visitors ran towards the cubicles, desperate not to lose even a second. I saw my parents. They stopped when they saw me. Their faces filled with pain as they entered the cubicle. I felt sick and anxious when they arrived. I grasped the phone in my hand and my mother picked up the phone on her side. My father just couldn't hold back his tears. I was able to control mine as I asked my mother, 'How are you?'

'We were very worried. We're better now. How about you?'

'I'm good. Is everyone all right?'

'Yes, we are now. Before you phoned, we thought they'd killed you.'

I could see my father was trying to stop crying so he could speak to me. Eventually he took the phone from my mother and asked, 'Did they hit you?'

The line went dead.

A guard came to my cubicle and said, 'Your phone will be reconnected this time, but watch what you say.'

I could see that my father realised he shouldn't have asked about my being 'hit'. I wouldn't have answered him even if I had been allowed to talk freely. How could I tell my parents that I'd been tortured – and might be again at any time? They wouldn't be able to bear it.

So I just said, 'Don't worry. I'm OK.'

'How long are they going to keep you in?'

'What do you mean?'

'When are they going to release you?'

Anguish filled my heart. I said, 'I'm sorry, but they're not going to release me. They execute people like me.'

This time we were not disconnected. The Islamic regime would not admit it tortured prisoners, but it had no problem admitting it executed them. In fact, names of executed men and women were published in newspapers.

Every muscle in my father's worn face started to shake with anger. Rage and sorrow poured out of his eyes. Yet he still managed to splutter, 'I won't let them kill you!'

I tried hard to hold back my own tears. I'd never seen my father like this. I could see he was engulfed in terror and grief at the thought of losing me, and I was so sorry that I'd just told him so curtly that I expected to be executed. I was used to the idea, but he wasn't. I couldn't give him false hope.

'Look,' I said, 'I didn't give them the information they wanted, and I refused to participate in that television recantation and confession jamboree. They execute people for such defiance!'

'But you haven't done anything. They can't kill you. I'm not dead yet. I'll fight.'

My father was so overcome that my mother took the phone from him and asked, 'Can't you do something to please them so they don't execute you?'

'No, I can't. Try to understand.'

Incredibly, the time was up and the phone was cut off. I felt forlorn. I'd had so many questions to ask, and now it seemed my last opportunity was gone. The guards ordered all the visitors to leave. As he went, my father put his lips on the glass as if to kiss me. His tears soaked the glass. My mother did the same. I kissed the glass back at them. For a while, they didn't move, but just stared at me as I looked back at them. Finally, a guard pushed them towards the door, and I watched them leave in tears. For the first time in my life, I felt utter sorrow for them. They were so sad and hopeless. I wished I could hold their hands.

The guard took us back by car to the interrogation centre and soon we were back in our small and airless cell.

Two days later, after searching them for contraband, the guards handed over the presents our families had brought us on visitors' day. Soraya's family had brought some lovely clothes for her and Arash. My parents had given me some new clothes too, including underwear, and a very pretty white dress with blue flowers. Even though I expected to be executed, I felt joyful to get out of the ugly prison garb I had been wearing ever since my arrest.

CHAPTER 8
The Suffering of Others
Joint Committee Interrogation Centre, 1983

Little Arash was already asleep, and Soraya and I were getting ready for bed. The city was quiet, so we could clearly hear the sound of a car arriving into the yard. It stopped abruptly and a guard shouted, 'Blindfold!'

Soraya and I looked at each other. Someone else had been arrested and brought in for interrogation. Soon, in the silence of the night, we began to hear terrible sounds of flogging and a man screaming in agony. We lay down, but no sleep came. How could it? With every sound of the lash, not only the horror of the man's agony but our own pain shot through the soles of our own feet again. We felt every lash along with this new unknown prisoner. We hoped this new prisoner would have the victory of enduring, of not betraying his comrades.

Eventually the morning came and Tehran awoke. We could hear the sounds of cars buzzing in the air and all the other noises of life being lived outside. The prisoner from last night was still being flogged. His screams had changed into deep hoarse croaks, which we now barely heard through the noises of the daytime.

That evening, when Tehran became quiet and deserted

again, we recognised the same prisoner screaming even louder, but there was no sound of lashing. They were using some different, silent, gruesome torture on him. His ordeal continued throughout all that night and for another whole day. The following evening he was still being tortured, yet though we recognised his cries, they no longer sounded human. With all our hearts, we hoped his torture would end, yet it went seeming without reprieve. Finally it stopped and we heard, resounding through the night-time prison, the man give out one great primeval cry of anguish. His suffering seemed to shake the entire prison.

We then heard men's boots running into the yard and a car speeding off, and we knew the tortured prisoner could endure no more and that he had betrayed his comrades.

I wished I could comfort him in his despair.

His torture had ended. We didn't hear him any more. It was as if the whole earth was silent. We could not sleep, but waited for the car to return, hoping against hope it would not bring one of the tortured man's comrades. An hour or so later, we heard a car sound its horn. The heavy iron gate of the prison opening and a car revving into the prison yard. The engine was switched off. Once again, we heard the harsh voice of a guard shouting, 'Blindfold!'

CHAPTER 9
Children in Prison
Evin Prison, 1983

One spring day, six months after my arrest, Soraya, little Arash and I were told to gather all our belongings. This meant we were being transferred. Although no one told us, we suspected we were being taken to Evin for trial and sentence and that Soraya and I would probably be condemned to death, and that little Arash might finally be freed and released to Soraya's family. As we got into the waiting van, Soraya and I arranged our chadors and blindfolds so we could see a little. I immediately spotted my comrade Raz sitting in a corner of the van. She also saw me, but we were too far apart from each other to talk.

Despite the macabre circumstances, I was happy to see her. I hadn't had the chance to speak to her since she was pointed out to me in the corridor some six months earlier, and now she was here almost next to me. I now hoped we would be able to talk or even be put in the same cell or wing.

The journey took about an hour. We were greeted at our arrival by a host of chador-clad women guards. In the confusion, as we all got out of the van, Raz and I managed to stand alongside each other, as if we had been cellmates.

I knew she hoped as much as I did that we would be put together. We were lucky – we managed it, but it was a bittersweet victory as in my anxiety to be placed with Raz, I was separated from Soraya and Arash. They were sent to another wing, while Raz and I were put in the downstairs section of Wing Four.

Wing Four was made up of six large cells arranged around an L-shaped corridor. Our cell had two barred windows. The panes were painted cream so no one could see in or out. The cell was about three metres by four, and it had originally been intended to house five or six prisoners. Yet each of these cells now had to house forty to sixty of us. The wing had six toilets and three shower cubicles. We were not 'locked down'; theoretically we could go to the toilet whenever we wanted, but as there were some three hundred of us, the chances of finding a toilet free when we wanted were never good. Still, it was much better than being 'locked down'.

We also had access to a yard for recreation. With so many of us, it was usually crowded, but that had some advantages, as the trusties could not observe us very effectively. And so, when I first went out into the yard with Raz, the trusties didn't see us when we smelt oranges and followed the magical scent. The smell brought us to a pile of boxes, all filled with oranges and covered by an army blanket. Raz immediately warned me that the oranges must be for the trusties and that I'd be beaten for theft in front of all the other prisoners if I was caught. Before she had finished speaking, I had grabbed an orange. Without peeling it, I took a large bite out of it, right through the peel. I hadn't even seen fruit since my arrest and nothing could stop me. I ate two whole oranges, peel and all. They were unbelievably delicious – the most wonderful oranges in the world. They smelled and tasted of the world outside, of freedom. As I ate them, I looked up and saw the tip of a mountain. It must have been part of the Alborz Mountains as Evin Prison was built in 1972 under the reign of Mohammad Reza Pahlavi, in the foothills of the mountain range.

That first day at Evin at lunchtime, we were called to eat in our cell. A tablecloth was spread out on the floor. There were two little girls about one and three years old sitting on one side beside a woman who must have been their mother. A thin, malnourished-looking woman, her daughters were thin as well. We could see the smallest was trying to fight back tears over something or other. The sight was just pitiful.

Two prisoners served the food: just a thin yellow liquid followed by some mashed-up red beans, chickpeas and potatoes. We'd had better food at the Joint Committee Interrogation Centre. I wondered why the food was so bad here. Perhaps they wanted to weaken us.

I went back to the yard after lunch, just to walk about and feel the beautiful spring sunshine. A woman I didn't know came up to me and warned me to be careful as some of the prisoners were 'anti-revolutionary'. Her use of this term revealed she was a trustie, as the Islamic regime called itself 'revolutionary', and to confuse things even more, anyone like me who wanted a real revolution was dubbed 'anti-revolutionary.'

I played a little dumb. 'How do you know?'

'They give themselves away by what they don't do. They don't read the Koran, and they only talk to other infidel prisoners like themselves.'

I said, 'Can you point some out to me?'

She indicated two women walking together and another very beautiful young woman who was walking alone, seemingly deep in thought. 'Those three are infidels.'

I laughed inside as the trusty was showing me some possible new friends and allies. When she'd gone, I went up to the beautiful young woman. 'I was told you are an infidel,' I said.

She laughed and asked my name.

'Nasrin. I was transferred from the Joint Committee Interrogation Centre just this morning.'

'Ah, we know each other already. It was me you talked to through the wall about the bloody handprints in your cell. I'm Pari. I was transferred here last week.'

We hugged each other like old friends and I apologised to her. 'Were you interrogated and tortured because of me talking to you?'

Pari shrugged, as if it didn't matter, and then we talked for ages. She was Kurdish like Raz, and had been with a left-wing group called Komalah.

Night came – my first in Evin. Just as before at the Joint Committee Interrogation Centre, we each had to sleep on a thin blanket on the floor and we had another thin blanket to cover us. A trusty made a point of finding Raz and me a place beside two other leftists. It turned out all the trusties at Evin were Mujahidin and they didn't want to mix leftist infidels with believers.

Even so, we were all so close up to each other that it was difficult to turn or even breathe. The thin prisoner with her two little children was with the Mujahidin in a corner. It was safer. We needed to climb over each other to go to the toilet at night, and in a corner the children were less likely to be stepped on. Incredibly, I saw the thin woman was still breastfeeding the youngest. What milk she might still have was a mystery.

It was impossible to get comfortable; we were crammed in like sardines. In desperation I called out and asked how many women were in the cell. One of the prisoners shouted back out from the darkness. 'Fifty-two!'

I soon got to understand the make-up of our wing. Most of the prisoners were very young, many less than twenty years old. They were either Mujahidin or closely connected to them. They were all Muslim, 'believers', while all we leftists and Tudeh Party members were atheists, infidels and unclean.

As devout Muslims, the Mujahidin had originally supported Khomeini, but the Islamic regime refused to share power with them and they had adopted a policy of urban terror, planting bombs and carrying out assassinations. And on 20 June 1981, they actually took up arms against the Islamic regime. Yet in prison they adopted a policy of becoming penitents. It was not genuine, but a tactic – the Mujahidin wanted to save its members and supporters from execution and perhaps even get them released so they could join the struggle outside again. Some of these faux 'penitent' Mujahidin had been made trusties. Obsessively religious, they hated us 'infidel' leftists with a passion.

A very small number of women in the cell were members of the Tudeh Party, which supported Khomeini, yet they were atheists and pro-Soviet, and the Islamic regime had no interest in being supported by them and imprisoned and executed the Tudeh.

At Evin we were also permitted to buy a few things with the money our families were allowed to give us, but clubbing together was forbidden. There was logic to this: the Islamic regime didn't want us co-operating with each other in any way, and they certainly didn't want to see richer prisoners helping the poorer. Even so, Raz and I, along with couple of other prisoners, quietly managed to make joint purchases and later shared the goods out among ourselves.

Randomly, every now and then, a guard would tell us to draw up a list of things we wanted. We weren't allowed some items like chocolate and biscuits, but we could buy fruit – dates and raisins – as well as basic necessities like washing powder, soap, shampoo, toothbrushes, toothpaste and the cleaning materials for the room and the wing, as cleaning was our responsibility.

We had a rota for tasks – cleaning the cell and the wing – as well as for distributing food and tea, but only the fit and healthy worked; the ill and disabled were excused. Because we were infidels and the believers thought we were unclean, we were not allowed to wash the dishes unless a believer rinsed them afterwards, so Raz and I usually swept the cell.

There was very little space and we all had to be extremely tidy. We stored our everyday things, our toothbrushes, combs and few toiletries, in individual bags we made out of old clothes. Some of these bags were stitched beautifully. On two of the walls there was a high up narrow shelf. We used to hang these bags under them and we piled small sacks of our bigger belongings on top of them.

The cell also had a small bookcase filled with religious and anti-socialist books. There was also a TV. It was on most of the time, broadcasting the recantations and confessions of 'penitent' prisoners. We also received two pro-government newspapers a day, Kayhan and Etelaat. They still gave out some information about the outside world and I wanted to read them. As we were not allowed to read the articles out to each other, the sheer number of women in the cell meant I always read yesterday's news.

When I had nothing to read, I sometimes used to just sit and observe the other prisoners. In one corner there might be a few women sitting together talking and even having a quickly surreptitious laugh. In another corner, some Mujahidin might be gathered whispering with their heads together so no one could overheard them.

Occasionally I spotted the thin woman trying to calm and comfort her young children, while another prisoner might be praying alone. A couple of women might be reading the Koran. But among all this more or less normal activity, there were women who would sit for hours just holding their haunches, their hands on their knees and their eyes downcast looking vacantly into space. Other prisoners carried tasbih beads and stroked them constantly as they walked or talked. I thought they were religious at first, but I learnt that playing with the tasbih was just a nervous habit. The repetitious movements somehow calmed them.

Bedtime was at ten o'clock and at eleven the lights in every room were switched off centrally from the guards' office, but lights in the corridor and toilets were left on. A strange silence descended over the wing and transformed it into a different world. If we couldn't sleep we were allowed to walk in the L-shaped corridor. I liked doing this, but sometimes I would just sit up and watch the women's silent sleeping bodies, all lying beside each other. Sometimes a low moan or a sigh told you that there was life. I wondered if in their dreams, they felt free and lived again in the outside world.

During the day the wing was always busy and noisy, and there was no privacy, but at night there was rest from the daytime sounds and the endless loudspeaker announcements which meant interrogation, execution or separation.

Often, to get some air I used to stand beside the door to the yard. It was barred but I could see the pale-yellow moon and shining stars and sweet memories came back to me. I remembered my last summer of freedom, seeing the same sky with my friends when we went walking high up in the Darakeh mountains. Darakeh was not far from Evin, and yet the times I had had there with my friends seemed to belong to another world.

Waking-up time was seven, and though I often had a strange feeling and felt I needed to sleep more, I made myself get up even earlier so I could use the toilet before a queue formed.

In the morning, tea would be brought round. It was laced with camphor to dampen sexual energy. Breakfast was bread and cheese or bread and some watery carrot jam.

Once a week, but only during the night, everyone was allowed to have a warm shower. Three of us had fifteen minutes to use a cubicle intended for one person. Showering once a week was hardly enough, and when I could bear it I also showered in cold water. But the water came straight from the mountains and it was like ice.

After only a few days, I realised that the lack of

food was affecting me in a peculiar way that I could not understand. On many mornings I woke up with feelings that my head was heavy, and I had such extreme forms of dizziness that I could not talk or walk until I had had my breakfast. Feeling sick, I would sit in a corner, trying to remember if I'd had a dream during the night before, but I would remember nothing. At these times I used to rest my heavy head on my knees, hugging my legs and hide inside myself. Some days the uncomfortable feeling would not go away after breakfast, and a kind of pain throbbed between my eyebrows. I asked to see a doctor and she said it was sinusitis and my sinuses were infected. I was given a course of antibiotics, but it didn't help. Sometimes I felt my head was going to explode, and sitting in a corner with my eyes closed didn't help. On these days I wished I could lie down for a couple of hours until my foggy head became clearer, but the room and the wing was so cramped that it was not possible. This 'sinusitis' pain and heavy head stayed with me and visited me frequently, especially when I became tired or stressed out as well as when I was hungry. The pain shot from between my eyebrows to my forehead and slowly clouded my brain. I did not understand what was happening inside my head, nor could I adequately describe it to a friend. I only knew that I should always save some food such as raisins for those moments when the throbbing between my eyebrows visited me. At these times, I thought of the hungry children among us.

The children imprisoned with their mothers were heart-breaking to watch. There were boys as well as girls, and in their play they copied what they saw in the prison. Often a little boy took the role of a blindfolded prisoner and another boy would act as the guard taking him to interrogation. He would order the other boy not to move his head or look around. Yet this did normalise prison for them, as when an order came over the loudspeaker telling us prisoners to put on our chadors, which meant a man was coming into the wing, the children, boys and girls alike, would be terrified. They knew all the interrogators were male and they must have associated even the male electricians or plumbers with the possibility of their mothers being tortured. What memories these children had of a life before, and what scarred lives they would live when they went out again into the 'normal' world was beyond comprehension.

Meal-times were the happiest: even though the food was meagre and poor, everyone's mood lifted, the wing came to life, prisoners shouted, 'The food has come! Bring your pots! Spread the tablecloth!' and the children would rush to the main gate and hold onto the bars with anticipation. As the food was ladled into the separate pots for each room, their eyes would be glued to the big pot. They were hungry, we all were hungry, but the hunger of children is terrible to behold.

There was a little baby boy just at the crawling stage in the next cell. He was called Abbas, and his mother was a leftist like us. As soon as the food was on the tablecloth, his mother had to hold him tight to restrain him, otherwise in his hunger he just jumped at the food. All sharing, including sharing with somebody else's child, was forbidden, but once a week, when we were each given two eggs and a potato, we secretly gave our eggs to Abbas's mother. If we had been discovered, we would have been punished.

Before I had been imprisoned, I never thought of the

physical and psychological effects of constant hunger. Some prisoners talked about what food they missed and how it tasted. Prisoners reminisced about food.

'My mother made ghormesabzi with fresh vegetables and lamb.'

'My favourite is kebab.'

'What about aubergines? I miss them so much.'

'I want shirini more than savoury food.'

But the children were the most affected. They openly cried for food while we adults denied we were hungry, even when our empty stomachs betrayed us by rumbling.

At Evin, whenever a new prisoner came onto the wing after being tortured, with bloody dressings on her swollen feet, the children stood still and stared with eyes filled with a fear and horror that defies description. And although they played, the imprisoned children were pallid, ill-looking and always wary.

One day, the thin mother with the two little girls beat her three-year-old for crying out of hunger. Her friends went over and stopped her. Later on I heard that she had just found out her sister had been executed. How strange that in her agony she gave grief to her poor little daughters, whom we all knew she loved with all her heart. A few days later, when the thin woman was praying, she collapsed on the floor, her whole body shaking. Her one-year-old didn't realise anything was wrong, but the older one looked at her mother, frozen with horror, watching women gathering around her mother and one putting a spoon in her mouth to prevent her biting her tongue.

Every six months our parents were allowed to bring us new clothes; the poorer prisoners never had enough, and so secretly they were given clothes by other prisoners. Even so, everyone could still see who was rich and who was poor. Yet women from vastly different backgrounds lived alongside each other. There were women in Evin who had never worked in their lives and others who had worked hard since childhood.

Unlike outside, in prison respect was not bestowed to anyone simply because of their money or social class; rather it was given to moral strength or how different prisoners behaved in prison: whether they compromised or collaborated or became penitents to save their lives, or whether they preferred to die rather than recant and confess.

CHAPTER 10
Resistance
Evin Prison, 1983

I'd been in the wing for more than a week when, while walking in the corridor, I saw a familiar face. It was Huri, very pregnant, sitting by a radiator. I stared at her in disbelief. She was with the Peykar; I had no idea she had been arrested and now here she was imprisoned. Speechless, I sat down beside her. She told me her story. It was like mine, but worse.

'I knew you were here, but I didn't want anyone to realise we were friends. I was looking for a way to make contact with you without letting on we knew each other from outside.'

'But why haven't I seen you? I have been here a week.'

'I'm in Room five, and I can't move around very much.'

Huri told me about her arrest. One winter morning, she had gone to meet a Fedaian (a left-wing group believing only in armed struggle) to get news about two of her friends who'd gone to join the Peshmerga in Kurdistan. Anxious, she arrived ten minutes early to check the area out for guards, but immediately two men caught hold of her hands from behind. At first she thought there'd been a mistake and asked them what on earth they were doing and why didn't they let her go, and so on.

Because they thought she was with the Fedaian, the plainclothes guards opened her mouth to see whether she had a cyanide capsule and searched her to see if she had a weapon. One of them sat next to her in the car and said, 'Now we'll go to Evin. This woman will tell us about you.'

Huri wondered who they meant and then she realised that a chadored woman was sitting in the corner of the car.

Huri was blindfolded and her head was pushed down into her lap. They brought her direct to Evin and took her to a room for a thorough body search. An old woman told her to undress, and she searched Huri very carefully. With her still blindfolded, they took her to Wing 209. Her interrogator was called Ali. He tied her hands and feet to the gurney and asked her a few questions. When she told him she had nothing to say, he started flogging her feet. There were two other men in the room – one of them, Rahim, became her interrogator later.

They flogged her for ages, and then said they thought they should use a thicker whip. Huri was in so much pain already; she couldn't imagine that the thickness of the whip would make any difference, but it did. They beat her feet again endlessly. Eventually they stopped and left her in the corridor with a blanket to sleep on. The pain and nausea kept her awake. In the morning, they gave her a glass of water, a piece of bread and an egg. She drank the water but she found she could not urinate. The next day, and the following day as well, there was only flogging and agony. At night, she developed a terrible pain in her kidneys. She still could not sleep and she was still unable to urinate.

The third night, while she was lying in the corridor with her untouched food beside her, Ali came and kicked her in the ribs, asking her, 'Are you on hunger strike?' She said no, she just had a severe pain in her kidneys. He took her to the prison clinic, where a doctor examined her and said she was in a critical condition. He warned her that if her kidneys didn't start working in a couple of hours, she'd have to go for dialysis. He gave her a shot of something for the agony and attached a drip. It took three hours, but finally she was able to urinate.

In the middle of the night, Ali came back for her. She could hear him talking to the doctor, who, it became clear, was also a prisoner. He was explaining to Ali that though Huri's kidneys were now working, they might stop again. Ali said that didn't matter, Huri had to be interrogated. The doctor tried again and said Huri still needed more treatment. After a long pause, Ali said, 'All right, I'll bring her here after every session.' The flogging continued all that night, but Huri was taken back to the clinic afterwards. When she had the opportunity, she told the doctor she believed she was pregnant. One of the women guards took a urine sample, but Huri was told that it came back negative. Huri did not believe that, and when she saw the doctor again Huri told him she was certain she was pregnant and that she didn't want to lose her child.

At lunchtime, Ali came and kicked her in the stomach, saying she'd lied about being pregnant and that he'd whip her on the back a hundred times as an extra punishment. After they'd finished, he'd start on her feet again. Her kidneys stopped working again and they took her back to the clinic. They put her on a drip. The doctor explained that she had to urinate naturally as she'd lose her child if she went on dialysis. After a few hours on the drip, Huri found she was able to urinate again.

The doctor told her that the lacerations on her feet were so deep that she needed stitches under a general anaesthetic. She objected as she was worried that an anaesthetic would harm her child. The doctor reasoned, 'If you're pregnant, it's better if I operate on your feet because you won't be taken for interrogation until they get better. By that time, it will be clear you're pregnant – if you are – and they won't take you for interrogation if they know you're having a child.' So Huri agreed to have her feet stitched.

After the operation, they put Huri in a small ward with three other patients. A guard was stationed beside her. When she came around from the anaesthetic she worried immediately that she might have given some vital information away in her sleep, but one of the women in the room reassured her that she had said nothing incriminating.

Huri was in the clinic for a week, and the doctor did another pregnancy test. Before the results had come back, she was taken for interrogation again, this time in a wheelchair as she couldn't walk at all. Ali told her she'd wasted their time, as she hadn't given them any information and they hadn't been able to arrest anyone. And even though the doctor had stitched her feet just the week before, Ali still beat them. He stopped eventually and everywhere was silent. The interrogator returned, put Huri into the wheelchair, and took her back to the clinic. When she arrived, all the female guards quickly gathered around her, wreathed in smiles. 'Congratulations, the test has come back positive. You're pregnant!'

Huri didn't respond. They put her on the bed, but her entire body was in such extreme pain she couldn't lie on any part of it. Yet it was clear the torture had been stopped because she was pregnant.

CHAPTER 11
The Sound of Execution

Evin Prison, 1983

Whenever we could during the long summer days, Raz and I would sit in a corner of the yard and talk. I was aware of the Kurdish people's struggle and I had distributed Komalah's pamphlets on my party stall, but I really didn't know that much about what had been going on in Kurdistan. And Raz spoke to me about the struggles of the Kurdish people against the Islamic regime. They were fiercely opposed and boycotted the referendum in 1979: 'Islamic Republic. Yes or No'. They successfully raided army barracks for arms and ammunition and they set up a provisional council in the city of Sanandaj led by the Komalah Party. It was a time of great solidarity and hope.

'The radio news bulletins were read out by Sedigh Kamangar, whose little daughter was held as a hostage at the Joint Committee Interrogation Centre. You met her, didn't you?' Raz asked.

'Yes, I did. She was a lovely little girl – she used to come and play with Arash, the son of Soraya.'

Anyway, the council survived for five months, and then after some false pretence of negotiations, Khomeini ordered an all-out attack on Kurdistan. This was July 1979. It was a proper invasion with an air assault, thousands of Islamic regime troops attacked with tanks. The Kurds had no chance with just the light weapons they had taken from the army barracks. In victory, the Islamic regime massacred the Kurds: men, women and children alike. Anyone who was young and able, escaped to the mountains to join the Peshmerga, the women fighting alongside the men.

I went to the corridor to walk and saw Arezou, with whom I was friendly with; she'd been in prison for eighteen months and was under sentence of death. She hadn't been given a date for her execution and could be called to it at any time. She was several years older than me and the mother of two little children. They hadn't been told. Her family would tell them when they were old enough to bear it.

She was deep in thought when I went up to her. We walked together for a while. There was a lot of noise coming from somewhere, and I wondered whether the prison was being extended. 'What makes you say that?' she asked.

'Didn't you hear the sound of iron being offloaded out there?'

She looked at me with amazement. 'Nothing is being offloaded. That's the sound of bullets being fired. It's a firing squad. Executions are taking place.'

My mind froze and I broke into a cold sweat. I'd heard exactly the same sounds the week before, but no one had told me they came from a firing squad. Everyone must think everyone else knows.

Arezou was calm. 'After the volley of bullets, if you listen you can hear the sound of single shots. One of the guards always goes up and gives a final single shot in the head to make sure they're dead. We can work out how many are killed by the number of single shots. Last week they executed eighty of us. We'll soon know how many they've shot tonight. Last year, hundreds were executed every night, but the executions are only once a week now.'

I was stunned by the mixture of routine and horror.

Arezou told me to follow her. She went into room six and up to a prisoner standing by the barred window. 'How many?' she asked.

'Ninety,' the woman replied.

I was speechless. Arezou said, 'Don't be upset. We're in prison. This is what happens in prison.' She went on, 'Some of the executed were women. One of them was from our wing and two from the wing above. We don't know yet how many were taken from the other female wings.' And then she said to me in a calm voice, 'I've heard you'll be sentenced to execution too. Is that true, Nasrin?'

'Yes it is. I refused to take part in the big TV recantation and confession.'

Arezou just nodded. 'They wanted my husband and me to participate in it as well but we also refused. They told us it was our last chance of escaping execution, but I just don't want to do something I know to be wrong. I don't want to go and say the Islamic regime is good. Is there any bigger lie? I've struggled for equal rights and justice all my life, and this Islamic regime is the enemy of all human freedom and equality. So how can I say it's good? There are people outside who know me and supported me through my struggle. I don't want them to feel betrayed. But you are in a different situation. How long were you active?'

'Two years.'

'That's nothing. You shouldn't be killed. You're very young. People will understand. They won't make the same judgment about you as they would about me. It was good you didn't agree to appear in the mass television recantation and confession, but in your case, there's nothing wrong with writing a repentance letter so you won't be executed. You mustn't allow the Islamic regime to kill you. People outside need people like you – when you get out you can still do some good.'

I was horrified, and I argued with her. 'But I am the same as you. I can't recant and confess any more than you can. I can't lie and say my opposition to the regime, my political activity, was wrong. What could I do when I was released? Nobody would trust me ever again. I simply can't do it. If they execute me, so be it.'

'But you are so young. You have all your life ahead of you. No one will say you've done wrong by writing a confession. People will understand that you had to.'

I couldn't understand Arezou's reasoning, and I changed the subject.

'You know,' I said, 'if, back in 1976, someone told me that in just three years an Islamic regime would be running Iran, I would have said it was impossible. I just don't understand how after ousting the Shah, people voted in the referendum for the Islamic regime. It was if people had no memories. They had forgotten that the Islamists killed Kasravi in 1946 for his opposition to the clergy.'

Arezou smiled. '1946 is a long time ago. Very few people remember Kasravi. You know the Shah never had the killers of Kasravi arrested, though he, and everybody else, knew who they were. It is all denied now, of course, but the Shah tried to have a good working relationship with the mullahs. They hated Kasravi's ideas and wanted him dead and the Shah found it convenient to turn a blind eye to his murder. It was politics. The Shah thought the mullahs were controllable and that the leftists were his biggest enemy, and so he put the leftists in prison, or they fled into exile and the mullahs were left free. Ironic, isn't it?'

Arezou went on. 'As for your point about the referendum, there was only one question: yes or no for the Islamic regime. People voted yes because Khomeini had promised them free oil and electricity if they did, and nobody had any idea what would happen if they voted no. It was all confusion. And don't forget, to please the middle classes, Khomeini also promised freedom of expression, but what is free speech when the government and the wealthy elites own all the media?'

Arezou then asked me about myself and I began to tell her.

'I was in England in 1979. I lived in a small town, Cheltenham. I tried to find out what was happening in Iran from the BBC News and The Guardian and any other European paper I could get hold of. I came across an interview of Khomeini, where he was questioned about what he meant by an Islamic government. He actually claimed that women would be as free as men, including free to wear whatever we wanted.'

Arezou interrupted me. 'To get power, Khomeini said what he thought people wanted to hear. And you know people are busy with everyday life and they have short political memories. They should have remembered

Khomeini's opposition in 1963 to the Shah's "White Revolution". It gave women the right to vote that really enraged Khomeini.'

Arezou went silent for a few minutes, and then she asked me, 'What made you decide to come back to Iran when you were safely in England?'

'Would you believe it?' I said. 'I only came back for the holidays. When I got back here, I enrolled in a summer course in drawing at some little college near Tehran University. One day, on my way home from class, I got caught up in a demonstration in Revolution Avenue. I turned the corner and there was such a sea of men and women in front of Tehran University. The crowd was demonstrating against the closure of the Ayandegan newspaper. I felt such hope and energy. It changed my life. It made me stay in Iran.'

Arezou said, 'I was at that demonstration with my husband. We knew that if the Islamic regime succeeded in stopping the publication of Ayandegan, a liberal newspaper, our publications would be next.'

'And how right you were, yet then it seemed that all Tehran was there and that we would win. Everyone was shouting slogans, demanding freedom of expression. Until suddenly from various directions a barrage of stones and bricks began to hit the demonstrators, and the regime's gangs poured into the crowd with broken bottles, sticks and knives. All of them shouting, "Allah o Akbar, Khomeini rahbar (God is great, Khomeini is the leader)." A young lad was knifed in front of me, and when the girl with him protested, her face was sliced open.'

Arezou interrupted me with a whisper, 'They knifed a friend of ours too.'

Arezou and I talked long into that night. When we finally went to our beds, I couldn't sleep. My mind was too crowded with thought of the men and women executed just a few hours earlier.

As I lay down to sleep, memories of the summer of 1979 came back to me. The Islamic regime had only been in power for a few months, and we all thought we could transform the struggle against the Shah into the struggle against the Islamic regime. To us, the real revolution was still alive and gathering momentum. And then, in 1981, the Islamic regime began its butchery.

A few days after Arezou and I had our long talk, she was called for execution. We kissed each other's cheeks as we said goodbye, trying to contain our grief. As she went, Arezou asked me if I had changed my mind about recanting and confessing. I shook my head and she told me to think again. As Arezou was on her way to be executed for refusing to recant and confess, she urged me to do just that to save myself from the fate she was about to face.

CHAPTER 12
Family Pressure
Evin Prison, 1983

One morning I woke up feeling strangely elated. For the first time since I had been in prison, I'd had a pleasant dream. I was swimming in the sea; the water was bluish green. And now I was wide awake, I began thinking of when I was a child and of family holidays by the Caspian Sea. How we had all swum and played together.

Since my arrest, as far as I could remember, I'd had no previous dreams about the outside world or my life before. Every night when I went to bed, I thought of my family and friends, of the music I'd heard and the books I'd read, and told myself to dream about them, but it never seemed to happen. Either I didn't remember my dreams, or I never had pleasant ones.

That very morning the guards came to the room bringing three prisoners with them. They were wearing chadors and covering their faces with pieces of cloth. We were told to stand in a line while they stood about a metre away from us. They looked at us closely one by one. We realised they were informers, and they were trying to remember if they had ever seen us in a meeting or in any other political setting. We were all nervous, frightened of being identified. Everyone had something they were still hiding from the interrogators.

They left with the guards without revealing if any of us had been identified. We would find out later if we were called to be tortured. We began to talk about them, calling them the KKK.

One of the prisoners told us that this sort of a line-up had happened a few months before. That time, after the KKK had finished examining everyone's faces and were leaving, a prisoner called Shirin stood on one of their chadors. It came off, revealing the informer was not only a man, but her cousin. He ran out of the room, disgraced in front of prisoners. The guards were furious and demanded to know who had stood on the chador. Nobody owned up or gave Shirin away.

Shirin only told her friends that the man was a cousin of hers after the guards left. She said that she'd known him from childhood and even though he was covered up from top to toe, she'd recognised him by his build and the way he moved. She'd known he was a prisoner but she hadn't known he had become a trusty. She had just wanted to make sure it was him. Shirin's cousin betrayed her and told the guards she had stood on his chador and exposed him. Shirin was taken to solitary for six months or so.

Not long after this, another prisoner was called for interrogation. She came back a few hours later, ashen and aged about twenty years. I heard her tell another prisoner what had happened.

'After beating me for I don't know how long, they told

me to wait as they were going to take me to see my brother and my husband. I felt so joyful that I no longer felt pain. I was blindfolded as a guard led me into a hall. My head immediately hit something that was heavy, but moved as if it was suspended. The guard then told me I could remove my blindfold. I adjusted my eyes and there were about forty bodies hanging from the ceiling. And I realised I was standing next to the swinging corpses of my brother and my husband. I felt my heart disintegrating.'

A few days later I was called for interrogation. I was blindfolded, but soon I heard a whisper. 'Take your blindfold off and look at her.' And I realised someone had been brought into room to identify me. I had no idea if they were a man or a woman, or why they had been told to try and identify me. Had anyone I might know been arrested? I had a sinking feeling, not knowing what was happening. The experience of being watched while not being able to see was disorienting.

No one said anything, but I could still feel eyes upon me. Then I heard, 'Put your blindfold back on. Come now.'

After my first family visit, I saw them regularly every twenty days. The rules were very restrictive – parents, spouses and children – but until they changed the rule only brothers and sisters over the age of forty could visit. This meant that among my seven siblings, only my oldest sister could come and see me. Friends were not allowed to visit at all.

Visitors' days were happy for everyone with visitors, but some prisoners' families, who lived far away, often found it impossible to make the long and expensive journey to Evin. I remember once a guard called out the name of a woman who had never had any visitors at all; I don't think I have ever seen so happy a face.

Some parents used the family visits to put pressure on their daughters to repent and confess just so they would be released. These parents were usually bewildered about their daughter's involvement in politics and believed girls should all live a traditional life, get married young and have children.

For family visits, I tried to appear reasonably content and animated. Once, just as soon as I was settled in the booth and had picked up the phone, my father asked me frantically, 'When the Iraqi planes come and bomb, is there somewhere you can take refuge? I am frightened that if they bomb the prison, you'll be killed.'

'We don't have a place to shelter from the bombs. But don't worry, the walls here are very thick. They can't be destroyed by Saddam's bombs.'

I reassured them, though I knew as well as they did that some prisons had been bombed and prisoners had been killed, but I wanted to calm my father's fears. My mother was also anxious and she took the phone from my father and said, crying, 'Why don't you recant and confess so they won't execute you. You don't have to mean it.'

'You know I will never do such a thing,' I said, 'So don't ask me again.'

My mother ignored me and went on. 'I've told people you've gone back to England to study. No one knows you're in prison. I can't tell anyone you're here. It's so embarrassing.'

I couldn't believe what my mother had just said. I should have, because being frightened of what the neighbours might think was so typical of her. I felt on fire with anger, but I restrained myself and said, 'Oh, Mother, I'm not ashamed of being in prison. And you shouldn't be either.'

'If only you'd married your cousin you wouldn't be here now.'

It was such an absurd remark that I almost exploded with anger. My father must have realised as he snatched the phone from my mother and told her to leave me alone. We managed to talk about nothing in particular for a while before the line was disconnected. I waved them goodbye, but I was still angry at my mother. Mentioning my cousin had reminded me of something she'd tried to do to me.

I'd been about sixteen when I learnt that my mother had arranged for me to marry my cousin. She'd talked to my uncle and aunt about it, and they'd agreed to the marriage without telling me. One day my aunt came to visit and my mother just said, 'Let's go out so they can buy you a wedding ring.'

I refused point blank. I wouldn't marry my cousin. I didn't want to marry anyone; I wanted to study.

My mother pleaded with me to get the ring, at least, assuring me that if I later regretted my decision, the wedding could be cancelled. I knew my mother was lying and that if I agreed to the ring, she would make me marry my cousin. She and my aunt waited while I went to get ready, but instead of going to my room to fix my hair, I sneaked out and went round to a friend's house. I came back very late that night. My mother was really angry. She felt humiliated in front of my aunt, who had travelled from Mahalat to Tehran just to buy the ring. My mother raged at me, but my father was silent and I realised he wasn't part of her marriage plot.

CHAPTER 13
Execution
Evin Prison, 1983

Night

Time froze
at the call of the first name.
The names always began
being called at noon
when the air was dank
with hundreds of women
confined
breathing each other's breath
longing for the darkness
for no one was ever called
for execution at night.

Out of the blue, Pari was taken for interrogation. When she came back she told us that she had been informed again that if she agreed to recant and confess in the Assembly Hall, her sentence would be reduced from death to fifteen years' imprisonment. She'd refused.

Pari couldn't sleep that night, and she kept several of us

up late, talking to us about her need to die for her beliefs. I'd wondered later if she had been trying to convince herself, or if she had been hoping one of us would contradict her or urge her to stay alive for the sake of her little child and her husband, but no one did. Not one of us told Pari that she should accept the regime's offer.

Perhaps waiting for our own executions had made us numb, but we felt there was no choice and that we would rather die than recant and confess.

A few days later, Pari came up to me in the prison yard and we walked about together. At first she laughed and talked as if everything was all right, yet we both knew her execution would take place soon and her eyes had the colour of deep sadness.

'I need to confess something to you,' she said. 'But I'm frightened of your reaction.'

That puzzled me. The worst anyone could do in prison was to collaborate with the interrogators, and I was convinced that Pari would never do that. So what had she done?

Pari hesitated before beginning. 'When I was arrested, I was in shock. They took me directly to the torture room and started flogging me. They wanted me to give them the address of my handler.'

Pari started to weep and her words were almost inaudible. 'I told them where they could find her.'

My brain suddenly went heavy and I felt dizzy. It was like a big wave hit my brain. My legs went weak and I had to find a place to sit down.

'I know what I've done,' Pari said. 'Even execution won't wipe away my betrayal. But it will put an end to the terrible guilt devouring me.'

I was bewildered; when prisoners gave up information under torture, they always behaved in a cringing way. They were broken and never did anything to provoke the guards or the trusties. Yet Pari had not appeared to be broken.

I found myself saying, 'You'd never have betrayed her if the guards hadn't tortured you.' Pari knew that herself and my words gave her no comfort.

'You wouldn't believe how strong I felt when I first joined the resistance,' she cried. 'Yet you know I never really thought I could be arrested and tortured.'

'Did any of us?' I said. 'Look, Pari. You've managed to remain cheerful and that has given others strength.'

Pari just shook her head. 'The woman I betrayed has been sentenced to death.'

Saddened by Pari's sorrow at her comrade's execution as well as her own, I said nothing more for a while. And somehow the thought came into my head that in a way we were all actors. And in Evin, Pari had been the best actress of all. She had presented herself to us all as an indomitable fighter and she had managed to appear cheerful, content and at peace with herself, while underneath she had carried so much guilt and remorse. I felt that Pari must not give into her grief now, as her bravado had actually helped to make her really brave, and her bravery had helped make us all courageous.

A few days later at lunchtime, the loudspeaker came on. It silenced us, not just Pari and me –three hundred and seventy-nine women all stopped eating at once, and the few children with us stopped talking. We knew that names were going to be called out for execution. Filled with fear, we searched each other's eyes, silently asking,

'Whose turn is it today? Mine or yours?'

I looked at Pari. I studied her face, as it could be the last time I ever saw her. Even in prison she was still stunningly beautiful, and I thought of her husband and child and hoped the Islamic regime would not find them.

Pari's name was called.

Before she was led away by the guards to her death, she was allowed to kiss and say goodbye to us. She was so tall that I had to stand on tiptoe to kiss her cheeks.

As Pari walked towards her execution, she called back to us, 'Stay alive.'

Her voice was still in the air when she disappeared from our sight for ever.

That evening eighty shots were counted and I wondered which one had killed Pari. None of us cried at execution times, but I felt my heart bleeding.

CHAPTER 14
The Shah
Evin Prison, 1983

One day as I passed by the toilets I saw a large pool of vomit and blood on the floor near the toilet door. Then I saw Goli on the floor, slumped against a wall with other prisoners around her. My legs shook and I felt sick. Goli was a cellmate, a Mujahidin supporter, but she wasn't friendly to anyone. Yet on seeing her plight we were all instantly concerned. One woman had already gone to the guards' office as it was so obvious Goli needed to be taken to the clinic.

Goli had been in prison for about a year. She came from a wealthy family; they all supported the Mujahidin financially. We knew her family had tried to buy her freedom, but though Lajevardi, the prison governor at Evin, sometimes took bribes from rich families, he was not able to in every case, and Goli remained in prison.

Later that day, I saw Goli just sitting in the cell. She was very white and her face was full of pain. 'They didn't take you to the clinic?'

'No. They didn't refuse to take me, they just didn't take me and they won't.'

'But vomiting blood is serious?'

'So? Who cares?' she replied, with a cold smile.

For a whole day and a night, Goli didn't have the strength to get up and she vomited continually in the bowls we brought her. She became even whiter, like a death mask. And yet she recovered. Her body healed itself; weak and malnourished, her body still struggled for life.

We shared the yard with the wing upstairs, and when it was not our turn to use it, we were forced to stay inside. I longed for an interesting book to read. There was only the Koran and some Islamic books. I argued with myself and decided that as all the laws were based on Islam, I should read the Islamic texts, just so I could understand the law. The last time I had read Surah al Nesa in the Koran had been as a school assignment when I was thirteen. The contempt it showed for women had made me very angry, and I'd asked my father if he thought my brothers were more intelligent than I was?'

'In no way,' he replied.

'Then how come the Koran says men are more intelligent than women and that women must be subordinate to men? I've no faith in a god that declares men superior to women. And if god was as powerful and merciful as you all say, he'd pronounce men and women equal.'

My father was surprised at my vehemence, and tried to persuade me not to judge god by his word, as it was written one thousand four hundred years ago, before people were civilized. That seemed a poor argument to me, and I argued with my father, but neither of us would bend. From that day on, I didn't believe in god. It gave me a kind of freedom, as the fear of god had no effect on me any more. For a little while longer, before an exam, I'd pray to do well, just as a matter of habit, and if I made a mess of the exam I'd swear at god and tell him he was useless. He couldn't even help me with my exams, even when I'd asked him nicely. Then I'd tell myself again, See, there isn't a god, if there was, after all your swearing at him, he'd have turned you into a frog by now.

Now, eleven years later and in prison, I reread the Koran to see how accurate my childish understanding had been. I turned to the Surah al Nur, where I found among its other advice that it told men, 'If you fear desertion, first admonish your wife, then confine and beat her.' And 'Your wives are a tilth for you, so go into your tilth when you like.'

I felt nauseated reading just Surah al Nur. I didn't know how any woman could read such misogyny and not become enraged, but with culture reinforcing religion, most women in Iran take on the mindset of their oppressors and see men as superiors because that is what they are continually told. Certainly, men look down on women as their inferiors. This misogyny did not enter Iran with the Islamic regime. It is intrinsic to the religion of Islam. It conflicts with official Western ideas, and to please their American and European backers the Shahs, father and son, had paid some lip service to improving the status of women. Even so, all laws concerning women were still based on Sharia, and though Reza Pahlavi forced women to remove the veil, neither he nor his son Mohammad Reza Pahlavi believed in gender equality. They wanted women out of the house so they could work as cheap labour, not to give them personal freedom or legal equality with men. Also, as women started to work outside the home and stopped wearing the hijab, they became an easy target for Western make-up and clothing fashion.

I remembered an interview the Italian journalist Oriana Fallaci had had with the Shah, in 1973. She'd asked him questions about the women's struggle for equal rights. Although Fallaci's article was to be published in the West, the Shah could not hide all his true feelings.

'What do these feminists want? What do you want? Equality, you say? Indeed! I don't want to seem rude, but … You may be equal in the eyes of the law, but not, I beg your pardon for saying so, in ability …You've never produced a Michelangelo or a Bach. You've never even produced a great cook. And don't talk of your lack of opportunities. Are you joking? Have you lacked the opportunity to give history a great cook? You have produced nothing great, nothing!'

The Shah had also talked about his religious apparitions and visions. Such talk must have looked insane in the West, but the Shah had two audiences; he was also talking to the mullahs.

Fallaci had also pressed the Shah on democracy. He had told her defiantly that 'Iran is more democratic than your countries in Europe and that the imprisoned communists in Iran were not political, but criminal prisoners as communism was against the law. But even though it was illegal to be a communist, no one was executed just for being a communist. They always had to have done something extra to be executed, and so they were executed for terrorism, not communism.'

The Shah meandered on and eventually he described his White Revolution as socialist, as it 'gave incentives to work'.

'... believe me, in Iran we're far more advanced than you in the West and we really have nothing to learn from you. But that's something you Europeans will never publish because the international press is infiltrated by left-wingers, by so-called progressives. The Left in the West is even corrupted by the clergy.'

The Americans had overthrown Mosaddegh in 1953 to put this confused Shah as their satrap. He served them well for years, but by the early 1970s, there were worldwide economic difficulties which affected Iran as well. And the Shah started hinting that when the twenty-five-year oil contract he had signed was due for renewal in 1979, he wanted a better deal from the West for Iranian oil.

I wonder whether Khomeini had been America's first choice; they must have imagined they could control him like they controlled the kings in Saudi Arabia. All that is known for sure is that as the Iranian unrest began to turn into rebellion, the West feared revolution in Iran and hatched a plan to foist Khomeini on the Iranian people. Timing is everything. I remembered the Guadalupe Conference in the first week of January 1979, when the Western leaders met to discuss the critical situation in Iran. Just two weeks later, on 17 January, the Shah left Iran, and just two weeks after that, on 1 February, Khomeini returned to Iran after fifteen years in exile. If the West had not wanted him, would they have allowed Khomeini to get on the plane?

CHAPTER 15
Trial
Evin Prison, 1983

Raz and I made friends with Mother Mastureh. She was in her sixties, possibly older, and we used to wash her clothes and help her generally. She'd been arrested to put pressure on her sons. They were Peshmerga freedom fighters with the Komalah. They were fighting in the mountains along the Iran-Iraq border, so Mother Mastureh felt safe, confident that they were beyond the reach of the Islamic regime.

Mother Mastureh was sometimes called for interrogation, and although the regime had nothing on her, they constantly postponed her release. Although she knew that the trusties were watching and informing on her relationship with us, and that it might delay her release even more, she still preferred to be with us. She used to call the trusties 'microbes'. Once, when they warned her that we were infidels and that she shouldn't talk to us, she'd replied, 'There are only two real human beings in here: Raz and Nasrin.'

While we were walking together one day, Mother Mastureh asked me about a headband I sometimes wore. 'It's very pretty, with all its stars.'

'Pari made it for me.'

'I'm sorry they killed her. Did you see how jealous the microbes were of her? They couldn't stand her because she was so beautiful and so confident and so strong and brave.'

I never told Mother Mastureh that Pari had betrayed her comrade under torture – and that this comrade had been arrested and executed too. It was better that she remembered the best of Pari, not the worst.

It was four o'clock in the morning and my turn for bathing. It had been a full week, but finally I could use warm water for fifteen minutes. The shower room was very crowded; no one would have believed it was the middle of the night. We were showering ourselves when someone shouted that Raz and I had both been called for interrogation. We dressed and went to the guards' office. They did a body search and told us to put on our blindfolds and chadors and wait in the corridor.

After a couple of hours, a male guard arrived and told us to follow him. We passed the central office and went down the stairs. I could just make out from under my blindfold that all the steps were covered in fresh blood. As we reached the yard, I saw a pendant on the floor. The guard was walking in front of us with his back turned, so I picked it up and put it in my pocket; perhaps it belonged to whoever had owned the blood that was on the stairs. We carried on walking. After some fifteen minutes, we reached a large building. The guard took us up one flight of stairs into a hall filled with prisoners, all waiting for something. The guard told us to sit on the floor, in a corner away from the others, until our names were called. He did not tell us, but we guessed we were waiting for our trial. We'd come out of the initial torture queue and now here we were in the trial queue. While we waited I took the pendant out of my pocket, keeping it inside my chador. I tried to look at it.

It was a small white stone shaped into a tear drop, with a word inscribed: Tomorrows. It looked as if it had been made by a man for the woman he loved.

After about two hours, my name was finally called and a guard led me into a room. He told me to remove my blindfold. I saw a mullah sitting behind a table and another man next to him, who said, 'This is your trial and this is the judge, Haj-agha Neiri.'

The mullah looked at my file and said, 'You didn't disclose any information.'

I said nothing.

He lifted his head up from the file and looked at me. 'Are you willing to recant and confess in the Assembly Hall in front of the other prisoners? Admit that you were wrong to fight the government?'

'No.'

'So you want to be executed?'

I said nothing.

The secretary spoke instead. 'Yes, she's happy to die for her infidel beliefs.'

The mullah dismissed me with a flick of his wrist and the guard who had come in with me told me to put my blindfold back on and follow him.

I had been given a death sentence yet the mullah hadn't even bothered to announce it with any formal words.

I returned to the corridor thinking that I didn't want to be a martyr, but I just couldn't recant and confess. My mind was clear. I could not denounce myself and play the role of penitent in their theatrical Assembly Hall, so instead I would be executed in their Theatre of Violence. I preferred to die free rather than live as their grovelling slave.

Raz had also gone into courtroom. She came out just as quickly. We sat for a while. Then the guard came and told us to follow him back to the wing. When we got outside he told us to wait while he went off to fetch another prisoner. Under our blindfolds we could see a garden full of large and beautiful dahlias. Raz kept watch as I picked some of them. They reminded me of my friend Kokab, because the word for dahlias in Farsi is kokab. Kokab was still outside and free, perhaps still struggling against the regime. I hid the dahlias under my chador before the guard returned with the other prisoner. He put her at a distance from us to make sure we couldn't talk to her. Back in building 216, I felt that the stairs had been washed until no blood remained.

CHAPTER 16
Recantations
Evin Prison, 1983

Anahid came up to me in the yard and asked if she could join me. I said yes happily. I enjoyed talking to her. She was witty and made jokes about the trusties and gave me news about them. She was only fourteen, yet she'd been arrested two years earlier when she was twelve. As the court had no evidence against her they couldn't sentence her. And, like Mother Mastureh, she'd be released sooner or later.

Anahid always walked barefoot in the yard. When I asked her why, she said, 'Since they knew I had no information, they didn't beat me on my feet. But while I'm here in prison, there's always the possibility they will decide to anyway, so I strengthen my feet by not wearing shoes.'

'Didn't they torture you at all?' I asked.

'After I was arrested, they tied my hands so tight behind my back, I thought my shoulders were being torn apart. The pain was unbelievable. I was lucky they didn't hang me up with my hands tied. They did that to another girl my age, and her shoulder kept on dislocating and she'd scream with pain. They wouldn't take her to the doctor. So she learnt how to get her shoulder back in place herself. It

117

was frightening to see her spin herself around on the floor screaming until her shoulder clicked back in.'

We walked in silence for a while. Anahid continued, 'Did I tell you I am waiting for them to call me to make a public recantation and confession in the Assembly Hall? I have to say the regime is good. I need to lie in front of all those prisoners. You've never told me it's wrong, but I know you're going to be executed for refusing to recant and confess.'

I found myself using Arezou's argument. 'My situation is very different from yours. You were not political, you are here by accident. I was political and for me, saying the regime is good would make my life meaningless. It would be like killing myself. Why kill myself? Let them kill me!'

Anahid said, 'I'm not happy at all about lying and saying the regime is good, but I don't know what else to do. I really want to get out of here and live.'

'Then lie, confess. You were only twelve when they arrested you and you will be recanting and confessing things you never did. Outside, if you want, you can join the struggle in reality and fight for justice, better wages, a fair society and women's equality. You can still have a long and happy and useful life. Confess and stop worrying.'

Occasionally, guards entered the wing and told us to go out into the yard. They'd body-search us at the door and as soon as we vacated the cell, they'd start searching it for forbidden items. They'd confiscate anything that helped us to forget prison: a book, a note, some handicraft work, a needle, a pen, paper.

These searches usually took about three hours. The

guards left a mess, with everything they hadn't taken strewn about on the floor. It would take us several hours to put everything back in its place, and it was tiring work. I was generally lucky as I had found a hole in the wall where I could hide my small precious things. It was one of those places that is right in front of everyone's nose, but no one ever sees. However, not everything could be made small, and on one of these sudden searches, the guards confiscated a little bag I'd made for Huri out of small pieces of dark green leather, cut from a torn bag that one of the prisoners had wanted to throw away. Huri kept it on the shelf with her valued things inside it.

CHAPTER 17
The Assembly Hall
Evin Prison 1983

Sometimes, usually on a Thursday evening, the guards would come into the wing and call us to the Assembly Hall to listen to the prisoners who had buckled and decided to recant and confess.

Raz and I usually managed to avoid going, but the women with husbands, lovers or some other male relative in the prison always wanted to go. Although there was a curtain separating the men and the women, there was always a chance they might get a glimpse of the men they loved. Very rarely they might even be able to say a word to them or exchange a note or small present. If the guards spotted them they would be punched and kicked to the floor, or taken to be tortured, but they felt the terrible risk was worth the brief remembrance of love.

One particular evening, Raz and I were forced to go with the others. The guards led us all to the Assembly Hall. It had a stage at one end, where the prisoners who were going to recant and confess were already sitting on chairs. The prison governor, Lajevardi, was also on the stage. Looking every inch the bully he was, he walked up and down glowering at the prisoners with real hatred.

There were many stories told about Lajevardi. As an Islamist, he had been a prisoner of the Shah in Evin. When the Islamic regime made him governor of Evin, he went on a tour of inspection. Visiting the solitary cells, he recognised a Marxist prisoner, who he knew from when he had been imprisoned in Evin himself. Lajevardi asked this prisoner how long he had been in solitary. 'Eight months,' the man said. Then Lajevardi asked him how much longer he thought he could bear solitary confinement.

The Marxist replied, 'More than three days.'

The following day and for ten days the Marxist was tortured. Unable to walk, he was finally brought back to his solitary cell in a wheelchair.

Lajevardi ordered the torture because of what 'three days' meant. When they had both been prisoners of the Shah, Lajevardi and the Marxist had both been put in solitary confinement until they agreed to some condition or other. Lajevardi had given in after three days.

Once Assembly Hall had slowly filled up, Lajevardi began to harangue us. He had pet ideas and used to tell us that all the Islamic prisons were 'factories' for mass-producing 'penitents'. It was a threat more than a statement. He was telling us that one way or another we would all be broken and on this same stage we too would recant, confess and beg for mercy.

I rested my head on my knees and tried to sleep. I felt really tired and my head felt heavy. I was dozing off when I heard Lajevardi reading out the names of prisoners who were going to recant and confess. When I heard Taher Ahmadzadeh's name I could not believe my ears. I raised my throbbing head with horror and asked Raz to make sure that I'd heard right. My heart was racing and I couldn't breathe. Taher was the father of Mojtaba, my handler, until he had been arrested.

Taher had also been arrested many times under the Shah. The last time he was imprisoned was seven years ago. He was released by people's uprising in 1978 and the Shah had executed two of his other sons.

He began, 'I hope my penitence has been accepted by god and Khomeini.'

It was terrible to see Taher so defeated. I tried to listen to him but I couldn't; a strong sad memory of Mojtaba had come into my mind.

I had just come back from a group hiking expedition on Darakeh. I only wanted to go home and rest as I had to go to work the next day, but I'd promised Mojtaba that I would meet him and Mehrdad later. Mehrdad wanted to see me, but I had only agreed because Mojtaba thought it would do some good. Mojtaba and Mehrdad were waiting for me in Mojtaba's car. Mehrdad got out and offered me the front passenger seat as soon as I arrived. He sat in the back.

In silence, Mojtaba drove us away from the city up to the foothills of Damavand. There were small fields, trees and wild flowers; everything was beautiful. No one talked. Eventually Mojtaba broke the silence. 'Why don't you say what you want to say?'

Mehrdad then asked me directly, 'Why won't you accept my marriage proposal?'

We'd been through all this before. 'Because I don't love you, and I don't want to get married.'

'Do you think our parents loved each other when they

got married? When you get to know me, you'll come to love me.'

'I don't want to get married, and I'm not your parents.'

'Where do you think you're living? This is Iran. Eventually you'll be forced to marry. Why are you running away from it? I'll be a good husband.'

'I shan't marry you, and I don't even want to see you any more.'

I could not have been clearer, but Mehrdad kept on.

He was the head of our small group. I'd had no problems with him in the first few months, but after a while he'd asked me to go out with him. I didn't have any special feelings for him, so I'd always said I had work to do and couldn't see him. Yet he wanted me to marry him.

That evening in the car, Mehrdad kept on talking, determined to persuade me to marry him. After a while I didn't even respond. Finally, Mojtaba interrupted Mehrdad's flow. 'Nasrin's heard it all, you have heard what she's said. Why not give up?'

My mind came back to the Assembly Hall. Sometimes the recantations and confessions were not accepted, but today all of them including Taher's were and presumably they all got out of prison. Yet between the Shah and the Islamic regime, Mojtaba's father had lost three of his sons.

The only other time Raz and I were forced to go into the Assembly Hall, the outcome was horrific.

On this particular evening, Lajevardi ordered just four male prisoners – two Mujahidin and two leftists – to come forwards, who shuffled up onto the platform. Utterly dejected and utterly broken, they each recanted and confessed. Like all the others before them, they had only agreed to this abject degradation on the promise of their death sentences being commuted or even of their being released if they had already served their sentences. Yet there was always just a little doubt and the possibility their recantations and confessions would not be accepted. It gave the ritual tension, as 'we' in the audience had to accept the prisoners recantations and confessions. Of course under orders from Lajevardi, the trusties sometimes objected. They would shout out, claiming the recantations and confessions were not genuine, and they would demand that the grovelling penitents should have their original sentences reinstated.

A group of trusties shouted out that this penitence was false and they screamed a litany of denunciations.

'Death to the Marxists!'

'Death to America!'

'Death to Russia!'

'Death to the Mujahidin!'

Desperate, the four 'penitent' prisoners grovelled even more, and swore their confessions were genuine and that they now supported the Islamic regime completely.

After a frenzy of denunciations, Lajevardi stopped walking on the stage, sneering at the two leftists. 'If you are so penitent, give me the names of five leftists in your wing who have said or done something hostile to the regime that we don't already know about. If you are truly repentant you will give me names so we can deal with them.'

'We would, but we don't know any,' the leftists prisoners pleaded.

The trusties cried out again in unison. 'Death to the Marxists!'

The hall felt as if it was about to explode with dread as Lajevardi turned sneering to the two Mujahidin penitents. 'Why did you only give us the names of leftists in your reports? Now give me the names of some of the Mujahidin in your wing who are only pretending they are penitent. That will show us how repentant you really are.'

The two Mujahidin cried out, 'I don't know any, I swear.'

'How come you have information about the leftist infidels, who don't speak to you, but no information about the unrepentant among your own Mujahidin cronies?'

The trusties all bellowed out again in unison. 'Death to the Mujahidin!'

Lajevardi now refused to accept that the 'penitent' prisoners' confessions were genuine. They were all ordered off the stage, knowing that their self-abnegation had been in vain, fearing that they would receive more punishments. Perhaps more years of imprisonment or even execution, though sometimes when recantations and confessions had been rejected in this way, the 'penitent' prisoners were later allowed to recant and confess again.

Yet that day their sufferings were not yet over.

As soon as four young men came down off the stage, their shoulders hunched and their faces full of shame, the trusties fell on them. They were so totally outnumbered and the punishment they would get if they hit the trusties back was so beyond imagination that they just had to try to protect their genitals and their faces as best they could. As the blows rained down on them, Lajevardi and the guards revelled in the scene, roaring with hate and laughter.

Once the four 'penitents' were all beaten to a bloody

pulp, the trusties turned and started attacking the male prisoners in the audience. It was now a scene of total mayhem and terror; a sickening show. The trusties endlessly punching unarmed, defenceless prisoners with their fists. The prisoners writhing in hopeless agony, winded and bleeding.

Then the female trusties stood up and faced us, as if they were going to attack us too, but the guards told them to sit down, as Lajevardi had not given the order for the women prisoners to be beaten.

Finally, when many male prisoners were a pulpy mess, Lajevardi called for an end to his entertainment.

I heard years later that Lajevardi had been assassinated, shot point blank on one of the few occasions he ever left the Evin Prison, in which he lived for his own safety.

CHAPTER 18
Suicide
Evin Prison, 1983

Anahid and I were walking and talking in the yard. She'd made a public confession a few days before in the Assembly Hall. She hadn't been given a hard time and we both knew she'd be released fairly soon.

She was deep in thought and said, 'Although I've been here for two years, I feel I've been away from the world so long. I feel alienated from my family, and I don't know how I'm going to face my aunt. She's sent friendly messages to me here, through my parents, but I don't know how she'll react when she sees me.'

'Why does this aunt of yours matter so much to you?'

Anahid took a deep breath. 'Because I was arrested with her daughter. They searched us in the street and found socialist papers in her bag, so they arrested and interrogated us. My cousin told the interrogator that I knew nothing about the papers, which was true, and I wasn't tortured anywhere near as much as she was. They even raped her. They put us in two solitary cells next to each other, and we managed to communicate.'

Anahid told me about her cousin's rape and how she

had felt so dishonoured she wanted to die. She told Anahid that she was going to kill herself.

'I wept and begged her not to. I loved her so much and didn't want to lose her, but she could not live with the shame and she committed suicide. I banged on the cell door, screaming to the guards to stop her, but no one came. The next morning, I could hear the guards' comings and goings. I even sensed when they took her body from the cell. My aunt's family knows everything. The regime told them she'd committed suicide, and I told them she'd been raped. But how can I face them? I'm alive and their daughter is dead.'

Anahid was beside herself and couldn't talk any more.

I wanted to hug and comfort her, but dared not touch her because if a trusty saw us, we might be accused of lesbianism and flogged in front of the other prisoners. I said, 'Why feel guilty? You didn't do anything anyone can blame you for. It's the Islamic regime that drove your cousin to suicide – that and the Islamic culture of honour which values a girl's virginity more than her life, and which she had not freed herself from, though she called herself a socialist.'

Anahid looked at me, astonished. 'I don't understand you. Are you saying that a woman shouldn't commit suicide after being raped? I have always thought what my cousin did was morally right – when I pleaded with her not to kill herself, it was because I didn't want to lose her, not because I thought she was doing something wrong.'

I shook my head. 'A woman's life is more important than her virginity. Tradition and religion says a women's honour is everything, but that is to look at a woman just as a commodity, whose exchange value has been reduced.

Women are human beings; we are more than our virginity before marriage or even fidelity within it. So to answer your question, Anahid, no, I don't think a raped woman should kill herself. The punishment should fall on the rapist, not his victim.'

Anahid stayed deep in thought as we walked around the yard, then after a long while she told me that she knew of some other girls who had committed suicide simply because they were threatened with rape.

'I always thought they did the honourable thing, yet you are saying they were wrong.'

'Rape is just another form of torture. Nothing more. We mustn't hurt ourselves because of it – that's what they want. They want to destroy us inside and out. We mustn't do their work for them.'

'I've never heard anyone talk like this before. I wish my cousin had heard you.'

Anahid's new understanding did not give her any comfort. If anything, she was more upset than she had been before, because she now felt her cousin had fallen into the regime's trap and had died for nothing; whereas before Anahid had seen her cousin as heroic, she now saw her as a victim.

CHAPTER 19
Infidel Washing
Evin Prison, 1983

Soon after this, two new women, Zahra and Roya, both leftists and hence atheists, were transferred to our wing. They had been upstairs in Cell Six where there were so many non-believers that they had a washing line area all to themselves, and there had been no fuss about keeping believers' and non-believers' washing separate.

Our situation was different: we atheists or non-believers were in a small minority and we had a special washing line allocated to us to keep us from 'contaminating' the believers' washing. Raz and I had never had a problem with this and neither had any of the other leftist 'infidels', but when the trusties in our wing told Zahra and Roya they had to hang their clothes on the washing line set aside for 'infidels', they took exception to the order. Ignoring it, they put their clothes out to dry on the believers' washing lines. The trusties were furious at this defiance and threw Zahra and Roya's clothes on the ground, shouting out that they were 'unclean infidels! Non-believers! Atheists!'

Defiantly, Zahra and Roya shouted back, 'You're the ones who are dirty – not us!' They had to wash their clothes again, and when they put them back on the believers' line, the trusties just threw them back onto the ground again. We couldn't see what Zahra and Roya hoped to gain, but they continued putting their clothes on the believers' lines, and the trusties continued throwing them onto the ground. After this had gone on for a few days, Zahra came to me and said, 'Why don't you side with us? Why don't you hang your clothes on the non-believers' line?'

I explained our thinking. 'We agree with you and Roya. The very idea of having separate believers' and infidels' clotheslines is mad, but it doesn't really bother me if my 'infidel' clothes are kept separate from their believers' clothes. We don't give a damn about such an idiotic issue. It's not worth getting upset about. The trusties and their clothesline are not the targets of our struggle.'

'But shouldn't we fight them on every point?'

'Fight who? The Islamic regime or the trusties? The trusties are only prisoners themselves.'

'But doesn't giving in to them mean we're giving in to the Islamic regime? They're its representatives here in our daily lives,' Zahra argued.

I repeated. 'Where I hang my clothes to dry makes no difference to me, as long as they dry.'

Zahra replied, 'If we're not going to challenge the regime here in prison, then why do we refuse to confess and recant? We might just as well comply and get our freedom back.'

'Obeying petty rules about washing isn't the same thing as abjuring our own political activities. These quarrels with trusties take time and energy, and I'd rather spend mine on more important issues. We should be purposeful.'

'What do you mean by spending your time on important issues?'

'We were arrested for talking to people and encouraging them to organise. We can take back our freedom by teaching each other here – by discussion and debate. In prison we have the time to educate ourselves and learn from each other. It's difficult, but some of us meet and exchange our knowledge of history, politics.'

We walked about in silence until I asked, 'I heard you were in prison under the Shah. What was it like?'

'It was different. We were tortured for information immediately after our arrest, just as we were here, but after that, we were left to ourselves. I was there for two years and I was only tortured once again after that first time. They wanted us to celebrate some event of the Shah's. We refused. One by one they tied us to a tree and beat us as a punishment. Here, after the initial torture, there is always the random possibility of more. The unpredictability is psychological torture. It's part of the plan to destroy our hope, our spirit, our personalities.'

CHAPTER 20
Prison Baby
Evin Prison 1983

One visitors' day, my father told me confidently that my file had been sent to the Supreme Judicial Council, which had promised to commute my sentence to two years' imprisonment.

'Don't be too sure. Some parents thought they could buy a shorter sentence for their children or even save them from execution and lost their money as well as their children.'

My father refused to listen. 'I tell you your sentence won't be more than two years. We won't even let you stay here that long. I'll get you out sooner.'

I didn't argue any more; I always wanted to part on good terms with my father.

When our families had left, we prisoners walked back to the wing under guard. It was pleasant to be in the open air, and from underneath my blindfold I could just see the beautiful flowers in the prison gardens. That day, I noticed we had a new escort guard, with a thin, anguished body and a gaunt face. His hair and his stubbled beard were white. He was obviously too old to be working, and I asked the prisoner next to me, 'Why isn't he retired?'

'He has lost three of his sons in the war. Another was killed by the Mujahidin. He continues to work as he likes seeing all the prisoners as his enemies and he enjoys witnessing our misery, because his own heart is full of it.'

The tale didn't make me angry; I just felt sorry for the confused old man. Blaming us for the death of his sons when blame rested on the Islamic regime for which he was working.

After each family visit we always shared our news, and so I heard that my party, the Unity of Communist Militants (UCM), and Komalah, based in Kurdistan, had set up a new Communist Party of Iran, along with several smaller leftist parties. There had been talks going on between them all even before I was arrested, and Raz and I were delighted to hear that they had come to fruition.

The UCM was quite distinct from the rest of the Iranian leftist organisations during the Iranian Revolution. Most were opposed to the political and economic dependency of Iran and as such considered the conflict between 'the people and anti-people' and 'the people and imperialism' to be the main battle lines of the Iranian Revolution. Such an anti-American outlook brought them closer to Khomeini and hence into supporting him. In the aftermath of the revolution and once the Khomeini regime had embarked on suppressing the revolution, the most radical of these organisations reached an impasse and fell apart. In contrast, from the very beginning the UCM realised that the Islamic Republic and Khomeini were counter-revolutionaries who represented the interests of the bourgeoisie and were tasked with the suppression of 1978-1979 revolution.

The conflict between the revolutionary Marxism

represented by the UCM and the populist leftist organisations and the subsequent ideological and theoretical struggles over some of the key issues and theoretical matters such as the political and ideological independence of the working class and the party programme attracted a considerable number of socialist activists from leftist organisation to the UCM and to its revolutionary Marxism. The popularity of the UCM and its rapidly growing influence within the industrial workers' movement and among the socialist activists stemmed from this fundamental fact. Mansour Hekmat, a founder and the theorist of the UCM, played a vital part in leading this struggle.

The Communist Party of Iran (CPI) was founded in September 1983. The formation of this party was the direct result of the triumph of revolutionary Marxism over populism in all its political, theoretical and practical aspects and led to the formation of a number of revolutionary Marxist factions within the populist organisations and their subsequent affiliation to the party.

I felt that a similar theoretical and practical 'battle' took place within prison among leftists, no matter what their affiliations were.

A few days later, Raz came up to me and, pretending to wipe a spot off my clothes, dropped something into my pocket.

'Take it into the toilet,' she whispered. 'It's a report about us made by the trusties. We need to be more careful.'

'Where did you find it?'

'Roozhin somehow managed to pick it up from the guards' office.'

I shut myself up in the toilet to read the report. It was short, the main accusation was that Raz, Huri and myself had an 'organisation' in the wing and that we met regularly with a few other equally dissident prisoners. It said we wore red most of the time, which was true up to a point. It then said we didn't go to the Assembly Hall as we did not want to watch the confessions on television – this was also true – and then, worst of all, it said we didn't pray and our 'infidel' behaviour was influencing others.

The report also said that, as infidels, we made the trusties' lives hell, as we would splash water on them, forcing them as 'believers' to bathe and change their clothes to cleanse themselves of our 'contamination'. This was a total invention. We avoided the trusties, and even if we had wanted to do something so petty, we rarely got near enough to them to splash water or do any other pointless stupidity to them.

The report recommended that we should not be allowed to wear red and ended by recommending that we should all be put into solitary confinement. After we had all read the report, we destroyed it. Chances were it was the only copy and we would hear no more of it, although we knew that sooner or later the trusties would report similar things again. For a while, at least, we thought we had a respite.

In the meantime, Huri's expected delivery day was approaching, and we were preparing things for the baby. Her family also brought clothes. For no reason in particular, the guards refused to allow families to bring bed sheet or towels. So I asked mine to bring in some long cotton skirts to make into baby bedsheets and, because they were a little absorbent, to make nappies.

Huri gave birth to a beautiful little boy in the prison clinic. It was a cold autumn day when she returned with him to the wing. She was very weak and slept most of day with her baby snuggled up beside her. She only awoke when he needed feeding. To help her, we washed his nappies. It was painful to see a baby in prison, yet he made life beautiful. I never tired of looking at him or stroking his little fingers. I wondered whether he'd suffer from all the torture his mother had endured, seeing as he had been a baby growing inside her when she was being beaten almost to death.

One morning when the television was showing prisoners' recantations and confessions as usual, I was walking in the corridor, trying to avoid the broadcast. I would have gone out into the yard but it was closed, and I caught the voice of a young man coming from the television. It was clear just from its haunting timbre that he had been tortured beyond endurance. I was riveted and, despite myself, I listened. He was telling his story. He said he had been in Evin for a year and that he had recanted and confessed and had been released. He had immediately fled to Turkey, where he had been arrested by the Turkish police and deported back to Iran. He was sent straight to prison and now he was making this second recantation and confession before he was executed.

As he had been speaking, I had made my way slowly towards my room to look at the television. I wanted to see the young man's face. It was so consumed with despair and terror that I would not have recognised him if he had been my brother. My heart went out to him as I looked at his strange face, so etched with the tortures he had suffered. I

141

knew he was only recanting and confessing to avoid even more torture before he was shot or hanged.

My name was called out on the loudspeaker one morning, we all thought I was going to be executed that day. It was the strangest feeling. I felt no fear, but I remembered my father's last hopeful words and felt deeply sorry for my family.

I kissed my friends and said my farewells, put on my blindfold and chador and went to the guards' office. A guard took me to the interrogation building and led me into a room, where a new interrogator told me to sit down and introduced himself.

'I'm Ruhollah. Your sentence is execution, but in his great mercy, Ayatollah Khomeini has ordained that if you recant and confess in public in the Assembly Hall, we can commute your death sentence to life imprisonment. Your fate is now in your own hands: repentance or execution?'

I remembered my father, who believed my sentence of execution would be commuted to two years without me having to recant and confess. I was being offered life imprisonment only if I recanted and confessed. I did not hesitate.

'I won't confess.'

'Then you'll be executed.'

'When?'

'What do you mean?'

'When will you execute me?'

By way of reply, the interrogator kicked me in the back and out of the room. To the surprise of all my friends, I was returned to the wing.

CHAPTER 21
Pebble
Evin Prison, 1983

Next visitors' day I told my parents that my sentence of death had been confirmed. My father's face crumpled with pain and anger. His eyes became a waterfall of tears. The sight of his anguish was terrible.

My mother cried out, 'Can't you do anything to stop them executing you?'

'Yes, if I recant and confess, if I ask Khomeini for forgiveness, I can stay in prison for the rest of my life, but you know I won't. I'd rather die.'

'What's wrong with repenting if it will stop them executing you?' she asked, bewildered.

'I just can't deny my beliefs. My past actions are part of me, my life, and my future is a continuation of my past beliefs and actions. I can't recant and confess.'

My mother wanted to go on arguing, but my father took the phone from her and said, 'Leave her be.'

Growing up, I had witnessed my father give in to power, compromising himself again and again. We had clashed over it many times. Yet now he accepted my refusal, my resistance, and I was filled with new respect for him.

He said, 'As long as I'm alive, they can't kill you. I promise, I'll save you.'

My father's words were too painful for me – I couldn't speak, and even if I could, I wouldn't have been able to express the depth of my feelings. Time was soon up and the phone line was disconnected. We stood a metre apart, silently looking at one another through the glass divider, perhaps for the last time.

Looking at them with such intensity, I realised my parents had grown much older since my arrest and imprisonment. I felt so sorry for them. I thought perhaps I'd never understood them or loved them as much as I did now.

It was after this family visit that I learnt Hooshy had been executed.

It was now winter and the first snow fell. It snowed all day and all through the night. In the morning, I waited for the door to be opened so that I could go out and crunch my way through the snow. Only a few of us went out, but we played like children. We made snowballs and laughingly began to throw and dodge them.

We were stopped by the shouts of a guard. 'Aren't you ashamed of yourselves? Get inside now.'

We went back into the wing, out of breath but feeling really alive, somehow. Our mood was cut when we heard Roozhin's name called on the loudspeaker; she was to go for interrogation. She had only just been transferred from solitary confinement to our wing. The call probably meant she was going back.

We were all angry for her sake, but Roozhin only said, 'The same thing will happen to you later.' We kissed her cheeks as she left.

We all felt bereft and at the same time angry. Yet our faces were always expressionless, as we did not want the guards and trusties to derive pleasure from the sorrows they inflicted on us.

To calm our emotions, we instinctively looked to create something, which is why I got the idea of engraving pebbles. Little pleasures of this kind were forbidden, and so I found a place behind the washing lines where I would not be seen as I painstakingly etched a design on the forbidden pebble with an equally forbidden needle.

I was sitting behind the washing line when Sima came up and started to move her clothes on the lines as if making more space for them. She was a normal prisoner, not a trusty. One of those who just wanted to do her time and who would recant and confess so she would be freed. Even so, Sima had some principles, and she would never knowingly cause trouble for another prisoner, so I felt safe enough to continue working on my pebble while she went on rearranging the clothes on the line. As she fussed about, she whispered me some news.

'Have you heard the governor of Ghezel Hesar prison, Rahmani, has devised a new kind of torture to completely break the spirit? They call it the Graves. The prisoner is put in a wooden space like a coffin. The wall by the head is kept open so the prisoner can get in and out to go to the toilet. They go just three times a day and they have to eat in this coffin-thing. They are blindfolded and wrapped up in a chador all the time and there is nothing to do. Anyway, there is big hall with rows and rows of these coffin things, and hundreds of prisoners have been put in them. They are close up together, but there are lots of guards and trusties and there is no way anyone can speak to anyone else, and the prisoners are kept there until they give in, recant and confess.'

'Are you sure?'

'I am sure, and these Graves work. They are unendurable – prisoners who you never ever thought would give in are now begging to recant and confess.'

'How do you know?'

'I hear things, and I know some of the prisoners who were in the Graves themselves have become trusties and are watching the prisoners still in the Graves and suffering.'

'Do you know names of any these new trusties?'

Sima gave me some names. One was Zari, a cellmate of mine in the Joint Committee Interrogation Centre. I remembered Zari's story and how she had been arrested with her baby, who had been placed outside the room as her mother was tortured. And now, after all that suffering, Zari was a trusty.

CHAPTER 22
Death Sentence
Evin Prison, 1984

One day in February 1984, a year and three months after my arrest, I was called again for interrogation, and again we all thought I was about to be executed.

Would they shoot me or hang me? I wondered. I felt I'd rather be shot; I imagined I'd fall to the ground, and as my body became soaked in my own blood, I would feel I was flying away. I certainly knew I didn't want to be hanged and hear the sound of my own neck bones snapping.

My friends came with me as far as the guards' office, and we waited outside together, but my mind was too crowded with thoughts of meeting death to take in what they were all saying. I took in a little of what I saw, though. The corridor was full of women, old, young and in their prime, walking around, alone or in pairs. Only a few were talking, yet there was still a great buzz in the air. I also heard the faint cries of the thin woman's two little girls, and I felt sad for them as I always did. Finally a guard appeared and called my name again, and I kissed my friends on the cheeks and whispered 'Stay alive' with difficulty, as if my throat already felt the pressure of a rope.

I was taken, blindfolded and chadored to sit in a corridor outside the wing. I sat there alone all day, waiting to be executed. I thought about the life I'd had, and my mind went back to my stay in England – it was only five years ago, but it seemed so much further away. And now, instead of being at university in England as I'd planned, I was sitting in a corridor waiting to be executed.

I sat with my thoughts until the evening, when a male guard came and told me to follow him. We entered a room, and from beneath my blindfold I could just make out masses, maybe hundreds of folders and files spread out on two desks and on the bookshelves along the walls. I could see that there were two men, one at each desk. One of them showed me a sheet of paper. He told me coldly to read it, and I saw that it was the warrant for my execution.

I don't know why but I felt myself smiling. It was so unreal. The other man caught my smile and was amazed.

'Look at her! She's happy she's going to die.'

I tried, but I couldn't stop smiling. It all seemed so absurd. These ordinary-looking men working every day on this conveyer belt of death; no one would imagine they worked in this horrific prison unless they told people, and they would go home every evening to their families where they would live an ordinary life.

The first man took the execution warrant from my hand and gave me another piece of paper, telling me to sign it. I said I would read it first. And I realised with delight that my father's endless going backwards and forward from one government office to another had not been in vain. My sentence had been commuted to ten years in prison. I had to stop myself from laughing.

I was not going to be executed.

It was not a total victory as I had to stay in prison, but it was still a victory. I had not recanted and confessed, yet the Islamic regime had climbed down and commuted my death sentence. I felt joyous and I wanted to get back on the wing immediately, but the guards were not in any hurry to take me back.

It was hours before I was returned. My friends had all been imagining I had already been executed, and as we all hated the guards and trusties to see our pain, had been struggling all day not to show emotion or cry. They were so amazed when they saw me walk back into the wing alive and smiling that all the tears they had been bottling up burst out and they all started crying. It was a while before we could talk properly, and we spoke of how my father's endless pleadings must have saved me from execution.

I wanted to tell my parents the good news immediately, but that would have to wait until visitors' day. We not only had no access to phones, but we could only send pro forma letters so I couldn't tell my parents that I had been reprieved.

As well as my good news, there was also bad news on the wing. In the few hours I'd been away, some of the prisoners, including Zahra and Roya, had been transferred. All the transferees had one thing in common. They had already received their sentences, but like me, none of them had recanted and confessed. We suspected they had been sent to the Graves in the prison of Ghezel Hesar to have their spirits broken. Perhaps if I'd been given my ten-year sentence just the day before, I'd have gone with them.

On the next visitors' day, when I told my parents that my life had been spared and that my sentence of execution had been commuted to ten years' imprisonment, I expected my parents to be as happy as I was; instead, my mother looked shocked and my father sobbed.

'They promised me you'd only get two years.'

'Who promised?'

'Montazeri. I went to his office, spoke to somebody important and Montazeri agreed not to have you executed. He approved of you just getting two years.'

Montazeri was the designated successor to Khomeini and tremendously important within the Islamic regime. I wondered how my father had even reached his outer office, let alone got him to save my life. I had always imagined my father going from office to office, pleading my case to men with deaf ears. Yet clearly his dogged persistence had succeeded. I was amazed, not recognising then that my father's persistent character had any similarity to my own. All I said was, 'Two years, ten years, what matters is that I won't be executed. I'm very happy. You should be happy too.'

'I won't let them keep you in so long. I'll get you out, I promise.'

Soon afterwards I had a birthday. My friends decided to have a double celebration because not only was it my birthday, but I was not going to be executed. Somehow they found a way to make a cake out of dates and raisins and dry bread. Amazingly, it was delicious. I sat with my friends in the corridor, eating and laughing as if I was free already. The trusties glared at us and we decided it was wiser to cut short our celebration and separate, but Raz and I stayed talking. Suddenly, about twenty-five trusties, all strong women physically, came towards us, thrusting their clenched fists in our faces, and shouting, 'Death to the Marxists! Death to infidels …'

All our joy evaporated. We thought we were going to be killed, but after about ten minutes of this intimidation, the trusties stopped as quickly as they had started, all of them walking away as if nothing had happened.

CHAPTER 23
Bourgeois Individualist
Evin Prison, 1984

Election Day was in April, and the head guard, Rahimi, came to our wing and read out our names, calling us one by one to go and vote. I was strolling about in the yard. Some of the women, who usually avoided me out of fear of being reported by the trusties, now came up to me and asked if I was going to vote.

'We'll soon be told prepare our own nooses,' I said. 'All the candidates support the Islamic regime, so why would I vote for any of them?'

As I was standing at the yard door I could hear Rahimi. When she read out my name, I didn't move, and she started swearing, describing me as a traitor. After her anger had subsided, she carried on reading out the other names. She called Raz, and when Raz didn't appear either, she started cursing her too. It was intimidating. Out of some three hundred women or so in the wing, only fifteen didn't go and vote.

A few days later, a guard told me and few other 'non-voting' women who didn't pray to collect our things and go to Cell Six in the upper wing.

I felt sad as I knew I would miss Huri and her baby.

When we got to Cell Six, which was reserved for women who didn't pray and otherwise avoided prison rules, we saw there were some eighty-five women in there already. Yet it had been designed for just five women in the Shah's time, and the women already there were obviously not too pleased to see us.

I'd always wanted to be in a room where there were no believers treating me as 'untouchable', but I soon realised that life wouldn't be easy here in Cell Six either.

The women here were all atheists and many were leftists, but that is a broad category, and some of the women had views I could not share. Many, for example, felt it was wrong to live better than the poorest worker, and this affected the way we lived, as everything was bought collectively, and out of policy, the Cell Six women refused to buy enough of the few things we were actually allowed. I objected to this immediately, saying we should buy as much as we were allowed to. I was quickly labelled a bourgeois individualist, and except for Raz and the other friends I had come with, I was shunned by most of the Cell Six women.

We were not on lockdown, so I met women from the other cells and made friends with a few.

One of these was Sonia. She had been arrested for her connections with the Peykar. Parivash was another new friend. She'd been arrested for being a Baha'i, and my new hostile cellmates in Cell Six now accused me of converting to the Baha'i faith, just because I spoke to Parivash.

Oddly, Cell Six women tolerated the Mujahidin, but their mindset could not accept that anyone claiming to be a socialist or an atheist could ever talk to a Baha'i.

This ideological rigidity reminded me of an incident

on International Women's Day in 1980, when I was on a demonstration against the compulsory veiling. The Islamic regime attacked the protesters, beating us women with sticks, shouting out that we were 'whores and imperialist scum'.

I managed to escape the fray and get to our bookstall at the Democratic Crossing, where I quickly wrote on one of our placards, 'The Islamic guards are attacking women defending Freedom of Dress.'

A man at some other socialist stall said, 'You can't put that up.' I asked him why not. He said, with a straight face, 'We don't know whether the women being attacked are proletarian or bourgeois.'

'What difference does it make? What's important is that they are defending a woman's right to dress as she wants and the Islamic regime's forces have attacked them.'

'That's ideologically unsound.'

This attitude was typical of male leftists at the time, who just didn't see that women's issues were part of the struggle against Khomeini and that opposing the imposition of the hijab was an important political battle.

Parivash was waiting to be executed. One day she told me, 'Last month, an interrogator called me. He asked me to insult Baha. I wouldn't. I know they are going to execute me whether I deny my religion or not. I was a teacher, and I gave classes at home. They call that belonging to an organisation.'

'You mustn't lose hope,' I said.

'I want to live, but I shan't be sorry to die. My blood will be added to the blood of all those who've died for their beliefs – all those who were burnt, and all those who lost their lives trying to make the world better, fairer, more just, more free.'

Although Cell Six was so crowded that we didn't have enough space to rest or sleep properly, the days went by very quickly. We had some small freedoms: there were no trusties to report on us, so we could make things, have political discussions and even joke among ourselves. I continued engraving my pebbles whenever I wanted to be alone with my thoughts. Though it was difficult to do, I enjoyed it.

CHAPTER 24
Untouchables
Ghezel Hesar Prison, 1984

In spring, several names were read out on the loudspeaker. Mine was among them. We were to go to the guards' office, taking all our belongings with us. That meant we were to be transferred. But again they did not tell us where. As I prepared to leave, Parivash was standing at the door to her cell, watching us getting ready to go.

'I'm losing a good friend,' she said.

'I'm losing a good friend and a teacher. I wish you were coming with us.'

'Try to be happy,' she said.

'You too.'

I kissed her and gave her the usual words of farewell – 'Stay alive.' The guard shouted at us and we separated. I left the wing knowing Parivash would soon be executed. I would never see her again. A couple of months later, I saw her name along with her husband's in the official list of the executed that was published in the newspapers. Killed simply because they were Baha'i.

We got on the bus, blindfolded and chadored, and the guards told us to bend down and rest our foreheads on the back of the seat in front to make sure we couldn't see anything out of the bottom of our blindfolds. But by moving my head into exactly the right position, and lifting the curtain just a little to one side, I could still manage to see something of the road, and I realised we were being taken out of Tehran and were soon on the road to Karaj, which led to Ghezel Hesar Prison, and possibly the Graves. I didn't feel fear, only immense sadness.

When we arrived, the guards took us to a big hall and gave us some bread and cheese. There were hundreds of us and there wasn't enough food. When we had finished, we waited, and eventually the prison governor, Haji Rahmani, inventor of the dreaded Graves, entered and walked about among us, occasionally stopping and asking a prisoner her name.

Haji Rahmani was tall and massive. His eyes brutal and lecherous. And like a pasha, we had heard that he had a few concubines among the trusties. Everything about him was revolting; we found out later it was his last day as prison governor.

I was placed in Wing Seven, one of the most infamous for its brutality, but I was told it was not as bad as Wing Eight. Raz and my other friends were sent to another wing. I kissed them and we parted feeling bereft.

Our new guard was a young woman wearing normal clothes under her chador. She asked our names and the groups each of us belonged to and whether we prayed or not. I was the only one to say that I did not pray.

She told me, 'You are an infidel, so you must wash your own dishes and cutlery. You mustn't mix with the believers. In the washrooms, you will find slippers of two different colours – the red slippers are for untouchable infidels and you must wear them so the believers will know who you are and can avoid you.'

To the others, she said, pointing to me, 'You're forbidden to talk to the infidel untouchable.'

She sent me to Cell Six. It measured just one-and-a-half by two metres. The cells all had iron bars like you see in American prison films. Outside in the corridor there was a television incessantly broadcasting prisoners' recantations and confessions.

There were fifteen women in each cell, but there was only one three-storey bunk bed so we took turns to sleep in them. When it wasn't our turn, we slept on the floor in the corridor.

Wing Seven was mostly Mujadahin, and there were only nine other 'untouchables' like me. Four of these 'infidels' had come from Evin just a few days before me; the other five had come from the Graves. None of them had recanted and confessed. It turned out that Haji Rahmani's departure marked the end of the Graves torture, and these five and the few other remaining prisoners who all still refused to recant and confess had been taken out.

I quickly came across Roya, who had been in my wing in Evin until about six months ago, and had been brought to the Graves. She had been let out earlier as she had agreed to recant and confess. She recognised me and said 'good morning' but rushed away quickly – terrified to be seen talking to a prisoner wearing the red slippers of an infidel untouchable. I didn't want to get Roya into trouble, so I did not try to talk to her. I could see she was broken; her face was so lifeless. I wanted to know what had happened to her, but I didn't seek her out. I thought she would find me and tell me, if and when, she was ever ready.

Roya was ready sooner than I imagined, as just a few days later she asked me to go for a walk with her in the yard.

'You know I was in the Graves. I don't know how long but after sitting alone, blindfolded, wrapped in a chador from morning to night, endlessly listening to confessions being blasted out on the loudspeakers, I began to feel there would be no end to it, that I would stay like that until I died. Then some prisoners with me in the Graves recanted and confessed and became our trusties. So one day when Haji came and did his usual inspection I told him I would also recant and confess. Haji took me into a room and gave me a list of names and some paper and told me to write about the people I knew. About a hundred leftist prisoners were on the list, you included.'

She paused. 'I wrote that you and I sometimes had a political discussion, and that you'd helped me to engrave pebbles.'

I was surprised, but I said nothing; there was no point. She was broken, and I didn't want to make her feel worse than she obviously already did. But she had lied. We'd never had a political discussion; we'd only ever talked about the best way to engrave pebbles. I knew Raz had discussed politics with her, but I didn't ask her whether she'd revealed anything about Raz or any of the other prisoners on the list. What was the point? Instead I asked about her family, and then about Zahra.

'We were taken from the wing together but they sent Zahra to solitary confinement in Gohardasht Prison. She's

162

still there. I know she's well – some people who came from there told me so.'

The five prisoners who had come from the Graves were very quiet and didn't mix with other prisoners, not even other untouchable prisoners like me. They talked sometimes, but only among themselves. They mostly read or they walked about the yard in solitude. The experience of the Graves was just too defining. So many months of isolation when they'd seen no one, spoken to no one, had eye contact with no one and had no idea if their sufferings would last until their deaths had made them ghostlike.

Some prisoners, mostly those who saw me as a bourgeois individualist, didn't understand that the Graves-women's aloof silence was a psychological response to what they had endured, and instead they interpreted it as a personal insult and criticised, even scorned them.

I looked at the Graves-women with awed respect. Bloodied but unbowed, they had not betrayed their beliefs. What strength! What integrity! There was something magnificent about them.

In the Graves, they had been blindfolded, even when they ate and slept, and I wondered if when they first woke up each morning, they thought they were still in their nightmare and only realised they were not because they were not blindfolded.

One of the Graves-women, Mahin, always walked straight towards the flowers in the garden when she went out into the yard. A beautiful but strange smile transformed her face as she touched the petals and the green leaves.

There were three other prisoners (none of them Graves-women) who lived in a similar solitary world, which no one else was allowed to enter. All three were thin and had no appetite, not even for the small amount of food we were given. Gity was about thirty years old but she looked sixty, her face was so full of wrinkles. Awake or asleep, she had her place by the yard door. Awake she was motionless, seemingly calm and serene as she sat looking endlessly at her feet. Asleep she was curled up so tightly that if anyone had not known she was there, she would have been mistaken for a bundle of rags. She didn't shower, and she smelt of urine, dirt and stale sweat. Every now and then, some of the women would drag her to the bathroom and give her a wash. She resisted as if it was torture, but the women were stronger than her and eventually Gity gave up struggling and was clean for a while.

Another of these three women, Shahla, was only twenty-four, but again she looked twice her age. In stark contrast to Gity, she was obsessed with cleanliness. She was either washing or praying. Sometimes she washed her clothes in the morning, hung them up on the line to dry and sat watching to make sure no one else touched them. If any prisoner passed by she'd jump up and curse them in whisper for coming too close to her clothes. She'd burst into tears and washed them and sat watching them again. This pantomime would continue late into the evening, until the yard door was closed. In the morning, she'd stand waiting for the yard door to be opened so she could be the first to go out and remove her clothes from the clothesline. Despite looking old, Shahla was somehow still pretty. Yet the lines on her face revealed great suffering. When she wasn't washing her clothes, she prayed, beating herself on the chest with her fist.

We only had warm water once a week, and each woman had ten minutes to wash in it, sharing a small shower cubicle with two other prisoners. Fearful of being touched, Shahla chose to wash herself every day in cold water, rubbing her skin so hard that it sometimes bled. She was always agitated and frightened, her face full of alarm. In the evening, when she wasn't praying, she wrapped herself up in her chador and sat in a corner of the cell, trembling, or she walked rapidly along the wall from one corner of the corridor to the other. Her cheeks were red, as if she had a violent fever.

I found the third prisoner even more heart-breaking. Behi looked like a young girl of eleven, though it was said that she was seventeen and that she'd been in prison for four years. She had a baby face with blank, innocent eyes. Her behaviour was childlike too, and she often tried to jump like a kangaroo. I asked some other prisoners about her, and they told me she'd been kept in the doghouse at Gohardasht Prison. The doghouse was a very small cell, without enough room for the prisoner to stand up or stretch their legs or hands.

I tried to talk to Behi, but she paid no attention. I never ever heard the sound of her voice, nor had I ever seen as much terror in any prisoner's eyes as Behi had when the governor once came to inspect.

At Ghezel Hesar we were not allowed to lay out our bedding before eleven o'clock, though I was ready to lie down and go to sleep at nine most evenings. Worse, at Evin we had been able to avoid watching endless TV programmes of penitents denouncing themselves as spies, criminals, traitors and sinners, but at Ghezel Hesar it was made very clear that if we tried to avoid watching recantations and confessions, we would be flogged or sent to solitary confinement. So everyone obeyed and watched. I tried to think my own thoughts, but it was impossible to block out the sound completely, and I began to realise that the penitents were ritually blaming 'illicit' sex for making them 'corrupt'. They were accusing their party comrades of being totally corrupted by having sexual relations with each other outside marriage.

The Islamic regime argued that as we leftists didn't believe in god, we also didn't believe in the family or sexual fidelity. Yet though I knew a few leftists who lived together outside marriage, most of the leftists I knew had married in Muslim wedding ceremonies with a mullah reciting the vows for them. Few of them even criticised religion, arguing it was better to leave it alone as the masses were not ready to renounce their faith.

Some leftist women prisoners had residual religious feelings and, worn down constantly by the emphasis on 'sin' in these recantations and confessions, they began to identify the left as sinful and to feel guilty about their involvement in politics. They abandoned their 'infidelism' and began to pray.

After a few days in Ghezel Hesar, with Raz and all my other friends placed in another wing I began to feel very alone. I was sitting by myself in the corridor, just thinking and feeling sad, when suddenly the curtain across the entrance door to the wing was drawn back and Raz and all my other friends from Evin came in. I couldn't believe it, but it was true.

They told me they'd been taken to Wing Four, where

the other prisoners were acting as penitents. As my friends all refused to pray, they had been sent to my wing as it was designated for untouchables.

I was overjoyed.

Trusties varied in their hostility towards prisoners; they could be almost indifferent to us, or despise and detest us, but at Ghezel Hesar some of them hated us with an intensity I had never experienced at Evin. I asked a prisoner who had been in Ghezel Hesar for a while if she had an explanation. She told me these trusties had all been in 'the Apartment' where they had been tortured in a particular way.

'They're all Mujahidin and about twenty of them were kept in the Apartment together along with their interrogators. They had to cook for their interrogators and ate with them. After a while of this odd domesticity, one or two were selected and told to flog their fellow Mujahidin. If they refused, they were flogged instead. And so to escape being flogged they all continually flogged each other. They didn't have visits from their families, but were kept in the isolated world of the Apartment for months. In the end, they lost all human feelings.'

CHAPTER 25
The Miner's Strike in Britain
Ghezel Hesar Prison, 1984

Raz and I were transferred to Wing Eight, while our other friends remained in Wing Seven. Our new wing was the same size and shape as Wing Seven, with six cells on either side, but it was rumoured to be much worse.

Wing Eight had different rules. We infidels no longer had to sit in front of the TV listening to recantation and confessions, but this was the only benefit. There was no access to a yard, and inside all the windows were covered so no fresh air or sunshine came in. We weren't even allowed to go near the windows, as the prisoners from our old Wing Seven used the yard, and although we had just been living with them, we were now not allowed to look at them through the windows.

I was in Cell One. It housed fifteen women, though it had been designed for three, and the wing was cramped and overcrowded. We spent the day sitting close together in the cell or the corridor. Trusties sat among us, listening to everything we said, so we couldn't have any kind of political or serious discussion. There was little to read, just a few school textbooks, but I read them, even though the light was so poor it pained my eyes.

Wing Eight visitors' day was on Monday, and when I had my next visit, I found my family was worried about my move. Unusually, a trusty came and stood behind me, listening to what my parents and I said to each other and watching to make sure we didn't use sign language to communicate anything forbidden. The trusty's presence ruined my limited precious time with my family, but I was still able to tell them that Haji Rahmani was no longer the prison governor.

One day, a guard told us to get ready as we were to be allowed to spend a couple of hours in Wing Four's yard. It was huge and full of flowers. I thought how wonderful it would be if we could use the yard every day. I wanted to run about in it, but instead, the sky caught my eye. I gazed up at it. It was so very beautiful, covered by red, yellow and pink clouds. The red clouds slowly became pink, then yellow and then grey before gradually disappearing. This wonderful sight made me think of how there had been many shades of revolutionaries and just as the red clouds became pink and yellow, and faded to grey when the sun set, some revolutionaries had changed colour until finally they had turned grey – the colour of the Islamic regime after the defeat of our hopes for revolution.

After about a month in Wing Eight, Raz and I, along with some other 'infidels', were transferred back to Wing Seven. The guard had changed; a trusty called Homa was now in charge as wing guard. I was taken aback when I was told her uncle, Sarhadizadeh was the Labour Minister, as Homa had been in the Graves and had been broken by it.

A few days later we were told to put our chadors on and

sit in our cell. This meant an inspection. It was the Labour Minister, Sarhadizadeh himself. He entered the wing with some male guards and his niece, Homa, wearing a black chador. Sarhadizadeh passed by all the cells, looking in at us. He said nothing and I wondered if he was comparing his previous situation in the Shah's prison with ours.

We were allowed to watch the news. I didn't usually bother as it was just the Islamic regime's propaganda, but in the spring of 1984, I was glued to it. The miners were on strike in Britain and scenes of them being attacked by police on horseback were continually shown to demonstrate Thatcher's brutal determination – so that everyone in Iran would understand that it was not only the Islamic regime that crushed working-class movements, but the so-called liberal democracies too. The intended message was clear – suppression was everywhere and opposition was hopeless – but as I looked at the miners in their struggle, I saw that resistance was everywhere.

My heart went out to the British miners and their families, caught in the juggernaut of capitalism but continuing to fight back.

CHAPTER 26
Iran and Oil
Ghezel Hesar Prison, 1984

One day Homa told the other trusties to gather their belongings and follow her. It was clear to us that they were going to be released.

I was very pleased. Not for them; in fact, I believed they would never truly be released from what they had done in prison. I was pleased for us, because without the trusties, we normal prisoners would be able to talk more openly to each other. Talking was a small but significant freedom.

A few days after the trusties had gone I was washing the big food pot. I placed it by the door for collection as normal. Homa was standing by the office, watching, as if she had been waiting for me. She shouted in a loud voice, so that everyone in the wing could hear, 'A Muslim must rinse the food pot, not an infidel. The pot is now unclean, and the Brothers can't pick it up to bring hot food to the wing.'

No one said anything, but it was obvious we wouldn't have any hot food unless a Muslim, meaning one of the Mujahidin, rinsed the pot. I sat by the cell door. I heard the sound of the food cart, but it passed us by, leaving our rinsed-out, but religiously 'unclean', pot uncollected. We got no dinner that evening.

The Mujahidin approached us and suggested that we take our 'unclean' pot to the wash place and they would bring it out for us. They wouldn't wash it, of course, but they would pretend they had. We refused.

The next day we woke up hungry. We had some dates and raisins and we were given some bread and cheese for breakfast, but our food pot remained uncollected and we received no hot food at lunch or dinner.

The food cart went past our 'unclean pot' for three days without leaving us any hot food, but, on the fourth day, our 'unclean' pot was taken and we were given hot food again, without Homa making any reference to our 'uncleanness'. It seemed to be a victory of sorts.

Now that the trusties had been released, we could not only talk more freely, but we also began to hold more formal discussions. We set about using newspapers and the few books we had, as well as our own memories, to try to work out the stark reality of our defeated revolution.

Did the Iranian people really stand up against the Shah only to willingly replace him with Khomeini, as the BBC had claimed in its broadcasts during the uprising? Or had the Iranian people, as we all believed, wanted something very different? And, importantly, what part did the international powers and their demand for oil play in our tragedy?

We all knew that in the first half of the twentieth century, the other colonial powers had torn Iran apart, stealing and looting everything of value. And it was no coincidence that just a year before the long anticipated First World War broke out, the mass production of Persian oil began at the Abadan Refinery (soon to be the largest in the world) and that same year – 1913 – Winston Churchill, First Lord of the Admiralty, abandoned the use of the British-produced coal in favour of Persian oil.

Britain acquired the controlling stake in the Anglo-Persian Oil Company (later British Petroleum) by the D'Arcy Oil Concession Agreement, drawn up by Britain and signed by Ahmad Shah. Iran was only to receive sixteen percent of the profits. There was widespread opposition to the grossly unfair D'Arcy Oil agreement among sections of the Iranian elite. Yet the D'Arcy concession was extended in 1933 by Iran's new British-backed Shah, Reza Pahlavi. Under the conditions of the extension, the Anglo-Persian Oil Company committed itself to paying higher wages to its Iranian workers, to build schools, hospitals, roads and a telephone system. These commitments were not kept, and the Shah began to be attracted to the new Nazi regime in Germany. This became critical for the Allied Powers during Second World War when, to protect their oil supplies, Britain and the Soviet Union invaded and occupied Iran in August 1941, forcing the pro-German Reza Shah to abdicate in favour of his son, Mohammad Reza, who was willing to co-operate fully with the Allies.

The Second World War ended with an Allied victory, yet during the war, all the colonies of the Western powers had been gripped by nationalism and were demanding independence. This mood also affected Iran. Its elites demanded a fairer agreement with Britain, and in April 1951, the parliament of Iran chose Mosaddegh to be prime minister – by the 1906 constitution the Shah was duty bound to ratify parliament's choice. Mosaddegh came to power determined to take control of Iranian oil and to use the profits to develop the country in the interests of the Iranian people.

The Iranian parliament voted unanimously to nationalise the Anglo-Iranian Petroleum Company, which set it on a collision course with Britain. The Anglo-Iranian Company was Britain's largest and most profitable holding anywhere in the world. Churchill, who had lost office in 1945, returned to power in Britain as prime minister in October 1951. He was determined to stop the Iranians nationalising their oil. Churchill imposed crushing economic sanctions on Iran and established a naval embargo around Abadan. He argued that the Iranian oil industry was private property, which Mosaddegh was stealing from its shareholders. Britain now took Mosaddegh to the United Nations and the World Court. Mosaddegh responded by closing the British Embassy in Tehran and sending the British diplomatic corps home.

Thwarted in stopping the nationalisation, Churchill was now utterly determined to overthrow Mosaddegh. He was handicapped initially by US president Harry Truman's equivocations. There were presidential elections in America in 1952 and the new Republican president, Dwight Eisenhower, promptly sent an elite CIA agent, Kermit Roosevelt (grandson of the Republican president, Theodore Roosevelt) to Iran in the summer of 1953 on a mission code-named 'Operation Ajax' to organise the overthrow of Mosaddegh. The Shah, meanwhile, left Iran to wait until he could return in the CIA's baggage train.

Orchestrating riots and using bribery, 'Operation Ajax' took just three weeks to overthrow Mosaddegh. The Shah returned and immediately revoked the nationalisation of the oil industry. Agreeing to govern Iran as a satrap of the West, the Shah imprisoned all potential opponents from Mossadegh's nationalist supporters to the communists.

Having successfully carried out the coup, the Americans now demanded that the British allow American (and some Western companies) to participate in the exploitation of Iranian oil. From 1954, when the Shah signed a new twenty-five-year contract with this new international cartel, it dominated the global petroleum industry and controlled some eighty-five percent of the world's known oil reserve.

The oil crisis of 1973 completely upset this equilibrium, and the Shah announced that when Iran's contract with the oil companies came up for renewal in 1979, he would not extend it on the old unfavourable terms. The Shah was over-confident, with all his known domestic opponents in prison. He mistook Western backing for personal friendship and he just did not imagine they could replace him, just as readily as they had replaced Mosaddegh, if he got in the way of their aims.

Ironically, the US was helped by the unemployment and attendant social discontent in Iran, which had escalated over the Western-backed 'White Revolution' the Shah had instigated in 1963. The White Revolution was a series of reforms intended to modernise Iran. Women were given the right to vote, which offended the mullahs, while the peasants were forced, by various subterfuges, off the land and into the cities where, as the Shah's White Revolution intended to industrialise Iran, they were now required to work in factories. This dislocation of the peasants from their land to the cities, where they now lived in appalling conditions in shanty towns, working long hours for low pay, created huge anger with the Shah's regime, which was not lessened by the ostentatious and opulent display of the Shah's 'Ruritanian' coronation in 1967. This popular anger, discontent and opposition were all sharpened by the world economic crisis of the early 1970s.

As the Shah had operated through a one-party system, with all other political activity banned, and he had criminalised and imprisoned nationalists, liberals, trades unionists, socialists and communists, public anger and discontent began to be funnelled through the mosques by the Islamists, who were organised. It was now, when the Americans and the West were looking to replace the Shah, that the name Khomeini came to the fore.

There was a real people's uprising against the Shah in 1978. Workers all over Iran went on strike. The great Abadan oil refinery was closed down by the striking oil workers, but the well-funded Islamists were able to deflect and take over the uprising, as after years of oppression by the Shah there was no real trade union organisation, and only the Islamists could fund long-term strikes. Once the Shah fled to Egypt, deserted by the Americans and the West, and Khomeini arrived to take power, the Islamists not only stopped funding the strikers; they soon began rounding them up and executing them. The militant workers and the other dissidents had been useful in getting rid of the Shah, but there was no place for them, except prison or the gallows, in the new Islamic regime.

I remembered the day in early November 1979 when I heard 'students' had occupied the American Embassy and taken fifty-two hostages. Like so many people I rushed to the theatrical scene, where the regime's supporters were chanting slogans in favour of Khomeini. The Mujahidin, Fedaian and Tudeh party all supported the occupation of the American Embassy. Yet it was not revolutionary; it was an action taken by the Islamic regime to buttress its support internally in Iran, as everyone had become anti-American because the Shah was seen as pro-American. Three years later, the Americans backed the Iraqi invasion of Iran.

CHAPTER 27
Poems in the Graves
Ghezel Hesar Prison, 1984

I met Nazli for the first time in Ghezel Hesar. She was tall with curly black hair, funny, playful and friendly. She always volunteered when there was work to do. She was a hoarder and gathered things other prisoners discarded. She had collected an extra bag of things that she thought might come in useful someday. Some prisoners complained because her extra bag took up space and we were so cramped already. Yet when anyone needed anything, a needle or pin, they would always go to her.

I knew Nazli had been in the Graves and I asked her what they were really like.

'When I was transferred here to Ghezel Hesar from Evin, I expected to be placed in solitary confinement, so I'd hidden some poems. I'd put the paper inside my clothes, so if I did end up in solitary I could read them. When we prisoners arrived here, the governor, Haji Rahmani, welcomed all of us with a brutal beating. We were told to undress for a body search. I managed to hide the poems between my buttocks. After the body search we all had to dress and put on a chador and a blindfold again. They took us into a big hall, full of large coffin-sized boxes, open at one end and deeper than a coffin and without a top.

'We were each led into one and told to sit down. We were ordered not to try to speak to each other. The side walls were about a metre high. The width was about seventy centimetres. The length was about 180 centimetres. Sitting inside, silent, it felt like being in a grave. We were allowed out to the toilet three times a day and were given a shower once a week. We had no exercise. We had to eat in the coffin. We were only allowed to lie down at night to sleep. The rest of the time we had to sit, chadored and blindfolded, listening to recantations and confessions or readings from the Koran.

'We had no idea how long we were going to be kept in these coffin-boxes. At first, I comforted myself that it might last just a few hours, perhaps – or a few days at most, but no longer. It was too cruel. After a while, when I felt sure the trusties had gone, I Morsed a few words to the woman I knew was next to me. She didn't reply; perhaps she was scared that the trusties were still there. I didn't Morse again. Some hours later, it could have been a day, a guard came and took me to Haji Rahmani's office. He told me to remove my blindfold and began to lecture me about rules and conditions, and he told me that I was to be confined in the coffin box indefinitely. He called it the Graves. The horror of what he said was only just sinking in when he began to hit me. He kept hitting me until he got tired or perhaps just bored. I was then taken back to my "grave".'

Nazli fell silent for a moment. I just looked at her and wondered if I could survive in the Graves for months and still come out of it sane and militant, as she had done.

She began talking again. 'During the days, we had

to sit up in our grave, unable to move our bodies much. We battled with pins and needles and we were always in pain. Our backs, legs, and necks seemed to take their turns. Sometimes every part of our bodies would be in pain. It was only eased a bit at night when we were allowed to lie down in our grave.'

'Did you ever have a chance to read the poems you'd hidden?'

'Even though we were always blindfolded, after a while I did manage to loosen mine so I could see just a little from underneath. I don't know how they missed my poems on the first body search but they did. They found them after about a month. I was reading them, listening out for the footsteps of a trusty, but for some reason I didn't hear, and one of them found me reading them. Haji Rahmani came about an hour later, and without getting me out of my grave, he started kicking my head and shoulders, demanding to know how I had kept the poems hidden for a whole month. He was beside himself with anger.

'Haji Rahmani beat me at other times as well, often just a matter of routine terror. Once I caught a cold and couldn't stop sneezing. I was given nothing to blow my nose with, so I was using my chador. It was disgusting. Haji Rahmani didn't beat me for that, though; he beat me for the noise I made sneezing and blowing my nose. We just weren't allowed to make any noise. Women were even beaten for moaning in their sleep. They found reasons to beat one woman or another every day. After about four months in the Graves, I was suddenly given a broom and told I could sweep out my grave. I was now allowed to do this regularly. The broom was traditional and made of sorghum.

Once I removed a few twigs and put them as a decoration in a makeshift vase I had shaped with some soft leftover bread. The guard saw me and reported what I'd done to Haji Rahmani. As he was beating me, this time he laughed, saying, "She's been making flowers for her grave." In the long daytime hours, I thought of my family and friends and wondered if they knew where I was. I tried to imagine how each of them would behave if they were in my situation. I thought some of them would be able to bear it, but others I was sure would give up and confess.'

Nazli said she thought part of the reason she had stayed strong was that she had never believed the torture of the Graves would be permanent. She had always felt that the regime would let them out, eventually, even without a confession.

I was still listening to Nazli, but at the same time I was thinking of Roya and how she hadn't been able to bear the Graves as she had thought the torture of it would never end.

I asked Nazli if she had known she were such a strong person before she was put in the Graves.

'No. I didn't. Once I was in the Graves, I discovered a part of myself that I had not been aware of before. At one point they took me to be interrogated about my Marxist views again. Before when I'd been interrogated about Marxism, I'd been evasive. Now, after being in the Graves, I defended Marxism.'

No explanation was ever given of why the Graves were ended. It was a puzzle as the Islamic regime got the results it wanted with all except a handful of prisoners finding it so unendurable that they recanted and confessed. Yet after nine months the constant psychological and physical torture was just stopped as suddenly as it had begun.

Nazli spent six months in the Graves, and she was one of the few that came back into the normal cells without having succumbed. And now here she was, after all that bodily and mental anguish, talking to me, lively, intelligent and unbroken.

CHAPTER 28
Scabies
Ghezel Hesar Prison, 1984–1985

After a few months at Ghezel Hesar, some prisoners began scratching themselves. Soon it was obvious that the prison was infected with a contagious skin disease.

I got it too. It was awful. We would all scratch ourselves red raw. If I could, I would go to the shower cubicle, undress and, in a vain attempt to get relief, scratch myself until my skin bled. Some women got it worse than others. But all of us became scarred and sore. Anyone still free of infection avoided the infected out of fear of catching it.

We kept telling the guards that we needed to go to the clinic to get treatment.

Finally, a guard took us to be examined by a doctor. She was young, chadored and completely out of her depth. She knew nothing about skin disease but wanted to hide her ignorance. We were seen one by one. She told each of us that our sores came from shaving our legs. I burst out laughing when she said this to me. I couldn't stop myself; it was so absurd. She glared at me in disbelief when I told her we had no razors, and none of us were given any treatment.

Next visitors' day, we decided we would have to tell our

families about our skin conditions and ask if they could exert some pressure on the authorities in order that a skin specialist could come and treat us.

When I told my parents, my father asked me to pull up my sleeve to show him my arm. I refused as I didn't want him to see it and get upset. He insisted, and I reluctantly pulled up my sleeve. At the sight of my arm, he burst into tears and started swearing at the regime. 'These scum torture you – they're determined to break you bit by bit. Why didn't they just end it with one bullet?'

He calmed down after a while and said he would go and see people and make them do something about it.

I knew my father would do his usual rounds of every government office he could think of, and eventually Maysam, the new prison governor, got to hear of our skin disease. He called me into his office and asked me about it. I told him, 'We need a specialist to diagnose the condition.'

'I could send you to Evin for treatment today if you wanted.'

'It's not just my individual problem, it's a problem in the entire wing.'

'In that case you must all wait until we've found a specialist.'

This was an absurd remark as Iran is full of doctors, many of them specialists. Maysam could have 'found' one in half an hour.

I returned to the wing to tell my friends about my inconclusive interview with Maysam.

They all said they understood Maysam's trick. Whenever a prisoner's family complained about some medical issue, the prisoner was ostensibly offered treatment, as I had just been, and was taken back to Evin only to be kept in solitary confinement instead of being treated.

A few days later, Homa told the worst-affected that we were to go to the prison clinic to see a specialist, a middle-aged man. I was the third prisoner to go in and see him. I told him how my whole body itched – even my neck and some parts of my face. He asked to see my arm and one of my legs. I pulled up my sleeve and I lifted my trouser cuffs. His face changed the moment he saw it and he left the room. I heard his voice in the corridor.

'I've seen three of them now – I don't need to see anyone else. Where is Maysam? You must disinfect the prison. They all have scabies.'

The doctor seemed to walk a long way off and soon I couldn't hear his voice any more. Back with the others in the waiting room, I worried that Maysam wouldn't allow him to treat us. But eventually the doctor returned and talked to all of us.

'I don't need to see each of you individually. You all have scabies. To get rid of it, you must treat your skin with a special medicinal lotion. After bathing, you must put it all over your skin, on both the obviously infected parts and the parts that seem clear.

'You must all do this for three consecutive days. Then for fifteen days do not put the lotion on. Then put the lotion on again for three consecutive days. Follow this pattern until all the itching stops. The lotion will make you feel your skin is burning. It isn't, it just feels as if it is. Unfortunately, there's no other more agreeable treatment.'

It took a week for the guards to bring us the lotion, and just as the doctor had warned, it made our skin feel as if it was burning and we cried out in pain when we put it on. Raz and I put it on each other; somehow that made it easier, but it was still awful.

Every fifteen days, I used the lotion for three days as the doctor had ordered –but it took several months before the scabies went completely. After the itch went, our skin was rough and scarred.

The doctor had told us that when we were free from the scabies, we would see him again so he could prescribe something new for our damaged skin, but no matter how many times we told the guards that we needed to see the specialist again, we were ignored and we never saw the skin specialist again.

Sometimes I liked to separate myself from the busy wing, and I would squeeze myself onto the small windowsill, where I could think without any distractions. The sky above Ghezel Hesar was beautiful; it was full of rainbow colours, and each coloured cloud seemed to push against another. The sunsets there were spectacular, and I would watch as the clouds took the redness from the sun and the sky became gold. I loved seeing the slow play of colours before the night brushed over them and covered everything. The sights of the sky fired my imagination; they made me feel free somehow.

One evening I was in my little place by the window watching the sky and thinking about my family and my friends, when from what seemed a long way away I heard Homa telling me to go for interrogation.

Homa was one of very few prisoners, out of thousands, who had been promoted from trusty to guard. It isolated her among the guards and trusties, yet we shunned her as we shunned all the trusties and guards. But clearly the Islamic regime felt they could rely on her.

I turned my head to Homa when she spoke; she was standing at the cell door. Raz and my friends surrounded me, worried that I might be taken to solitary. As I followed Homa, two other women prisoners joined me, and I realised they had also been sitting at a window.

Homa took the three of us to the governor, Maysam, and told him, 'These prisoners were sitting at the window contacting Wing Eight.'

This was a serious accusation as contacting Wing Eight was forbidden. We were at risk of a flogging or solitary.

Haji Rahmani would have just slapped us across the face, but it was a different time, so Maysam asked us if what Homa said was true.

I replied, 'Haven't you seen the iron mesh in front of the windows? We can't see anyone there, let alone talk to them.'

'Then why were you sitting at the window?'

'To watch the sunset.'

Homa repeated that she was sure we had been contacting Wing Eight, but Maysam refused to listen to her and told her to return us to the wing.

I was concerned by Homa and her attempt to get us tortured. Why had she wanted to do this?

About a week later, it was very hot in Wing Seven's yard with its small garden of flowers. Unusually, I was inside as I felt unwell. I was just idly looking through the window, watching as some women filled the washtub with water from the tap in the yard, when suddenly I saw some of them begin to playfully flick water at each other, shouting and running around like happy children. Homa appeared and ordered them to keep quiet.

After years in prison, we could always sense trouble. It was suddenly in the air now – we could smell it. Homa ordered everyone to leave the yard and put on their chadors. Once everyone was back inside, Homa called out the names of the women who had been throwing water and playing. She told them to go and wait beside her office door. We others stayed in the cell, but we could see into the corridor, and after about half an hour we saw male guards arrived with whips and a large pallet. So this time Homa had got her way; she was going to torture prisoners.

The guards called out to us to come and watch the flogging, but we stayed inside the cell. We heard a woman being told to lie down on the pallet. It was easier for the guards to aim sure if the women's movements were confined.

Except for the sound of the whip cutting the air as it struck each woman's back one after the other, there was silence in the hot afternoon. None of the women being flogged cried out, but a middle-aged woman in one of the other cells could not restrain herself and started to weep loudly.

The lashings seemed to last for hours, but they finally ended, and the door to the yard was opened once again. Although I still felt unwell, I went out like everyone else and wandered around dazed. I wanted to cry, but knew I couldn't.

I was just walking around when Shahrzad came up to me and gave me a flower she'd just picked from the garden. She'd also endured the Graves, and like many who'd been there, she usually spoke very little and only to one or two people. I took the flower from her, but fearing I wouldn't be able to hold back my tears much longer, I said nothing and just walked away. Looking at the beautiful flower, I felt life had never been so painful.

I thought of how, just as the Islamic regime had reintroduced public executions as a theatre of oppression, so they also performed public torture in prison as a macabre theatre. And even though we prisoners were forced to be the audience, we still felt complicit watching the infliction of acute pain that we had all suffered and knew well ourselves. We witnessed collectively, humiliated, fearful and traumatised with feelings of aching guilt as the 'other' endured.

One afternoon, a few days after the public floggings, the wing suddenly filled with guards and trusties, who ordered us to go out into the yard. One of the trusties saw Nazli attempting to hide something, and when we'd all gone out, Nazli was called back in for interrogation. When we came back in, I saw that a pencilled sketch I'd drawn of a mountain had been torn off the wall and confiscated. It was painful, but it was nothing compared to the dread I felt at what might be happening to Nazli.

She did not return. We assumed she had been sent to solitary confinement.

Around this time, Huri was transferred from Evin to Ghezel Hesar, and she was brought to our wing. It was seven months since I'd seen her and I was delighted by her return. She told me she had been allowed to give her baby boy to her family. But though she knew it was for the best, she was still very upset at being separated from him. He was going to join his father in Europe, which was also for the best, but it meant Huri would not see her son again until she was out of prison – if she ever was. After talking about her son, Huri also told me that her brother Hamid had been executed.

I now spent most of my time reading books and discussing politics with Raz, Huri and one or two others. There were only a couple of good books in the wing. Ivan Pavlov's book about conditioned reflexes was one, but since everyone wanted to read it, each of us took turns to read it for an hour a day. This was frustrating, so we decided to make a copy of it. It didn't take us that long and then we were able to read it together and discuss it. We thought to explore our situation and the way the regime was treating us with the aid of Pavlov's conditioning theory.

CHAPTER 29
The Fight for Coloured Chadors
Ghezel Hesar Prison, 1985

One visitors' day, the guard announced that everyone had to wear a black chador. Up till then, we'd been able to wear any colour of chador we liked, and we all began talking about the new rule.

The prison authorities often announced new rules. No matter what the new rule was, the change always created disagreements among us prisoners. Some prisoners, the Fedaian among them, argued that we should always oppose rule changes no matter what. To them, it was matter of maintaining our rights.

Predictably, the Fedaian now took the position that we should continue to wear our coloured chadors. I couldn't see the point of this as a coloured chador is still a chador. I'd always hated the chador. I wore it because I was in prison and had no choice. Before my arrest I'd occasionally used it as a disguise – or, rather, I'd used it to hide myself. Yet even then, I'd carried the chador in my bag and put it on in the taxi at the very last possible moment, and I'd taken it off again the moment I thought it was safe, putting it back in my bag.

Now I not only felt the Fedaian position was wrong,

but I also thought they were rushing headlong into a trap. Obviously the new rule had been imposed to provoke us. Among my friends, I argued that we shouldn't rise to the bait. Before we had time to discuss the issue properly, Homa read out the names of prisoners who had visitors and told us that we could only see our families if we put on a black chador.

A number of the women on our wing already wore black chadors, but now that it had been made obligatory, many of them wanted to show their opposition by wearing a coloured chador. Everyone was so agitated that although Raz and I were willing to wear a black chador, we decided not to have our family visit until we'd discussed it thoroughly with everyone else. Raz and I hoped to get everyone to agree that the colour of the chador didn't matter and that it was fruitless to confront the Islamic regime over such a petty issue. We wanted to argue that we should preserve all our strength for the more important struggle of refusing to recant and confess.

We were all still debating the issue when visiting time ended and the women who'd put on a black chador and had been allowed to see their families came back onto the wing. They told us that all our families had been very upset when we hadn't appeared and had told the guards they wouldn't leave the prison until they were able to see us.

We were still debating it in the afternoon, when Homa told us that all the women who had not seen their visitors were going to be allowed to talk to them on the phone. When I spoke to my parents, they told me they had been worried as they had imagined I was being punished. I couldn't say much to reassure them as the line was disconnected after just a couple of minutes.

Back in the wing, Huri came up to me and told me that she had decided to fall in with the Fedaian and refuse to wear a black chador. I knew she had friends among them and was torn on the issue, but I still tried to persuade her not to join this particular struggle.

'What's the use of resisting on this issue? I can understand fighting not to wear the chador at all, but fighting just to have a choice of colour is surely as ridiculous as fighting for them to beat us with a particular colour of whip! Look, Huri, in the end, you know as well as I do that they'll torture everyone who refuses to wear the black chador. Do you really think it's worth it?'

Huri didn't argue with me, but I couldn't change her mind. Roozhin and Sonia also decided to wear a black chador, and I couldn't change their minds either.

It reminded me of a battle I'd had with my mother when I was about nine years old. One day my mother, who always wore a chador when she went outside, came to me and proudly told me that I was growing up and that it was time I started wearing a chador when I went outside. She told me that she had made one for me to wear when I went to school. She brought it to me and asked me to put it on to see how beautiful it looked. She must have seen the anger in my eyes, but she believed she was right and she said firmly, 'You're a big girl now and that means you must cover yourself up. If men see your hair, or any part of your body, you'll go to hell and burn everlasting.'

I said nothing, but I seethed. I couldn't accept what my mother said. Why should I cover my body when my older brothers didn't cover theirs? But I couldn't argue with my mother, so I remained silent. The next day, when I was getting ready for school, my mother came up to me and put the chador over my head and around my body and said, 'My darling, now off you go.'

I felt belittled and humiliated. My mother was so old-fashioned. It was the late 1960s; the chador was still worn in the villages but less and less so in Tehran, and very few girls my age wore it. Outside, as soon as I had shut the door behind me, I took the chador off and put it in my school bag. I did the same routine every day. No one saw me wearing it in the street or at school. I always put it back on just at the front door before I rang the bell, but one day my mother caught me. I'd come home at the usual time, but the front door was already open and I just went in and put my chador on in the courtyard. As I arranged it around my head, I saw my mother standing about ten yards away, watching me with an open horrified mouth.

I said 'Hi' to her, as if nothing had happened. I took the chador off again and folded it under my arm. I was nervous inside, though, as I knew that once she recovered from the shock, she'd explode like thunder. Later, I was in the sitting room doing my homework when my mother finally came in. She said, 'If you won't wear the chador, you can't go to school any more.'

'I shan't wear it,' I shouted.

My mother went into a rage. Yet somehow I knew I'd won the battle. That night, when my father came home from work, my mother told him what had happened and tried to get him to force me to wear the chador. But my father didn't say a word, either to me or to my mother. Although I was only a child, I realised his silence was his way of refusing. Without my father's backing, I knew my mother couldn't force me to wear the chador, and the next day I went to school without it.

In the Shah's time, neither the hijab nor chador were compulsory, and my sister even had a wedding dress which left her arms and shoulders bare. But when the Islamic regime took power in 1979, on 7 March, Khomeini announced that women must wear the chador. The next day, International Women's Day (8 March), thousands of women marched in Tehran and other big towns in protest against the new edict. The men just stood on the pavement, watching; they didn't back the fight that their wives, daughters, sisters and mothers were taking to the streets to win their rights, and the scene of women marching and chanting slogans for their rights was something new, just as the regime was new, just as this oppression was new.

Seeing the women's resistance, the regime modified its position. It now said that Khomeini had only meant to 'suggest' that women should wear the hijab and though, of course, women could wear the chador as well if they wanted to, it was not intended to be compulsory.

Khomeini said this to gain time, and very soon women were told that if they wanted to keep their jobs they had to wear the chador at work, while outside they had to wear the hijab and a long overcoat no matter how hot it was. There was resistance, but the regime used all kinds of techniques to enforce compliance. Outside in the street, the Islamic guards encouraged little boys to throw stones at any woman not wearing a hijab. Shop-keepers were threatened with closure if they sold anything to women who did not cover their hair. To counter this, some of the shops kept scarves by the door for women customers to put on. Yet altogether the pressure to make women comply was relentless. Women who did not comply were sacked, but most women did comply through economic necessity, and within about two years, the Islamic regime had managed to impose its will. During this two-year period, women who exposed their hair were physically attacked by the regime's gangs, who threw acid on women's faces or knifed them.

To ensure its victory was permanent, the regime passed a new law in 1983, imposing a punishment of seventy-four lashes on any woman who failed to adhere to the compulsory Islamic dress code. A year later a special patrol, Moral Police, was set up to hunt for women who might have a stray hair showing. Women's hair was a particular obsession of the regime.

The compulsory wearing of Islamic dress made the inequality of men and women very visible, yet most men didn't take up the women's cause. They didn't seem to understand or care that their mothers, sisters, wives and daughters were being branded as lesser humans. In reality, men not only became accomplices in the sexual apartheid, but benefited from it: polygyny, as well as inequality in marriage, inheritance, court testimony, custody, and compensation are lawful.

CHAPTER 30
Dead End Resistence
Ghezel Hesar Prison, 1985

The prison authorities might appear to impose random rule changes for no reason, but they had a deliberate plan. They always wanted to stir up dissension among us, and they now watched us as we quarrelled about whether to accept or resist the new compulsory black chador rule. This created tension in the cramped wing, where we could not escape from one another, adding yet another pressure.

Another example of these sudden rule changes was that one day out of the blue we were told we couldn't keep our newspapers for more than a week, when up until then we had been able to keep them for as long as we wished. The Fedaian prisoners reacted immediately, saying they wouldn't buy any newspapers if they no longer had the right to keep them.

I felt differently; although Etelaat and Kayhan were both pro-government papers, reading between the lines it was possible to glean some news, and I wanted to read them. I didn't see the point in keeping them indefinitely and so I didn't see the point of protesting about the new rule. Others felt differently, and soon there were two opposing camps: one that was dominated by the Fedaian, who were always ready to fight over anything and everything; the other was made up of prisoners like myself, who argued that it was best not to engage in struggles that would drain all our energy for no good reason. There were also prisoners like Huri, who oscillated from one side or the other.

But the chador issue dominated. We all just talked incessantly about it. In the end, out of about a hundred and twenty women on the wing, half decided to accept the new black chador rule and half decided to resist. This made the few undecided prisoners very important, as whichever side got them on board would have a majority.

The Fedaian tried to win over the undecided by argument, but they used low-level intimidation against those of us who had decided that the battle of the black chador was not worth fighting. To me, enduring torture and more torture as the price for keeping silent and not betraying my comrades was one thing, but to actually invite torture over the colour of a chador I hated wearing anyway just seemed senseless.

Angry at my stand, two Fedaian, Mona and Niki, made a point of coming up behind me, calling me coward and a traitor continuously like a mantra. They did it to other women opposed to them as well. It may seem a small thing, but it ate at the nerves.

Huri came up to me one day very upset. 'Mona asked me how I could be friends with you, Nasrin, when you are a traitor. I told her it wasn't true, but she just kept saying that you don't believe in the struggle, so you are a coward and a traitor.'

'Look, the problem is not the colour of the chador – the problem is that we have to wear a chador at all.'

'You might be right, but, oh, I don't know.'

'Huri,' I repeated, 'the Fedaian are just confused. They don't believe in religion, and the chador is the symbol of the religion they reject. Yet they fight over the colour of the chador, which is incidental, when the chador itself is the problem. What is the point of this particular struggle? Today, the regime gets us fighting over the colour of our chadors. When it wins, as it will, because in the end it will flog every woman who continues to resist, it will impose a new rule about some other stupidity. And Mona and her friends will start battling the regime on that as well. They're just wasting their energy.'

Before the chador furore, visitors' days had always been welcomed, but not any more. The women who refused to wear a black chador were denied visits, while those of us who had agreed to wear one saw our families as normal. It divided us totally, as prisoners in one camp often refused to speak to the prisoners in the other, even though all of us had friends in both camps.

This went on for weeks until some of the women, who'd been wearing the black chador on visitors' day, now suddenly refused as well. I asked Huri the reason for their sudden change of mind. She told me, 'Mona and Niki have convinced them all that they should struggle, except for Parvin. She has decided to refuse to wear the black chador under pressure from her father. He said she made him feel ashamed because she hadn't joined the struggle.'

I knew some of Parvin's brothers and sisters had been executed, and I could imagine her father's hatred for the regime, but getting his daughter flogged seemed an absurd attempt at revenge.

Months passed and Parvin changed her mind back again, and despite her father's exhortations she agreed to wear a black chador. Everything else seemed to remain at stalemate. The black chador 'resisters' were still being denied family visits, but no other punishment had been given to them. Then, suddenly, one day Homa came and read out the names of all the women refusing to wear the black chador. The guard told the women to come out of the wing with all their belongings. I hated to see Huri go. I didn't want to lose her again and inside I was distraught, but I kept calm as I watched Huri and the other women gather their things and go off to be flogged.

CHAPTER 31
Reflection
Ghezel Hesar Prison, 1985

Although we were opposed to the decision of the Fedaian to fight for the right to wear a coloured chador, we were downhearted that they had gone and hoped they could endure their sufferings. I feared for Huri and missed her, yet the tension created by the presence of the 'resisters' was also lifted, and without it, we remaining women relaxed; we read more books and had serious discussions with each other.

I found again that I could take pleasure in simple things. With yet another pebble I picked up in the yard, I used some small tools I'd improvised – a sewing needle, the blade from a pencil sharpener and a pen – to engrave Van Gogh's 'Peasants Digging'. It was very small precise work. The engraving could not have been bigger than two centimetres by one. Concentrating on this small work gave some rest to my mind. Yet I still mulled over our lives in prison and the way we handled things. We needed solidarity, yet we had such different ideas that it proved easy for the Islamic regime to engineer conflict between us.

I thought of the Mujahidin. There were more of them than any other group. They were disciplined and had a strict hierarchy. It was their party policy to recant and confess so they could get out and continue their struggles, but though they were made trusties, they remained loyal to their cause. I knew somehow that they were in touch with Mujahidin outside, maybe through Mujahidin trusties, or maybe through their visitors. We all knew as sometimes news was whispered through the prison that could come from no other source.

There were far fewer members of the Tudeh. They puzzled me. In Evin they knitted sweaters for conscripts on the front. This gave help to the Islamic regime, which had imprisoned them, yet they knitted. We saw them as slavish.

Both Tudeh and Mujahidin were highly disciplined; it was we leftists who argued and differed among ourselves. We came from so many different groups, and we lacked solidarity, not only on the chador issue, but on many others.

It was clean-up time on the wing. The weather was cold, and for some reason I had no energy, but despite this I joined in the collective washing of the cells from floor to ceiling. We were all busy when Homa came in.

Everyone stopped working as she read out some names. This time Raz and mine were among them. We were told to gather our belongings. I wondered if wherever we were going we would have family visits. We had a practical reason for worrying. Raz and I had given all our money to Huri and the others when they'd been taken off to be tortured and who knows what else, and now we'd be unable to buy soap or sanitary towels ourselves unless we received money from our family on visiting days.

Parvin had never been a friend, but she came and gave me some money. I was amazed by her kindness, and Raz and I embraced her.

CHAPTER 32
Solitary Confinement
Evin Prison, autumn 1985

W<sup>e were transferred from Ghezel Hesar back to Evin and put in a cell in Wing One, Building 216. We were told we were on lockdown and we would be taken to the toilet just three times a day. If there was time we could shower as well. Food would be given to us to eat in the cell. We were to have no exercise. The cell was very overcrowded – designed for five, when there were thirty of us.

As we were only allowed out to the toilet three times a day, we were careful about what we ate and drank and when. I only drank water just half an hour before I knew the door would be opened. Life was hardest in the mornings; we all awoke thirsty, but as we were not allowed out to the toilet until eleven o'clock, we struggled not to drink. I felt thirsty all the time and my lips were always dry. I rubbed Vaseline on them, but they often bled.

There was a bucket in the room for emergencies; few prisoners used it but it made the life in the cell even more intolerable.

The day after we arrived, the cell door opened unexpectedly, but rather than a guard, we were surprised to see prisoners. It turned out that though we were locked in, the cell door could be unlocked from the outside without a key. The guards had gone off somewhere just after these prisoners had been let out for their toilet time, so they had come to talk to us.

I asked them right away if any of them knew Huri.

'Yes, isn't she one of the women who wouldn't wear a black chador? All of them are in Wing 209, in the basement.'

'How are they?'

'They're not in a good state.'

We heard the guards coming back and just as quickly as our visitors-prisoners had appeared, they vanished. The last prisoner shut the cell door quietly as she left. It was all done so expertly.

When our turn came to use the toilet, the guard told us we had half an hour and could shower as well, then she went back to her office. Raz and I took the opportunity and went and opened one of the other cell doors, just as ours had been. We wanted to get some more information about Huri if we could.

I stood where I'd be able to see the guard if she came back, while Raz opened the cell door and went in to talk to the women. When I saw the guard coming back, I shouted out our agreed code – 'Bring my toothbrush'. Raz rushed out of the cell, closing the door quietly and locking it from the outside, and we went to use the toilet and shower without the guard realising anything.

We talked when we were back in our cell. Raz said the prisoners had told her that just a few days earlier, Haji Halvayee, the prison governor, and some guards had gone to the basement where all the women protesting against wearing the black chador were being held. They were brought into a hall and told to sit on the floor and watch as a guard flogged some of them. They'd responded by turning their backs to the torture. So some guards had started hitting them with cables while others kicked and punched them. The blows had fallen mostly on the women's heads and backs, but soon blood was everywhere, and nine women had their heads split right open. The women who told us had such details as some of them had been there, as they had been refusing to wear the black chador, but now, as they had finally agreed to wear it, they were in a normal cell and were able to talk to us.

'Where's Huri?' I asked.

'She's still with the other "resisters" in the basement,' Raz said.

I wondered again what sufferings Huri would endure before it ended.

The winter of 1985 was unusually cold. One day, at washing and toilet break, I was standing in the queue waiting my turn when a guard ordered us all to go back to our cell; I said I had to go to the toilet as I wouldn't be able to wait for another eight hours. She told us again that we had to go back to the cell, but no one listened to her as they too were desperate to go to the toilet. The guard went away and some of us managed to use the toilet before she came back carrying our chadors and blindfolds. She told us to follow her. As we passed along the corridors, one of the prisoners whispered in my ear, 'If you are being taken to the governor, Haji Halvayee, be prepared he hits prisoners on the back of the neck when they are not expecting it. If you stand up very straight you can keep your balance when he bashes you.'

We were taken to the main guard's office and were told to wait outside in the corridor. We were not allowed to sit down and we stayed standing there for hours; eventually we were ushered into the guard's office one by one. No one could hear what was happening until it was their turn. When I went inside, there was Governor Haji Halvayee. Blindfolded, I was expecting him to strike me on the back of the neck, but instead he slapped me full in the face. It was such an unexpected and strong blow that I just managed to put my hands out on the floor before my nose smashed on the ground. Haji Halvayee told me to stand up and to adjust my blindfold and rearrange my chador properly. My face was on fire, but I struggled to get up. From under my blindfold, I saw his huge and thick right hand, with one of the large opal rings that many Muslim men were wearing as a token of virility, and I could just make out that he was very tall with a big bulky body. Later on I heard he was very proud of his bull-like strength.

Once I was properly upright, Haji Halvayee shouted, 'Get downstairs. And wait – I know what to do with you tonight.'

I left the office, and a male guard told me to follow him down the stairs. We went out into a courtyard and into the open air where it was very, very cold. I was told to stand in the corner and just wait. I was only wearing slippers, and thin clothes under my chador and I felt the cold bitterly. Guards were going to and fro. One of them saw me trying to look from under my blindfold and shouted out at me,

'Don't raise your head. Don't look out from under the blindfold.'

When the guard had gone I still tried to look around, but I couldn't see any other prisoners, and I realised I was alone there. I wondered if Haji Halvayee had meant rape when he said he knew what to do with me tonight.

The time passed very slowly. I felt night coming as the light gradually faded and the cold intensified. I asked one of the passing guards, 'How long am I to stand here?'

'Haji Halvayee decides,' he said, and walked away.

My feet and legs hurt and I wanted to sleep. I wondered what had happened to Raz and the others. Were they standing somewhere in the cold too, or had they been taken back to the cell?

It must have been around midnight when a guard finally came up to me and told me to follow him inside. My feet were numb, and I moved with difficulty. After a long walk we arrived at the 209 solitary wing. He knocked on a door and handed me over to a woman guard. She took me to a cell. Before closing the door, she pointed to a card on the floor and said, 'If you need anything, push the card under the door. I'll see it. You must never bang on the door.'

The solitary cell was two by one-and-a-half metres. It wasn't clean, but there was the luxury of a toilet and a small wash basin, and there was also a small heater on the wall. I sat close to it, unthawing my feet. I was hungry, but even so I felt a little better, and after a while I lay down to sleep, putting one of the two blankets under me and another on top. They were grubby and smelt of torture. Still, I was so exhausted that I fell asleep quickly.

In the morning I was woken by intense pain in my

legs and feet. My toes had become ugly; they were red and swollen, and they were agony to the touch. I was also very hungry.

There was just one window very high up and so dirty that no real light came in. And I had no idea of the time. After a while, I heard the sound of cell doors opening and closing. Finally the door to my cell opened, and a guard asked whether I wanted tea. I said I did and she gave me a thick plastic cup full of tea. The cup had obviously once been red but the colour was mostly faded. There were names engraved on it with a needle, and I wondered how many of them had drunk from this same cup before execution?

As I hadn't eaten anything since noon the day before, I slipped the card under the cell door. After some time a guard opened it. Later, I learnt that her name was Akbari; she was large and tall about forty years old, covered with a chador, but she was wearing high heels and she had put on a lot of rosewater.

'Hello,' she said. I was astonished. It was the first time I'd heard a guard say hello to a prisoner; we never greeted them either. Akbari said hello again. I couldn't stop staring at her in amazement. She said hello for a third time, obviously expecting me to say hello back, but all I said was, 'I didn't have anything to eat last night, and today all you've given me for breakfast is a cup of tea.'

Akbari said nothing but just shut the door and left. I heard her swearing in the corridor about me not saying hello back to her. I got no food until lunchtime.

I didn't have any soap, and I asked another guard if she could give me a bar or if I could buy one. She said that I had to wait till the regular shopping time. But I soon learnt that one of the guards named Yosefi, who was old and exuded an air of poverty, would do anything for a bit of money. So I said to her that I needed soap and she agreed to get me a bar if I could pay. My few essential belongings had been brought to the cell, so I did have money. Yosefi took some toman and later, when there were no other guards around, she handed me the soap.

After my short spell alone in the blood-stained cell at the beginning of my imprisonment, I had always been with others. This was my first time in real solitary, but it was bearable as I was still allowed to see my parents on visitors' days and because I found I could entertain myself with thoughts and imaginings.

I woke up early one morning, but I stayed lying down on my blanket, looking up at the sky through the dirty window, when I heard the sound of a guard opening and shutting the cell doors, distributing cups of tea. I started counting to see if I could work out how many of us were in solitary. Last week, there'd been forty-nine of us. But today, at the ninth door, the routine was interrupted. I heard the guard drop something with a loud clatter. She let out a muffled cry, which sounded like genuine shock. Then I heard another guard running, and the sound of the two guards talking, and I thought I heard one of the guards sobbing. Getting up and pressing my ear to the door, I struggled to hear more. There were now several guards running about. I heard one of them say, 'I checked them all at five. It's now only six. She must have done it in the last hour.'

The other said, 'Don't upset yourself. These things happen. It's not important.'

Clearly a prisoner had hanged herself, probably with her own chador. She was not the first, nor likely to be the last. I wondered how long the woman had been in solitary and how long anyone can bear being alone.

It was well known that solitary could break prisoners who had withstood terrible physical torture, just as physical torture could break some prisoners who could stand solitary. While some prisoners could not tolerate either and broke and confessed immediately, others could withstand both physical torture and solitary. I used to wonder about this. What was it about the psychological strength of a character, their previous education, social class, political beliefs, that made some able to hold out and others not? And what was the role of other people's expectations of them?

In solitary, I thought of my family, my home, my garden, the streets of Tehran, the sounds. As well as longing to talk to some, most of all, I longed to hear music again. I wanted to learn to play an instrument. I wanted to live.

As night fell and even the guards went to sleep, I often heard the sound of tapping. I recognised it as Morse code used by prisoners to communicate. I regretted that I hadn't learnt it, but though I could not understand it, the sound of the tapping breaking the absolute silence made me happy. It proved the regime was not able to impose total isolation; the tapping represented freedom. It was prison music, and I decided that if I was ever back on the wing I would learn the Morse code. I wondered if it had been invented in a prison out of the basic human need to connect with others.

My cell walls had graffiti written by prisoners dating back to the Shah's time. Some prisoners had only written their names and the date they had entered the cell; some had had time to write their date of leaving. Some others gave the date of their expected execution.

One sadly said 'They kill those with brains, and crush those with hearts.' I did not believe that, not completely, as I felt the Islamic regime had still not crushed us all.

After I'd been in solitary for about two months, and the weather was getting warmer, I was woken one morning by two doves cooing in a nest they had built in the wall outside my cell. They must know that their eggs would give them fledglings. I could feel their happiness and it delighted me.

It was coming up to New Year Nowroz on 21 March, and the guard Yosefi came into my cell and asked me if I wanted to buy some biscuits.

'Yes.'

'How many boxes do you want?'

'As many as I can get.'

'There are lots. Some of the prisoners refuse them.'

I knew why; even though we were not given enough to eat, some of the prisoners saw biscuits as a bourgeois luxury.

I said I would buy three boxes: two to eat myself and one for my friends when I went back to the wing. I was sure solitary would not last forever.

CHAPTER 33
Learning Morse Code
Evin Prison, Spring 1986

After three months in solitary, I was taken back to the wing. It was no longer on lockdown. We prisoners were free to walk about in the corridor, and I saw Huri, back from her basement ordeal, and we embraced. Along with our other friends, we gathered round to talk. Huri told us that the Islamic regime had put her and some of the other women opposing the black chador, including Nazli, in solitary confinement and had interrogated them. And under the threat of more torture, she realised that their struggle for the coloured chador was defeated.

To end the battle in a show of defiance, she had announced a three-day hunger strike. For that she had been interrogated. She told us that non-political prisoners, including prostitutes, had been put among the black chador opponents in the 209 basement. This had made some of them capitulate and agree to wear the black chador, but some others had gone on hunger strike in protest. But most of them had given up their hunger strike after about a month and agreed to wear the black chador. Yet there were still ten women holding out on hunger strike in protest, in defiance of the black chador and at being mixed with ordinary non-political prisoners.

I was shocked. I could not see the problem with being placed along with ordinary prisoners; surely we believed in the equality of all human beings.

I argued that instead of starting a hunger strike in protest at being put with the non-politicals, they should have taken the opportunity to politicise them.

Soon after this discussion, one of the remaining ten women hunger strikers was transferred back to the wing wearing a black chador. She'd become dangerously thin, weak and pale, and her body was shaky. The struggle for the right to wear a coloured chador and the hunger strike both collapsed soon after, and all those who had held out came back on the wing wearing the black chador.

Some of them didn't see it as a defeat; rather they believed that their battle had been valiant, but all I could still see was that being tortured for refusing to give information had a real moral and political point, while courting torture over the colour of the chador you still had to wear was political theatre. And not long afterwards many, if not most, of the black chador resisters agreed to recant and confess so they could get out of prison.

It was around this time that I first met Farkhondeh Ashena. We instantly became friends. She'd been in prison since the beginning of 1982, but although she had been 'tried', she had not been sentenced. That meant the regime didn't have anything specific against her. They had still put her in solitary confinement. She knew Morse code and she now taught it to me.

'The Farsi alphabet has thirty-two letters. Morse divides

them into four rows of eight letters each. First there is a particular tap for the row, then for the position of the letter in the row. It's simple – all you have to do really is memorise the row and position of each letter. I'll show you.' She then tapped my name on my hand.

'There has to be a slight pause between the tap for the row and the tap for the letter,' she said. We practised together until we could sit silently in front of each other talking in Morse code. I was so happy to have learnt Morse; if I ever went back in solitary it would make it so much more bearable. Later on I adapted Morse and developed my own personal code which I shared with my close friends.

Farkhondeh had been nineteen years old when she was arrested. She'd already been working in the Merck medicine factory for six years. When she started aged just thirteen, she was still so short that she had to stand on a stool to reach up to operate her machine. It was illegal for anyone under fifteen to work, but there were no factory inspectors to check on anyone's age. As she was underage, she wasn't entitled to insurance, but luckily she didn't have an accident.

While Farkondeh was working there, some Merck managers came over from Germany to visit their Tehran factory. They wanted to take photos for their publicity brochures. Farkhondeh was told she couldn't be in the picture as she was so obviously too young to be working. An adult man was put at Farkhondeh's machine. Yet despite her youth during the 1978 uprising, she was elected a workers' representative.

'Were you active during the revolution?' she asked me.

'I was in England when it broke out. I came back after

the Shah had left and Khomeini was already in power. My revolution started with struggling against the Islamic regime.'

'England?'

'Yes. When I finished high school, I felt I wanted to travel and I went to study English in a place called Cheltenham. My parents weren't too happy, especially my mother, who just wanted me to get married. Anyway, I overrode them and I got to England, and after studying English for a while I got a place at university studying politics. I was due to start in September 1979. I came back for the summer break, and here I am, taking a crash course in real politics instead.'

'What did you think when you came back and realised that getting rid of the Shah was only the beginning of the battle?' Farkhondeh asked me.

'One thing I saw right away was that the media outside Iran was not reporting events truthfully. The BBC was putting it out that the Iranian people had willingly replaced the Crown with the Turban. What I realised afterwards is that when the Western governments realised that the Iranian people were in genuine revolt against the Shah, they set out to manage and contain this real revolution. Dressing up counter-revolution in revolutionary language, the lying Western media started hailing Khomeini as the people's saviour. Suddenly his face was everywhere.'

'Most people did not understand all of this. They could see no further than getting rid of the Shah and did not think about what came next or that tricks would be played on them.' Farkhondeh paused and asked me, 'So you came back to find the mullah sitting in place of the Shah. What did you think?'

'I had hope, though. We all did, didn't we? We

thought if we could kick out the Shah we could kick out Khomeini too, and what struck me most when I came back was how outspoken people, especially women, had become and how irreligious. It is a paradox but just as the Islamic regime was edging itself towards taking total control, people were openly expressing their disbelief in Allah for the first time. People no longer wanted to pray for food and happiness – they wanted a new political and economic system here and now on earth, not later in Paradise. And there was something else that struck me. Before the revolution against the Shah, the value and respect people gave to others depended on how much money they had. But when I came back, this had changed. Value and respect was determined by how much anyone opposed the Islamic regime and how many creative ideas they brought to the struggle against it.'

Farkhondeh agreed. 'Yes, I experienced that, and I wonder if it is still the same or people outside have changed back under the pressure of the regime's propaganda and oppression.'

Farkhondeh told me stories not only about her own political and trades union struggle, but also about the terrible living conditions endured by the working classes in Iran in the 1970s. To me, they sounded every bit as bad as Engels had described the Britain of 1840s in The Condition of the Working Class in England. Farkhondeh spoke of untreated sewage and dangerous pollution from factories running into the stream, which ran right through the centre of her district, ShadAbad in Tehran. In some cases this polluted stream lapped the front doors of the enclosed courtyards where the children played and they would get ill from the noxious gases.

'Our homes were surrounded by factories, each giving us a different problem. The match-making factory spread the smell of gunpowder. The paint-making factory gave out the smell of chemicals. The Persi gas factory was especially dangerous. Lorries carrying twenty-kilo gas bottles were going in and out of it all day. Before 1975, when it was asphalted, it was just a dirt track, and the dust affected visibility so badly that sometimes children were hit by lorries when crossing the road. When the road was asphalted, we were also given running water, but still the living conditions and the noxious smells in the atmosphere made daily life unbearable. The Shah's regime valued us working people less than donkeys, and the Islamic regime is no better.'

There were places in Iran even worse. Near where I lived in East Tehran there was a shanty town, Khak Sefid, which housed people from the country who had come to Tehran to work. The people made their own shelters out of anything they could lay their hands on: corrugated bits of roofing, oil cans, cardboard boxes. There was no running water or sanitation; the people cooked with camping equipment. Every so often the police came and destroyed the shanties, but as the people had nowhere else to go, they rebuilt them. Yet people wanted material changes, better living conditions, decent wages, health care; importantly, they didn't rise in favour of an Islamic state.

Farkhondeh and I talked often about all kinds of things. Once, in a quieter moment, she recited a poem to me. It had been written by one of her friends in honour of a mutual friend, Fahimeh Taghadosi, who was executed. Farkhondeh had memorised it in solitary.

Dear Fahimeh

That day,
that hot day in July,
when the Evin loudspeakers
called out your beautiful name and your lips
smiled, your eyes said to your friends,
'So today is the day.'
You went and your walk
was a perfume filling the corridor.
Everyone gasped, everyone asked with their eyes,
'Is today then the day?' The guard
flung back an answer: 'Where is her bag?
Where is her veil, her socks, her money?'
A rumour went round that you'd given a sign
that yes, today was the day:
'I don't need my food,' you had said.
So tonight is the night.
A silence hangs in the heart of it.
Friends look at friends and tell themselves
that perhaps you'll come back.
Fahimeh dear, tell us, spare
a word for your friends. Is
the sky sad where you are, does it weep?
And the wind, does it ruffle your veil?
Back here, the wing sweats for your news.
And a message gets through:
wind-blown breathless dandelion
comes from the mountains to say that clouds
are massing up there and they're big with child.
Head held high, you are standing and waiting for this,

for the clouds to open, for you
to be mother of change.
Rifles crack.
The moorland holds its breath
at a star shooting across it.
It would be good to sing and go with friends
to face the firing squad, to dance,
to float in the rain.
In the long sea-silence,
a wave lifts, oars clip at the water.
A young fisherman bringing his boat to land,
rice-growers trudging home,
they shape their lips to your name.
Your name is beautiful for young girls born in July.

One day, the loudspeaker told everyone in the wing to get ready for a transfer. It was bitter news. We all feared we'd lose our friends again. Friendship is everything in prison.

We were all in 216 corridor with our belongings waiting when a guard came and read out some names. Mine was among them and so was Roozhin's. The guard told us both to go and wait in another section of the corridor. The guard then led Raz, Farkhondeh and my other friends away somewhere else.

We only had time for a quick embrace and farewell.

Roozhin and I knew each other but were not close friends. She'd taken part in the great fight to wear a coloured chador, seeing it as central to the struggle, but after coming back from the horrors of Basement 209, wearing a black chador, she had become close to Raz. Now, as we were separated from our other friends, we gravitated to each other.

We waited in the corridor with some other women prisoners who were to come with us. Eventually some guards came and told us to go to Wing Four. A few of us refused as we knew Wing Four was for broken prisoners and trusties.

The guard left us alone for a while. We imagined that we would be flogged and then put into solitary. After a while, some other guards came and grabbed us by our hands. They tried to pull us, but we dropped down to the floor and they had to drag us towards Wing Four. The guard Hamidi had selected me. She was short and fat, but strong; I made it as difficult as I could for her. The corridor was very long, and Hamadi was sweating and breathless at the end and so angry she was apoplectic, her chador and headscarf all akimbo. I looked at her and couldn't stop myself; I began to laugh. Infuriated, she pushed me through the door and into Wing Four. When she finally caught her breath, still panting, she cursed me as an 'infidel', while another guard slammed the door shut.

We'd all been dragged to Wing Four in the same way. And now, locked up, we realised all our belongings were still outside in the main corridor. It wasn't immediately important, as in any transfer we always put our toothbrushes and other real essentials in our pockets.

In the morning, as we were eating breakfast, a guard read out a list of names through the loudspeaker. Some of us, including Roozhin and myself, were to be moved again. We managed to retrieve our belongings from the corridor and after a while we were herded outside and ordered to get on a waiting coach. We were not told where we were going.

CHAPTER 34
Hunger Strike
Gohardasht Prison, 1987

We were taken to a huge prison in a vast naked landscape outside Gohardasht, a town in the northern outskirts of Karaj, approximately twenty kilometres west of Tehran. The prison was built in a shape of a centipede. I knew that all the wings were connected to a main, long corridor, and that the prison was mostly made up of solitary cells.

We were all interrogated briefly on arrival, not by special interrogators, but by the male guards. They were better educated than most of the guards we had come across before, with many of them knowing surprising details about our different political groups. We were all asked about our political affiliation and whether we still believed in Marxism and what we thought about the Islamic regime. I refused to answer. This was my established policy whenever I was interrogated.

The guards were much larger, and they all seemed to have huge, thick hands that looked as if they could kill you with one blow. After our brief interrogations, we were taken to Wing Eight; I'd imagined we were going to be put in solitary and was surprised to find out we were going to share cells and that we were not going to be put on lockdown. Altogether, we were ten leftists, some eighty Mujahidin and a few members of the Tudeh party. Roozhin and I found we were sharing a cell with Shahnaz, a woman who had been connected to my party. She was Kurdish and struggle seemed to be in her blood. Three of us in a cell designed for one was difficult, but it was much easier than being on lockdown in the bigger cells at Evin.

A couple of hours after our arrival, a guard said we could use the yard. We were delighted. Our cell windows were covered with a metal grill, and there was no air in the cells or corridor. It was early summer 1987 and already very hot, and we longed for the fresh air. Once in the yard, we could sense some men prisoners watching us. We couldn't see them at all. We just felt their eyes on us, even though their windows were also covered by metal grilles. Suddenly, we saw fingers coming through one of the grilles. They were moving in a pattern and we realised we were seeing, rather than hearing, Morse.

'Hi,' the fingers said. 'Welcome to Gohardasht. Where did you just come from?'

Pretending to speak to each other, Roozhin slowly tapped a reply in Morse on my shoulder; she told the unseen man with the fingers that we had come from Evin.

A few days after we'd arrived, some female guards entered the wing aggressively, telling us to get out of our cells; when we did as asked, they shut all the cell doors and locked them. Our belongings were still inside and we asked them what was going on. They ignored us at first and then one of them said, 'We told you to write your names on the doors of your cells. You didn't do it, and the governor has ordered us to lock all the cell doors as a punishment.'

We were amazed; none of the guards had asked us to write our names anywhere and so we had never refused. We said this, adding that we had no objections and would write them down now.

'Too late,' they said.

'Why? You never told us. Who did you speak to?' We all asked this at once.

'We told the prisoners in the first cell.'

'They didn't tell us.'

'They should have told you,' the guards said.

'Maybe they should have, but you are the guards so it is your job to tell us things.'

The guards ignored us. 'The governor has ordered us to lock every cell door without names written on them and that is what we are doing.'

After locking all the cell doors, ours and Mujahidin and Tudeh's, they left. The Cell One prisoners were Mujahidin, and we all realised that although they had been told directly to write their names on the door, they hadn't done so.

We didn't think the oddity of this through immediately; we were too busy being infuriated by our own powerlessness. We had no idea when the cell doors would be opened again. We didn't have our things, and for all we knew we would all be left to sleep in the corridor without even a blanket to cover us.

Some argued that we had to demonstrate our anger and that we should go on unlimited hunger strike. Roozhin and Shahnaz asked me what I thought. I couldn't see how it would help and I just said, 'It would weaken us but place no pressure on the regime. They know we are angry!'

I was in a minority and even though I thought any hunger strike was pointless, I compromised with the majority and suggested a limited three-day hunger strike. I was surprised when everyone agreed as my views weren't generally taken on board.

We now banged on the door to the wing. A guard came, and once we surrounded her, I said, 'We are going on a three-day hunger strike in protest against the living conditions you have imposed on us – they are inhuman and arbitrary. We leftists have no problem writing our names on the doors.'

'Look,' the guard said, 'I told the women in the first cell, and they should have told you.'

'It was not their duty to tell us, it was yours.'

'I'll pass your message on to the prison governor.'

We began our three-day hunger strike, and then we realised that the Mujahidin, who were also locked out of their cells, had gone on an unlimited hunger strike until all our cell doors were opened. This reinforced our realisation that they had manufactured this confrontation, but we were still baffled as to why they should change their long-established policy of co-operation, even submission, to one of confrontation.

Two days into our three-day hunger strike, I developed severe stomach pains and blood started coming from me when I went to the toilet. The third day of our hunger strike was visitors' day, and we planned to tell our families to go and talk to the prison governor and get him to open our cells. But our family visits were cancelled. We knew this would make them worried, as this was the first visitors' day after our transfer and the prison had a very bad reputation. My family had to travel a long distance even to get to Gohardasht, and now they would have to go back without seeing me. I felt sorry for them.

We finished our hunger strike, the Mujahidin remained on their unlimited strike, but we all remained locked out of our cells. We had been given a few scanty blankets to sleep on, but we had no soap, toothpaste or toothbrush, no sanitary towels or clean clothes. We didn't have a comb for our hair, no books or anything else to read, and nowhere could we talk to each other without being overheard. It was miserable and it could have gone on for weeks, months or even years. None of us knew.

Then one day, a mullah came to inspect the wing. He did not speak to any of us, but half an hour after he had gone, the guards came and opened our cell doors, telling us to take our things and get ready for another transfer.

The Mujahidin and Tudeh were told to get their things too as they were coming with us.

We were taken across the main entrance corridor into something; except for the metal grille on the windows, it was like an ordinary flat. It had three rooms with a shower and toilet which we could use at any time. As there were only a few of them, the Tudeh party prisoners took the smallest room, we leftists took the medium-sized room, and as the Mujahidin were the biggest group, they took the biggest room.

I went to the barred window and managed to see that quite close on the left, there was a row of solitary cells. Again, we had no idea if they were being shared or whether their inmates were really being kept in solitary confinement, but I decided to take a chance and whistled 'The Internationale' to see if there were any leftist prisoner.

A man soon came to his cell window and hung out his shirt. He had written a message on it, telling us that he'd spent two years in solitary. He started talking to us, desperately. It didn't take us long to realise that he had lost his mind.

CHAPTER 35
Psychological Torture
Gohardasht Prison, 1986

Apart from opening the door to deliver our food and take the rubbish away, the guards came in occasionally for an inspection but otherwise left us alone. It took a while to adjust to this unexpected freedom. We were also allowed books from the library, and some of them were actually interesting; we could ask for Bertolt Brecht and Pavlov. With so much sudden and unexpected access to books, we decided we should make copies of them; if we were transferred back to Evin we could take them back with us and share them with our friends. So the moment we received a new book, we started copying it. We often stayed awake until midnight making copies in longhand.

The food was also much better than in Evin – and we were no longer always hungry. The store had more items in it too, and we could order some quite useful things. On the negative side we had no hot water so we had to take cold showers, but we could take them not exactly whenever we wanted, as there were so many of us, but more or less at will. It was hot and there was no air conditioning and the metal grille behind the window made the atmosphere so close that I used to take a cold shower as often as three times a day. We also had the great luxury of permanent access to the toilets.

Furthermore, we also had the freedom to change our rooms, but only one prisoner wanted to. Sarah, who had initially gone to the big Mujahidin room, came and joined us. She'd been arrested with the Mujahidin in 1981, but she'd since rejected god and religion and she now defined herself as a socialist. We welcomed her. She was young, only about twenty years old, she seemed so self-confident, beautiful and mentally very strong. We became friends very quickly as we talked about the Mujahidin and why she had rejected them in favour of socialism.

Although our living conditions were so much better, I suddenly developed severe pains in my legs and I could only walk with difficulty. I asked the guards if I could see a doctor. It took a few days, but I was taken to the prison clinic. The doctor examined me and said there was nothing wrong with my legs and feet. I laughed at him, which made him angry. When I came and talked to my cellmates, they said my leg pains must be due to the cold shower. So I learnt to clean my body a few times a day with just a wet cloth, and after a while the severe pain lessened and became bearable.

The big male guards sometimes appeared to take us to the yard for exercise. The first time they did this, I noticed the door to a small windowless room was open. Sarah whispered to me that it was called the sauna and was used for punishment. For the moment, I thought no more about it.

To get to the yard we had to pass along the main prison corridor, and occasionally our file of women prisoners going to the yard passed a male prisoner being taken somewhere by a guard. We would have loved to talk to them, but we were hurried along and all any of us could manage was a slight smile.

After about a month in the flat, we began to hear odd and disturbing sounds. We could make out that guards were bringing male prisoners and putting them into the sauna just outside our flat. Worse than that, the guards were putting so many men in the sauna at one time that the prisoners were so pressed up against each other that they cried out for air. The guards only closed the door with difficulty and once it was closed, the prisoners banged on the door, screaming that there was no ventilation and they needed air. We could hear the guards outside taunting them.

Just by listening we worked out that the men were kept in the sauna to the point of suffocation and collapse; then the door would be opened, sometimes for just a few seconds, to let in some air, and sometimes the prisoners would be let out, only to be replaced by a new group of prisoners.

This went on for a few days. It was mental torture to listen to it, but we had no choice, and over time we pieced together from the various shouts of the prisoners that the Mujahidin had started to exercise as a group. Any obvious collective activity was forbidden and so they were being punished for exercising as a group, rather than as individuals.

Once we understood this, the very next time we were taken to the yard, the women Mujahidin started to exercise collectively. This really surprised us, because most of them claimed to be penitents and some were even trusties. Yet just as they had been confrontational about 'writing our names on the cell door', they now sought to confront the Islamic regime on the 'collective exercise' issue. We leftists reasoned that they must somehow have received orders from their hierarchy outside.

The Mujahidin women did 'collective exercise' for the second time when we were allowed in the yard as well. But the next time we were taken to the yard again, a female guard told us to keep our chadors on. This indicated that a man was coming to inspect. A tall and massive man soon arrived. Sarah whispered in my ear that he was Lashkari, the governor. I had not seen him before, but I had heard a lot about him. Among his other brutalities he was a rapist. He looked at the Mujahidin women one by one and finally, he said, his voice icy, that any woman continuing to do 'collective exercise' would be beaten to death. After Lashkari left, the Mujahidin talked to each other and all agreed to stop their collective exercise.

Soon after this, men prisoners began to be brought in the corridor for interrogation just outside our flat, and if we put our ears to the door we could hear the questions: date of birth, date of arrest, etc. I listened and was horrified to learn that some of the prisoners were just boys as young as seventeen and yet they had been in prison for up to four years. These young prisoners were kept together in one wing, separate from the older prisoners.

Then one evening we heard the unmistakeable sound of flogging and men screaming in the corridor outside our room. The noise was horrific; bones cracked, arms and legs must surely have been broken, or feet and shoulders. After a few minutes of this extreme flogging, the men's screams became weaker. Then there were loud screams again as different prisoners began to be flogged and punched. Many men were flogged, creating a cacophony of horror I had never heard before. Not in all the five years I had been a prisoner of the Islamic regime had I heard such violence.

Eventually the guards stopped and left. We could still hear the muffled cries and groans of the tortured men who had just been left as they lay in the corridor. From the gap high above the door, we were able to use a mirror to look upon them in the corridor. About fifty or so men were lying on the floor, which was drenched in blood – as were the walls too. Some of the men moved, but others were immobile.

The day after and for every day for two whole weeks, the same floggings of different men took place in the corridor just outside our door. It was hell and it seemed eternal. For the men it was physical torture but for us women it was psychological. We were shattered by it. The horror went in so deep into our psyche. I felt my heart had been torn out.

One morning in the middle of this flogging terror, one of the male guards who used to take us to the yard came to collect us with his right hand bandaged. It turned out that as well as flogging the men, the guards had also kicked and punched them. It was poetic justice, but in punching the prisoners, this guard had hurt himself.

This particular day, the guard took us intentionally to a different yard, next to the clinic, where some of the flogged prisoners were receiving medical attention. Using Morse, we contacted one heavily bandaged man lying on the bed nearest us by the window. He told us that he was Mujahidin and that despite all the torture they had endured, despite some men actually losing eyes, they were all still demanding the right to group exercise. This man himself had lost one eye, yet he finger-Morsed us that he would not give in. Others clearly despaired as we learnt later that some of the tortured prisoners had committed suicide. It was one defeat too many.

After this epic torture had ended, all the wings went quiet. We still were taken to a yard for exercise where we were able to see the male prisoners in the yard opposite. Not the Mujahidin who had been tortured, but leftists. One of them stood watch to warn if a guard came, and they came as near to us as they could. We looked at them and smiled, and they looked at us, smiling. One of them started using Morse, but he was so excited that he used his whole hand instead of just his fingers, so we could not understand what he wanted to say. We all laughed at the absurdity of it and the men all started laughing too. Strangely, out of so much horror, it was a sudden moment of happiness.

CHAPTER 36
Cockroach Cell
Evin Prison, 1987

We were taken out of the flat soon after the torture of the men had stopped and transferred from Gohardasht back to Evin. On reflection, it was as if we had been deliberately taken to Gohardasht just so we could witness the men's torture. We had been the audience that every theatrical production needs, and we had suffered too in our minds.

By now it was autumn 1987; I was twenty-eight and I had been a prisoner for five years.

Back in Wing 209, once again we were divided into groups of three. Roozhin and I were placed in a cell with a Mujahidin. The cell was very small, one metre and half by two metres, and with all our belongings we could hardly find a space to lie down and sleep. The cell was just above the kitchens and very hot and full of cockroaches. We killed all the ones we could catch, but every morning, when we woke up, there were still masses of them in our blankets and our clothes.

After a month in the cockroach cell, we were told to get ready for a transfer again. Roozhin and I hoped we would be taken to our friends' wing, but we were transferred to a different wing in a newly built part of the prison which had had four hundred extra cells.

Our cell was built for one person, yet three of us had to squeeze ourselves and our belongings into it. I usually hated transfers, but this time I welcomed it as there were no cockroaches. The cell even had a window, and though it was high up, we could climb up on the heating pipe and see a bit of the sky. Of course we had to be careful not to be caught looking out of the window or we would be accused of trying to contact prisoners in other cells and taken for interrogation.

While arranging my things, I heard the sound of water running. I could have climbed up on the heating pipe to find out from where it was coming; instead, I imagined it was a mountain waterfall and that I could squeeze myself out of the barred window and stand under it. I used this fantasy to wash all the images of torture from my head and clean my soul. It seemed as if the running water was the first beautiful music I had heard in prison. It made my mind run wild.

The thoughts of a mountain waterfall took me back to my childhood to my grandparent's house in Mahalat, where a small stream ran through the courtyard. It passed through every house in the town. People kept their melons and watermelons by it, securing them with a few stones to keep them cool. These memories took away any urge to climb up to see out of the cell window. I didn't want to discover that the beautiful sound of running water really came from something mundane, like a broken pipe.

The day after I had first met Sorkh at my party stall, I had arranged to go hill-walking in the foothills of the

Darakeh with a large group of comrades. Sorkh joined us and attached himself to me. As we walked higher and higher, we chatted about everything and nothing. Every so often we all sang 'The Internationale' and other revolutionary songs. Our voices echoed round the hills, coming back to us more powerfully.

We sat and picnicked. Some came with delicious food they had cooked at home the day before. Some just with bread, cheese, or dates and some with nothing at all because they had no money, but we all shared everything between each other. While we ate we talked about politics and the new fair and just society we wanted to create. These were wonderful days, and finding Sorkh made them even more wonderful.

One day our walk took us on a path we did not know and we all had to jump from a height which was too much for me. Sorkh jumped down before me and put the palms of his hands at the same level as my feet. He told me to step onto them, so I placed my feet in his palms, and he brought me down gently till my feet touched the ground. And I felt he loved me.

Soon after this, the Islamic regime made it impossible for men and women who were not related or married to each other to go to the Darakeh or anywhere else. There was no way Sorkh and I could meet in a coffee shop, so we'd meet at a bus stop and take a double-decker bus from the city centre to Tajrish. We felt it was safe for us to talk upstairs on the bus, because there was a mirror on the stairs and if any Islamic guards got on we could separate just in time. We would talk about ourselves but mostly we talked politics, always with an eye on the mirror. When the bus reached the Tajrish roundabout near the Darakeh foothills, we took the bus back to the city centre, sitting upstairs and talking again as long as we could.

I wished we could have had a meal in a restaurant and drunk forbidden wine together, but as the Islamic regime tightened its grip, we had no such liberty. If an unmarried woman and man were seen together, they would be arrested.

I wanted to be with Sorkh, but I was terrified of marriage, which I saw as a trap. Once married, no woman could escape it. Yet we couldn't even be seen out together for fear of the Islamic guards and living together without marrying was impossible.

Now in prison, I wondered where Sorkh was and what he was doing. I hoped he would not get arrested and would live a long and happy life.

Taking one particular route up the Darakeh, we went past waterfalls, finally reaching a fresh mountain spring where we drank water as cold as ice. Our bodies were hot from the climb, and a chill passed through our skins as we drank. Another route up took us to a small plateau with cherry trees, and in May the scent and the pinkish colour of the cherry blossom filled the sky.

Once in 1980, as we were walking up the mountain, singing as always, we accidentally took an unfamiliar turn. We were suddenly confronted by some armed guards aiming their machine guns straight at us. They must have heard us coming. They told us to stop or they would shoot. It felt so unreal that we weren't frightened as we listened to one of them shout out that we had come too close to Evin Prison and must turn back. Without any question we turned round and went back the way we had come, singing our revolutionary songs again. It now seems so odd that I had no idea that I would soon be a prisoner in Evin myself.

Eventually I stopped thinking of the past and I climbed up to the window to see where the sound of the water was coming from. It was just an open tap.

In our little three-person cell, we were not given newspapers and we had no access to TV. The Mujahidin woman spent her time Morsing to her friends or sleeping, while Roozhin and I spent our time copying the books we'd brought with us from Gohardasht. On visitors' day, we planned to take the copies and try to give them to our friends. I put one section of the Brecht inside my socks and Roozhin hid another section in hers; when we met up with our friends on the way to see our visitors, without saying a word and in the blink of an eye, we handed the copies over to them. If the guards had seen us, we'd have been tortured, but the risk seemed worth it.

Our routine of copying books was only broken when, after family visits, we had Morse code conversations giving or receiving news with other prisoners. As it was forbidden, we developed a way of alerting each other to the sudden appearance of a guard. We poured some water under the cell door, as somehow the position of the light reflected any human movement coming down the corridor. Warned, we would stop Morsing, and though the guards knew some of us were Morsing they never identified who exactly it was.

After three months in our small three-person cell, a guard came and told us to gather our things as yet again we were being transferred. Roozhin and I were happy, believing that we were going to be put back with our friends. We'd now been away from them for nine months, and we missed them. Instead, the guards took us to Room Five, in Wing One, in a new building where we hadn't been before and locked the door. We were on lockdown again.

The transfer always made me very tired, and it would take a few days till I could recover and come back to my routine, while it didn't affect other prisoners as such. This time I felt the dizziness was stronger and I could not concentrate as my head was heavy and I had a kind of pain shoot through my forehead. When I got tired it was as if my forehead was the seashore and rough waves were beating onto a spot between my eyebrows. When I felt this disorientated I could not fight it, I just had to sit separate and alone, letting my mind submerge itself in this peculiar dreamlike state over which I had no control.

When I felt like this I could not sleep well, and I woke in the morning tired, sometimes with my whole body aching. My brain would feel unclear, as if I had drunk a few glasses of wine, or I felt my brain was inside clouds. Somehow I didn't mind, yet at these times, there was a kind of invisible distance between me and reality. I would become very sensitive and sad for no apparent reason. I didn't talk about these feelings to anyone as I didn't understand them myself.

The new building to which we were transferred was called the Sanatorium. We mocked the name, saying it seemed that the Islamic regime had put us in a 'mental hospital' as it saw our continuing refusal to recant and confess as a kind of mental illness.

Roozhin and I were not placed alone. The room was the size of a normal bedroom, and as well as us, there was

Sarah and two other leftists and thirty-five Mujahidin. We leftists had one corner; the rest of the room belonged to the Mujahidin.

There was a three-storey bunk bed in the cell. One of the bunks was used for storing our dishes. The cell had a window, covered with a metal grille. There were shelves in front of it but they didn't completely cover the window, and if we climbed up we could look at the prisoners in the yard. We were not allowed out there initially, and the yard was mostly used by the prisoners in Wing Two. They were all penitents, hoping their recantations and confessions would ensure their release once their sentences were over. They walked in the yard like the dead: each of them alone, their heads bowed. They rarely spoke to each other. And never laughed.

The day after our arrival, I heard some tapping on the wall. I listened and realised it was in the special code I had created with Farkhondeh. I was delighted to be in the next cell to her. We arranged where we'd leave letters for each other in the toilet when it was our turn to go.

I found out from Farkhondeh that she had been placed in a cell with the prisoners who had served their official sentences, yet they had not been released because they still refused to recant and confess. There were two other cells full of women who had completed their sentences but had not been released for the same reason. They were all kept away from us as we were still serving our sentences.

The Islamic regime had changed the procedures for recantation and confession. When I was first arrested these had been made publicly on TV or in front of other prisoners, but now recantations and confessions had to be in writing.

To-be-released prisoners who completed their sentences had to sign a declaration saying that they approved of the regime, condemned their past actions and would not be politically active in the future. Some women refused even though they knew it meant they might spend the rest of their lives in prison.

Huri, Nazli and Raz were all in Wing Three. They were allowed in the yard for a couple of hours most days, so when the guard wasn't watching, we would send each other messages by our special Morse code; sometimes they were able to come to our window and we managed to exchange letters. One of the letters contained a warning that there were elements in the wing very hostile to my particular grouping and a criticism of our politics was being circulated. Farkhondeh asked me how I wanted to respond. I said I didn't. 'Just ignore it'. A few days after that, Roozhin handed me part of something Zahra had written in response to our critics. It was not in code but in Farsi, so anyone who found it, a guard or Mujahidin, could understand it. I thought Zahra was risking torture for no good reason as her friends already agreed with what she was saying and her political opponents never would.

At toilet time, most women rushed out, but some of the Mujahidin stayed behind and would go to the toilet later. We leftists began to realise that the Mujahidin rifled through our things when we were out of the cell. We were angry, of course, but we also wondered what they hoped to gain from spying on us. We challenged them, but nothing was resolved.

One afternoon soon after this, when most of the other prisoners in the cell were asleep and I was writing a letter,

Roozhin was sending and receiving Morse messages from the next room. She suddenly stopped and told me her friend had just told her Zahra wanted to talk to me. I put my ear to the wall. Zahra did not know my special code so I had to use standard Morse, which most others could also understand.

Zahra tapped, 'Some elements are circulating wrong information about us. We have to defend our views.'

I tapped back, 'I know, but I don't see what we have to gain by writing a defence. Everyone here has already made up their mind about politics. We will not convert anyone – the guards could easily find our article and we could be tortured for it.'

Zahra replied passionately, 'You don't understand. Things are changing outside. Workers are striking. People are openly speaking out against the Islamic regime. Now is the time to defend party policy.'

I replied, 'How can we defend party policy? We have been here so long, we don't know what it is any more. All we can do is discuss our own views with each other, but we shouldn't write things openly. Anything we write in Farsi, rather than code, could get into the hands of the guards. What's the point?'

'If you're not willing, I'll do it on my own,' she said.

'You need to be careful.'

'Have you read my piece?' Zahra asked.

'I read the part I received,' I said.

'What do you think?'

I said, 'I can't exchange views using standard Morse. If we were in the same room, we could discuss things, but we can't like this, not properly.'

She tapped, 'I'm writing something new. Read it and tell me if you support or oppose it.'

I was now worried for Zahra. Out of nowhere she'd suddenly decided to represent the party in prison, overtly and alone.

A week later, I had a letter from Farkhondeh saying that Zahra had had an altercation with the guards about washroom time and had been taken to solitary. I was unhappy for her, but she'd been in solitary many times before, for long periods, and I thought she could endure it.

One morning, I was reading a book when I heard voices coming up from the yard. I felt certain I could hear Farkhondeh laughing, I climbed up the shelf to look out through the metal grille. I saw Farkhondeh and others from Cell Six talking and laughing. They looked up and I stuck my hand out, between the grilles and waved. They waved back. Although Farkhondeh and I Morsed, I'd not seen her or the others for about a year, but they seemed as alive and unbroken as ever.

I climbed down, thinking that now Room Six was being given yard time, then my cell would soon be as well, and that Raz and I could set up a system of leaving each other letters in a safe place in the yard.

Quickly, I wrote Raz a letter in our own code, suggesting we should bury our letters under the laleh abbasi bush in the small yard garden. I loved the laleh abbasi, the flowers opened in the evenings and closed at dawn like a fist, as if it was the night flower and wanted to fight the day. There were other flowers in the prison garden but I liked the laleh abbasi best of all because they reminded me of my home, where we had many laleh abbasi bushes. The laleh abbasi flower is able to adapt and survive in any situation. Not all flowers are like them; most die when displaced, but the laleh abbasi is resilient and strong. Laleh means tulip and this flower is often depicted on Iranian ceramics, carpets and old copies of the covers of the Koran.

Listening to the prisoners' laughter in the yard, I continued to write in code, explaining my idea to Raz. I'd tie my letter with red string, and she'd tie hers with yellow, and by pulling the string we could retrieve our letters from where we had buried them. Whenever I had a letter for her I'd hang my blue shirt out of the window, and when she had a letter for me she'd should hang her green skirt on the clothesline outdoors. When I'd finished writing these detailed instructions, I hid my letter inside a bar of soap, using spit to make the hole disappear. I placed the soap in a soap container, which I took out in the yard and hung up in the outdoor washroom. I didn't think the soap would raise any suspicions. In any case, if the guards or a person found my letter, he or she wouldn't be able to understand any of it.

The door opened, and just as I had suspected, a guard said we could now use the yard for half an hour. I passed by her with my soap container and walked over to the washroom, where I hung it up. Then I started wandering around in the yard with Roozhin and looking into the windows of Wing Three. Some of our friends were at the windows, calling things out to make us laugh. Roozhin and I were standing in a corner in such a way as to give the impression we were talking to each other, but using our special form of Morse I signalled to Raz that I'd left her something in the soap container, and she answered that she understood.

CHAPTER 37
Suicide
Evin Prison, 1988

It was almost our time to go to the toilets and we were all waiting for the cell door to be opened. I'd drunk my tea half an hour ago. The usual time passed, yet the guard hadn't opened the door. I started banging on it. The guard on duty, completely covered by her black chador, turned out to be Imani. That wasn't good. She had a real special hatred for us prisoners; it was as if we were all her personal enemies.

She asked me what I wanted.

'It's past our time to go to the toilet,' I said and walked out into the corridor.

'I know. Go back inside. I'll tell you when you can go to the toilet.'

I didn't go back and several other prisoners were now outside in the corridor with me. We refused to go back in, insisting it was our turn for the washroom. Imani grabbed my right wrist and twisted it. She was strong and she easily pushed me back into the cell. She did the same with the others, and then slammed the cell door shut.

I tried desperately to focus on something apart from needing to use the toilet, but it was impossible, and now my wrist hurt as well.

It was three hours before the door opened again. I bolted to the toilet but I couldn't hold it any longer and wet myself before I got there. I called to Roozhin to bring me some clean clothes. I didn't feel humiliated, and when Roozhin brought me my clean clothes, we both laughed as if it was funny.

After a quick shower, I went back to the toilet cubicle where Farkhondeh left her letters for me. There was a new letter, but it was too tightly wedged and I couldn't pull it out. I went to fetch a hidden pair of pliers that some workmen-prisoners had deliberately left for us when they were doing some small repair. I was careful to make sure no one saw me. Even with the pliers it was difficult to get the letter out and my wrist was painful because of how Imani had been twisting it that morning; somehow I lost control of the pliers and my hand hit the wall hard. I cried out with the sudden agony of it. Luckily the ventilator was making so much noise that no one could have heard me.

Instead of going away, the pain in my wrist grew steadily worse over the next few days. Simple actions like writing and washing dishes became intolerable. Roozhin and Sarah had to do some of my cleaning and tidying-up duties for me. I thought my wrist might be broken and wanted to see a doctor, but there was no chance of that so at my next family visit, I just asked my parents to bring me an elastic splint.

One night, when my wrist was still hurting and I couldn't sleep, somebody in Wing Three started banging, calling out to the guards, shouting, 'A prisoner here needs to get to the clinic. She's dying.'

My heart tightened as I wondered who she was and what had happened.

Soon I heard sounds of the guards running to and fro in the corridor. There was nothing I could do. I closed my eyes and just hoped I could sleep and dream of freedom, but I couldn't.

The next morning, Roozhin and I climbed up the shelf and looked over at the Wing Three prisoners who were out in the yard. They were all wandering about dejected. We sent a message in Morse; a message came back telling us that Parvin had tried to kill herself with some hair removal liquid.

Later we heard from a prisoner who'd been in the clinic that she had heard Parvin moaning in agony, saying she was on fire inside, yet she was refusing all treatment because she no longer wanted to live. Parvin died in the clinic on the third day. She was in her thirties.

For a while, I could think of nothing else but Parvin and her suicide. I wondered why, when she felt so much despair, she had not just given in and recanted and confessed, as so many defeated and broken prisoners had done, just so she could get out of prison. But I remembered Parvin's executed brothers and sisters and how her father was so consumed with rage that he pressurised her into joining the doomed coloured chador struggle, and I realised that not only her friends but perhaps Parvin's own family would have boycotted her if she had recanted and confessed, and that would have been unendurable too. Yet surely killing herself meant that she had no hope that her political views would ever triumph. She must have believed the regime had won or how could she have despaired so much to kill herself?

255

Some prisoners kill themselves to avoid revealing information under torture, which is a brave and courageous act, but suicide just to escape is always an act of despair and defeat. I also thought of the agonising manner of Parvin's suicide. It would have been easy for her to quietly slash her wrists at night when the other prisoners were sleeping and just bleed to death without anyone realising it. Others had killed themselves like that, and yet Parvin had drunk an acidic poison and died after three days of torment. It was as if she was punishing herself for committing suicide.

It was now coming to the end of the year and the beginning of a new one, and I longed to be transferred to Wing Three to be with my friends and have the simple comfort of going to the toilet when I wanted and regular access to the yard instead of only once a week, which was all we were allowed at the moment. My legs actually ached because I was not able to walk about.

As a child, the New Year on 21 March was always the best of times. It was spring and two weeks of school holidays and we had endless family gatherings with presents and special food, but in prison, New Year's Day was always the worst of times, as I remembered everyone I loved and how I missed them all so very much.

Suddenly, out of nowhere, the Mujahidin in our room started refusing to take delivery of our meals from the trusties. They would only take it from a guard. The trusties were Mujahidin and it was difficult to see what point they were making. When the trusties delivered the food and the Mujahidin refused it, we would take ours

but not theirs, but we would all take it from a guard. This
shadow play went on for some time in the background.
It turned out that they did have a point, but we did not
discover what it was until later.

I'd been closed up in lockdown for more than five
months when one afternoon, as most of the other prisoners
were sleeping and I was reading a book, I heard Morse being
tapped on the wall. I recognised the code I'd developed with
Farkhondeh. I put my ear to the wall. Farkhondeh told me,
'The guards just brought Zahra out of solitary for a couple
of hours to show her to us so that we would be upset.
They've now taken her back to solitary.'

'Why upset? What's happened to her?'

'She's skin and bone. She looked like she had been on
hunger strike, but she hadn't been. Zahra told us that she
couldn't eat because they had chained her hands and feet
and to eat she had to put her face down to the plate like a
dog. And that is not the worst of it. She was hallucinating.
She was telling us "the people have risen. Can't you hear
their voices? The people are coming. They're marching
towards Evin to free us. They're shouting slogans: Death
to the regime. Long live the revolution. Political prisoners
must be freed!"'

This news about Zahra horrified me. To be chained and
forced to eat like a dog must surely break even the strongest
soul. And Zahra had been so strong and optimistic,
circulating her political ideas on the small scraps of paper,
and she had been punished for it with a vengeance by being
dehumanised.

Some other prisoners who'd been in solitary but were
now back in the wing said they'd heard the guards beating

her, and they had heard her screaming and cursing back at the guards. I thought of her hallucinations. Wasn't it every political prisoner's dream to hear the people rising up to free them? Just possibly her hallucinations gave her hope and courage.

CHAPTER 38
A New Era
Evin Prison, 1988

Not long after the terrible news about Zahra, I was Morsed again by Farkhondeh: 'Nasserian is inspecting the cells one by one. He's transferring some prisoners. If you are moved to the upper wing, what hiding place shall we use for our letters?'

I tapped back and told her where I thought we could hide them.

'OK. I'll miss you, if they move you.'

'I'll miss you too.'

I quickly hid everything I did not want Nasserian or the guards to find. It was in time too as just a few minutes later, a female guard opened the door and told us to put on our chadors. After a few moments, Nasserian appeared in the door. A man of middling height, he wielded horrific powers. He was the prison prosecutor in charge of sentencing prisoners to torture. He told us leftists to gather our things as we were going to Wing Three. Although Sarah was now a leftist, she had been arrested as a Mujahidin so she had to stay. We did not know then that this was her death sentence.

We embraced. 'Without you, I'll be alone with the Mujahidin, it will be awful.'

'Farkhondeh will be a good friend to you. Morse her,' I told her.

Although I was sad to leave Sarah, I was so happy to be going to my friends in Wing Three. In prison it seemed you can never gain someone without losing someone else.

Huri, Nazli, Raz and Sonia were there in Wing Three. Roozhin and I were to share cell 102 with them. Although we had Morsed them, they now asked us for more details about our time in Gohardasht. Then they told us of their time in Wing 325 in Evin.

Raz said, 'It wasn't like a prison. It was like a beautiful little house. The regime only put us there for a few months because they were moving prisoners about. Now they have put the monarchists there. And did you know that Building 216 now only holds men?'

We talked about everything and Nazli told us, 'Huri's received a really pretty blouse from her husband in Europe, but she won't wear it.'

I asked to see it and Huri fetched it. It was very pretty, a beautiful midnight blue with a sheen to it. I asked Huri why she wouldn't wear it.

'It's evening not prison wear. It shines too much.'

'Wear it, or I will.'

Huri laughed and said, 'You can wear it, if you like.'

I tried it on. Huri was right; it was evening wear. I hadn't worn anything like it for years, and I remembered my time in England and how, wearing something very like it, I'd often gone out with my friends and danced the night away.

Wing Three had a very long corridor. After months of being in a locked cell, it was wonderful just to walk up and down it, and we were allowed in the yard as well.

There was a crack in the iron grille on the cell window and we could even see a section of north Tehran with people passing by, heading for walks in the mountains. Of course they didn't see us, and to us they appeared really small, but I loved watching them. They were freedom.

There was a TV at one end of the corridor, and during the evening at news time, we gathered and watched it. Usually it was heavily censored, but even we could feel that the long war with Iraq might be ending. We were able to meet together and have regular discussions, and I found myself becoming calmer; yet it was the lull before the storm.

On the way going down to the yard I saw a slogan – 'Eternal Light' – carved into the wooden banister. Later we learnt it was the codename for a military operation the Mujahidin started in late July 1988. Some Mujahidin must have carved it proudly and defiantly, unaware, as we all were, of the new horrors to come.

There was a young woman in Room 102, Mahin, who had been arrested with her husband in early 1982. I'd known her by sight but not to talk to; she always seemed to be alone. Before her arrest, Mahin had worked in Pars Electric factory. On arrest, when she was tortured she gave some information that had resulted in the arrest and torture of someone else. It was a terrible betrayal and, feeling guilty, Mahin had begun defending Marxism, hoping that the regime would execute her. Instead, she'd been given a life sentence and they had also sent her to the Graves. I'd first seen her in 1984 in Wing Seven at Ghezel Hesar prison, when they had just let her out. Mahin had not recanted or confessed, but she was traumatised. She just didn't talk to people; it was as if she could not break the habit of silence and solitude she had been forced into.

Sometimes I'd observe Mahin's face. She often seemed not to be fully present. At these times she looked transfixed as she stared straight ahead at the wall. At other times, she'd walk about in the yard on her own for hours or she'd sit on the middle bunk, where the space was similar to the Graves. She would face the wall, never speaking.

Mahin's husband had been released from prison as he had recanted and confessed. He visited Mahin, but his visits did not make her any happier. The only thing that brought a smile to Mahin's face was the sight of Jahan.

Jahan had also been in the Graves. A medical student before her arrest in 1982, she walked with her head held high and was obviously unbroken by what she had endured. Mahin would look at her with a strange longing as if she wanted to catch Jahan's spirit of unbroken-ness.

Early in July 1988, the TV news reported that the USS Vincennes patrolling in the Persian Gulf had shot down an Iranian passenger jet, killing all 290 passengers on board. There were film clips showing Iranian ships and helicopters searching for survivors but none had been found. Bodies were shown floating amid the wreckage. President Reagan came on to defend the downing of the plane, claiming it had taken 'proper defensive action', and the event was an 'understandable accident'. My mind went to the families of the dead, but I also thought angrily of the government of the USA, which felt it had the right to have its navy policing the Persian Gulf. What, after all, is the difference between the random executions in Iranian prisons and America's random 'executions' in the air?

Soon after this, the news showed clips of heavily armed Iranian Mujahidin based in Iraq heading towards the Iranian towns just over the Iraq-Iran border. The Mujahidin were watching with us. They did not seem surprised, but the rest of us were shocked. It seemed suicidal, as we could not see how they could beat the forces of the Islamic regime. Nor did we want them to, because the Mujahidin had only a slightly different ideology to the Islamic regime.

Every evening we now rushed to watch the news, and we were avidly following the Mujahidin advance into Iran when some male guards came and removed the television. We were told we were no longer allowed newspapers. After that, visitors' day was cancelled. We felt marooned and threatened.

The Mujahidin prisoners took all this as signs that the Islamic regime was losing against the invading Mujahidin army, and they found it difficult to hide their jubilation. They clearly expected that they would soon be freed by their victorious invading organisation, but we leftists did not believe the Mujahidin army would be victorious. Their victory would not have changed our situation anyway as the Mujahidin detested us for being infidels, just as much as the Islamic regime did. Instead, we felt dread.

After a few days that seemed like years, the Mujahidin began to be called for interrogation. A few of them went each day, until one of them returned, weeping. I heard her say, 'They're killing the men. Just after interrogation, they are all being executed and they are going to kill all of us.'

The woman was hurried away by a guard. She did not return, but her words hung in the air.

CHAPTER 39
Massacre
Evin Prison, Summer 1988

Lucky those who were executed first
they witnessed only their own deaths.
Those who were killed later
died over and over
alongside the comrades
as well as bearing their own deaths.

The next Friday, public prayers at Tehran University was broadcast on the prison loudspeakers. Rafsanjani, chairman of the Iranian parliament, was addressing the Faithful, declaring that prisoners who did not respect Imam Khomeini were all infidels, hypocrites and anti-revolutionaries and that they must all die; and that all prisoners who had not recanted and were not willing to confess were now to be executed. He said all prisoners would be given one last chance to reunite with the Faithful, who worship god and respect Khomeini.

The crowd screamed out in an agreement. 'Allah o Akbar.'

I looked at Raz, lost for words. After a long silence, she whispered, 'Will they really kill every one of us?' An immense sense of loneliness had taken over my whole being. It was clear from Rafsanjani's words that we were all to be slaughtered.

News somehow came that most of the male Mujahidin prisoners were being executed in batches. We leftists believed it, but women Mujahidin could not. They said desperately again and again that this could not be true and that the Mujahidin army were near to victory. They were sure their brother and sister Mujahidin were advancing on Tehran and that they would all soon be liberated.

But terror was in the air. It had no colour; it had a smell.

After the Islamic regime had killed most of the male Mujahidin prisoners, they did not call the women Mujahidin for interrogation and execution; instead, the regime turned on the male leftists. We heard that 'courts' were in session daily and the 'judges' of the 'Death Commission' were: Mustafa Pour-Mohammadi, Ayatollah Eshraqi, Hojatt al-Islam Nayeri and Hojjat al-Islam Mobasheri. It was said that the leftists (who in Iran were all atheists) were being told that their lives would be spared if they became Muslims. Those who refused outright were forced to pass a gauntlet of guards with truncheons. After this brutal horror, they were told they must accept Islam or face execution. Many just went to their death. To escape execution, others said they accepted Islam, but they still had to recant and confess. That was not all; they now had to agree to be taken to the United Nations office in Tehran to display their support for the Islamic regime.

The torture and executions of the leftist men took days and nights, and when we could sleep, we were often woken in the deep of night by the sound of shouting and the pounding of boots; 'Death to the Marxists' … 'Death to the socialists' … 'Death to Mujahidin' … 'Death to Imperialism' … 'Death to communism' … 'Death to America' … 'Death to Israel' … 'Death to Russia' … 'The only party is Hezbollah, the only leader is Khomeini.'

I used to wonder, as I lay with my blanket on the floor of the cell, if the shouting meant the guards were coming back from slaughtering prisoners and were going home to their wives and families. And whether after their day's work, they would have friends round and talk about anything apart from how they earned their living.

And I thought again of how I had heard Lajevardi state at public recantations and confessions, 'We shan't allow you to leave this place alive. We shan't make the same mistake the Shah made. He released prisoners, and once outside they organised themselves into an opposition. We won't let that happen to the Islamic regime. We'll kill all of you.'

Now it seemed Lajevardi's threat was coming true and that after everything we had endured, our only freedom would be death.

Despite what we knew was going on, the women Mujahidin in our wing began preparing themselves for solitary – not for execution. They cut their hair, as it was difficult to wash long hair in solitary. Then, one day, a guard came and took about fifty Mujahidin for interrogation, all of them young women. We hadn't shared their optimism about going to solitary rather than the gallows, and we doubted they would return. Nevertheless, strangely I found it hard to believe they'd really be executed. However we soon learnt that after enduring five, sometimes six years in prison, the fifty young Mujahidin women had all been executed. What a terrible fate, I thought, for us all to have been born at this time in this part of the world.

After this mass execution of female Mujahidin, fear was like lead in the air. Some prisoners began to sleep all day. This was a form of depression, as if something inside them wanted to protect them from a reality they had no power to change. We prisoners who managed to stay awake were not much better. We had no mental energy. Few of us even wanted to read. Some of us talked and told stories, but none of us could live normally, even by our own peculiar prison standards. We became death-like shadows of ourselves as we waited for death.

The prisoners who were already traumatised got into a worst state. We had to form a relay team to stop them committing suicide. Mahin deteriorated even more. She talked to herself and didn't eat. One day, after showering, she put on a pretty dress her husband had brought her, but somehow she couldn't bear to keep it on and she took it off after only a few minutes. Once, she tried to slit the veins in her wrist with a piece of glass; she was seen and stopped. Doctor Maryam, who was a prisoner with us, bandaged up Mahin's lacerated flesh.

Friendly and kind and always willing to give prisoners medical help, Doctor Maryam was in her late twenties. Her husband had previously spent four years in the Shah's prison and he was in prison again under the Islamic regime. None of us knew yet that he had already been executed in the massacre. They had a little daughter who was outside living with family.

One young Mujahidin girl on the wing, Rafat, was also in a very poor mental state. Her brother had been one of the prisoners tortured in the sauna and then flogged half to death at Gohardasht Prison. We all knew he had committed suicide after the defeat of the Mujahidin bid for 'collective exercise'.

Rafat now had so little control over herself that sometimes in the yard or corridor she exposed her breasts and walked about talking to herself. One day, a guard took her to Wing Two; she had no one to look after her there and we soon heard that she had killed herself.

Farkhondeh was still in Wing One in lockdown. Once, during her weekly exercise, she managed to get a letter to me. She'd written, 'They have taken all the Mujahidin women from Wing One. They also took Sarah, though the regime knows she didn't support the Mujahidin any more. None of the Mujahidin women believed they were going to be executed, but Sarah did. She was sure. I know for certain that they were all killed because I overheard the guards talking about it. Hamidi said that the smell of blood was making her sick and that she didn't want to do it any more. She was scared the spirits of the executed would haunt her. She was crying about having to throw the dead prisoners in the truck. The other guard with her told her not to be such a baby, that the mass executions would end soon and she mustn't make Haji angry by showing herself to be weak.'

Farkhondeh went on, 'We are all preparing for interrogation. Some I am sure will agree to recant and confess, but I believe most of us will refuse and we will all be killed. Love. Soon it will be over!'

After reading Farkhondeh's letter I went to the yard to get away from its suffocating news. I thought of the young Mujahidin women who'd shared our wing until just a few days ago. Now they were all dead. I didn't want to believe that Sarah had been executed – no, I couldn't believe it. Then a picture of the young, short, chubby guard Hamidi came to my mind; maybe she had taken Sarah's legs while another guard held onto her arms and they'd slung Sarah's still-warm body into a truck, which would be filled with young dead bodies and taken to a mass grave somewhere.

I began to think of my father, how he'd always said I must get out of prison and flee Iran. For him, my being in prison always carried the risk of getting killed. I'd laughed at him, but now? All these years I imagined I would one day see the autumn leaves again as I had seen them before my arrest. In my mind, I walked through the streets of Tehran on them, and I heard their crushing, crackling sound. I turned the seasons over in my imagination. I saw winter and pictured myself playing with the snow. I even felt the cold. I imagined going to a café again to have a coffee with a friend, climbing Darakeh up by the waterfalls. Looking at the new stems and shoots and leaves before the spring flowers come out at New Year. I tried hard to imagine the scent of the jasmine, just outside my room at home. Such reveries usually helped me to escape from prison, but now the reality was so harsh that even my imagination could not help me.

Still I walked in the yard and looked at the sky. How was the sky in England now? I wondered. And why had we been born in a country where the very words freedom and justice were tortured and killed. Our hopes had been so simple and so fair and now we faced so brutal a death. Soon it would be as if we had never been born.

A couple of days later, a guard came and told us to put

our chadors and blindfolds and come with her. We asked each other, 'Is it our turn?' No one had an answer. We were taken to another building, where some of the prison governors and senior officials were standing waiting for us. They asked all of us the same questions they'd asked the male leftist prisoners. Some of the leftist women, who thought they would be executed anyway for not being Muslim, now defended Marxism.

I decided to keep to my old policy of just saying, 'I won't answer'. It turned out not to matter. Instead of executing or torturing us for saying the wrong thing, they just sent us back to the wing, still blindfolded, still wearing our chadors. This cat and mouse unpredictability was more of the psychological torture.

Although this time our interrogation had not ended as we had imagined, we all still felt that sooner or later we would be executed too. No matter how much each of us tried to hide our fear of the firing squad, or of the noose tightening around our necks, we felt an ever-increasing sense of dread.

In the letters Farkhondeh and I wrote to each other, we affirmed we would not accept the Islamic regime's conditions for a reprieve. We would not recant or confess. We had demanded freedom of thought, and we had decided long ago that we were willing to die for it.

Oddly, in 1982, when I was sentenced to death, my senses had been frozen by the shock of my arrest and the brutal initial torture, and I would not have been sorry to die, but now, after six years of prison life, I realised I didn't want to die at all.

CHAPTER 40
The Call to Torture
Evin Prison, Summer 1988

Two months passed in this limbo. We were eating breakfast when the loudspeaker came on and a guard read out ten names, most of them members of the Tudeh Party. They were called for interrogation. We stopped eating breakfast as we watched the women make themselves ready. We knew that any of us could be called at any time, but today it was their turn.

We found out later that the Tudeh women were not executed but taken to solitary, and like the leftist women who were already there, they were all brought out of their solitary cells and lashed five times a day on their backs at prayer times.

Incredibly, when the women were 'unclean' from menstruating, they were exempt from flogging for a whole week: a gift from the all-merciful Allah.

Apart from this break, the women were told that the floggings would continue forever, or until they declared they were Muslim and agreed to pray. The women would also have to write a letter of recantation and confession, but in exchange, they were promised release from prison.

Now when we heard the sounds of Azan broadcast on

the loudspeaker, we thought of our fellow prisoners being brought out of their cells to be lashed. The call to prayer was the call to torture. It made the atmosphere on our wing even bleaker and more hopeless; it was the same in Farkhondeh's lockdown cell. This feeling of depression was in every cell on the wing, as we all felt we would soon be called to face the same flogging ordeal. Some prisoners said they hoped they'd be executed instead as death was much easier than being flogged slowly to death.

Around this time, I tried to read again. It was difficult to concentrate, and I became aware that Mahin was swearing and muttering angrily under her breath at two women sitting close to her; they were too deep in their own conversation and did not notice, but I was amazed by Mahin's behaviour. She had always been so quiet and kind to others. What she said made no sense.

I knew she had stopped eating as she was so terrified of the threat of torture hanging over her, as it was hanging over all of us, and I wondered if the lack of food, mixed with fear, was making her hallucinate.

I now often saw her sitting in a corner alone, hunched up, deep in thought for hours on end. She was clearly terrified, and I thought perhaps she was imagining herself being flogged again. After her initial arrest she had betrayed her friend under torture, yet afterwards she had survived the Graves, one of the worst tortures in any prison, but now it seemed that just the fear of being flogged again was breaking her spirit.

Soon once again we heard the voice of a guard on the loudspeaker calling out names of the women who had to go for interrogation. Silence took hold of the entire wing.

Another ten names were on the list again, most of them Tudeh Party or women close to them politically. This time, we already knew what fate awaited them.

Mahin was deteriorating even further and she had found some pliers and wanted to pull her teeth out with them. She said, 'My teeth are talking to me. If I pull them out, they'll no longer talk to me.' Some of us tried to get the pliers out of her hands, but she refused to let them go, and there was a struggle before they could be taken from her and hidden.

How strange the mind works and how little we know about our own brains. We now began to worry that Mahin would try to kill herself. Every time she went to the toilet she banged her head on the wall so hard that we could hear it above the normal prison noises. We started following her, telling her that if we heard her we would burst in and stop her.

Mahin now glared at us all as if we were her deadliest enemies. In a way she now had two different kinds of guard: the official prison guards who did not care if she lived or died, and us, her unofficial guards, who didn't want her to lose her life, no matter how hard it was for her to live it.

In the febrile atmosphere of daily expectation to be called for interrogation, the days seemed much longer, and a week felt like a year. For the third time, a guard called out the names of ten more women who had been selected for interrogation and torture. This time we didn't even ask each other any questions. The spectre of endless floggings had overwhelmed us.

We knew that male guards had taken over the floggings because the female guards weren't strong enough. I knew many of these female guards and none of them were physically weak, not even Taleghani, who was in her fifties and very old in our young eyes. Taleghani was particularly brutal and really hated us, and I heard she took real pleasure in lashing prisoners. She was one of those really devout Muslims who genuinely wanted to send all infidels to the abyss of fire, torture and death.

I'd always believed that women were different from men, that they were less violent and didn't do inhumane things. I'd thought the world was stamped with inequality, oppression, war and killings because men ruled it, and that Thatcher was an exception, but from what I saw of the female guards, like Taleghani in prison, I had come to realise that women can be equally as violent as men. And that it didn't matter whether men or women were in power; what mattered was the system and ideology and the ethics that governed them. It was self-evident that religious mania breeds cruelty, just like capitalism.

Somehow we heard that two of the women in solitary who had been unable to bear the floggings any longer had attempted suicide. One of them succeeded; the woman who failed was flogged as usual.

Some of the women, also unable to endure the floggings, had recanted, confessed and become Muslims and were now praying.

At around nine o'clock one evening, I was walking in the corridor, just thinking my thoughts, when I heard a cry for help resounding through the wing. It was Sonia's voice. She had been on duty watching Mahin and now she was shouting out that Mahin had slashed her wrists.

Women ran to the showers and tried to bring Mahin

out. She resisted fiercely yet said nothing. Her wrist was bleeding badly, but Doctor Maryam managed to tie it up and staunch the flow of blood a little. I watched her as she bandaged Mahin, and I was suddenly struck by Mahin's beauty and her childlike innocent face, so angry with us that we were interfering. She wanted to die and we were stopping her. When Dr Maryam had finished wrapping up Mahin's wrist, she said that it needed stitches and that Mahin must go to the clinic.

We all knew that if Mahin were to be taken to the clinic, there would be no one to keep watch over her and she'd succeed in killing herself. But what could we do? If we kept Mahin on the wing she'd soon die from loss of blood. We asked the guard to take her to the clinic. Mahin didn't want to go, but the guard took her just the same. As she went, I could see there was already no life in her eyes. I knew it was the last time I'd see her.

A few days later, we heard Mahin had killed herself in the clinic. She was about twenty-seven years old.

CHAPTER 41
The End of the Iran-Iraq War
Evin Prison, Autumn 1988

Khavaran
the mass grave
of the executed
is in south Tehran.
The young bodies lie there
hardly covered by earth
their eyes are wide open
their dead mouths frozen in defiant shouts.

After a third group of women prisoners were taken to solitary and were being flogged every day at Azan, we heard that the floggings had stopped. As the regime had taken away our television and newspapers and we hadn't had visitors since the massacres, we heard even less of the outside world than usual, but we felt something new must be happening. Out of nowhere, we were told we could write a letter to our families and invite them to come and see us the following week. This changed the whole mood of the wing.

Before breakfast one day, I was coming back inside from the yard when I saw a cyclamen in a pot just inside.

It was such a beautiful unexpected sight I felt drawn to it. I had a really strange impulse; I wanted to kiss it. It was the loveliest thing I'd seen for months, or even years. I touched it, feeling it with my fingers to convince myself it was real. Years ago, when I'd been in England at Christmas, I'd seen masses of cyclamens, but I'd never been so stunned by their beauty – the deep redness, so close to black, was lovely beyond what I could remember.

My mind went into reverie; unexpectedly, the cyclamen reminded me of a women's rights demonstration when all of us had been running from the Islamic guards and their hired thugs. Brandishing batons and sticks, all of them were shouting insults as they chased us. I saw again in my mind's eye the women in front of me, running with their long uncovered hair streaming behind them. I was deep in this memory when Raz came to get me.

'Where has this cyclamen come from?' I asked.

'One of the families came yesterday to visit their daughter and gave it to her. She put it here so that everyone could see it.'

Walking with Soraya in the yard, she told me her parents might bring her son, Arash, on their next visit. He was now ten years old.

'I'm not sure he'll come – he doesn't like coming back into a prison. He has so many terrible memories of his own. In the early years, you remember what it was like. When I first realised visiting made him unhappy, I told my parents to only tell him they were planning a visit on the actual day. If he wanted to come, they could bring him, but if he didn't, I told them not to force him. Sometimes I didn't see him for months, but it was better than him being upset at seeing me here and reminding him of everything he had suffered too. Still, I long to see him.'

The prospect of seeing my parents for the first time since the massacres worried me. I thought of other families who'd come expecting to see their sons or daughters only to be told they had been executed. Instead of seeing their children, they would be given their belongings. When I was called at visitors' time, I went into one of the booths and waited with my heart in my mouth. I heard the guards opening the doors and I saw husbands, mothers and fathers, brothers and sisters, running, looking desperately into the booths.

This scene was very different from other visits. Today there was panic in everyone's face. My family rushed so quickly that they nearly passed me by, then they saw me and stopped and looked straight at me, startled. I saw my father's face was wet with tears.

'We knew what was happening. The only thing we could do was ask whether or not you were still alive. We only found out you were a few days before we got your letter. We couldn't believe it.'

I told them that all the Mujahidin in our wing had been executed, but before I could say any more the phone was disconnected. A guard came to my booth and said, 'Only talk about yourself.'

The phone was reconnected and we talked more carefully. My mother asked me whether I was getting enough to eat and whether I was sleeping. My father stood behind her trying to silently tell me something. He obviously hoped I could lip read, which I usually could, but he was so agitated and excited that this time I couldn't.

My mother said, 'The guards are selling flowers outside.'

'Selling flowers?' I was amazed. The same guards who had just carried out mass executions, the same guards who flogged us, were now selling flowers.

'Cyclamens mostly,' my mother went on. 'I was going to buy one for you, but then some of the families said that after the massacres, it was like some kind of insult. So we decided to ask you if you wanted some.'

'No, I don't want any.'

We weren't allowed to talk long before phones were disconnected and the guards told us to leave the hall. But for once, no one took any notice. We all just stood in the booths, looking at our families. They didn't move either. We had no idea if the massacres would begin again, and we gazed at each other wondering if we'd ever see each other again. Eventually the guards came over and pushed the visitors towards the doors. As my parents walked away, they kept on turning back to blow kisses and look at me. It was as if they didn't want to lose their very last moments of seeing me.

Our poor families had stumbled into a tragedy.

From our visits we all learnt that the eight-year Iran-Iraq war was finished. UN Resolution 598, agreed on 20 August 1988, had established a ceasefire. Millions were dead and disabled. The war had destroyed many towns and displaced millions of people. As we thought of the suffering, we also wondered what the peace meant for us, if anything.

After that first visitors' day, many women learnt their husbands, lovers, brothers or cousins had been executed. Doctor Maryam learnt that after being imprisoned for six years, her husband had been killed. It was heart-rending.

Nazli also came and told us that her brother Mohammad had been executed.

'My sister told me. She went to collect his things, but she hasn't been able to tell our mother. She doesn't think she could bear it, not yet. My mother was hopeful that Mohammad had survived the massacre. She kept on saying that when they execute anybody, they give the family their children's belongings, but as they hadn't given her Mohammad's things she thought he must be alive.'

I was one of the very few who hadn't lost anyone I loved. Yet I also felt the heavy sorrow of bereavement. So many dead.

The atmosphere in the wing was filled with death. Yet not many tears were shed. Even a sea of tears could not drown that massacre.

Some older women who had all been arrested for belonging to the Baha'i religion came to give their condolences to Nazli and to the others in our room who'd also lost someone in the massacres.

Although Nazli didn't cry about her brother, she began to talk about him.

'Mohammad was born in 1948. He was a socialist and was arrested first during the Shah's time in 1971. The guards shot him in the foot, shattering it. Then he was sentenced to life imprisonment. He was released when the revolution began in 1978. He was rearrested for being a socialist in August 1982. His foot had never got completely better and he was flogged on his injured foot. He never received a sentence, and we thought he would be executed at any time. Now, after six years in prison, he was executed for being an atheist.'

Nazli read out one of her brother's letters, which he had written just a few months earlier in March 1988. In a concession to the New Year, a guard had been allowed to bring it to Nazli. Knowing it would be read by the prison authorities first, Mohammad avoided all open mention of politics and instead he had talked poetically, almost in riddles, but we understood his code. He had not despaired, and despite his own bitter experiences, he also had sweet memories and loved life and he still thought humanity would make a better world.

Slowly, other bits of information filtered down to us, and we heard that all the murdered Mujahidin prisoners had been buried in the cemetery at Beheshte Zahra, near Tehran, but because the socialists were all atheists, they had all been thrown into a mass grave at Khavaran. The soil had not completely covered them. Then we heard that some of the mothers of the murdered had gone to Khavaran to search for the bodies of their sons. They found them badly buried with legs and arms sticking out. They started to dig them up to give them a dignified burial. The Islamic guards attacked the mothers, dragging them away before bringing in more soil to cover the bodies properly. Every Friday, the families took flowers to Khavaran and, sitting together by the mass grave, they talked about their children to each other, wondering about how they'd died and what sufferings they had endured before they were shot.

The Islamic regime has created many mass graves, but Khavaran was specifically for atheists; its very name, like the others, symbolises resistance. Men and women are buried there together, including Parvin, who had killed herself the year before. Ironically, all the different socialist groupings, who had all been so divided in life, were now lying beside each other for eternity.

After the massacres had ended and things began to return to what passes as normality in prison, as well the reinstatement of visitors' days, we were also given our TV and newspapers back. When it was time for the news, we all gathered in the corridor and sat in front of the TV just as we'd done before. There were reports covering the period of the massacres, and we learnt details about the 'Eternal Light' offensive launched by the Mujahidin from their bases in Iraq. I now understood the meaning of the carved words I had first seen on the banister. The Mujahedin prisoners must have received instruction about the coming offensive. It had given them false confidence of their release; instead, it had sealed their fate.

TV footage showed the Mujahidin army crossing the border into Iran, marching obliviously straight into the waiting Iranian troops. The Mujahidin were utterly routed, and piles of men and women Mujahidin were shown lying dead on the Western border of Iran.

Another day soon afterwards, the news showed prisoners being bussed to the United Nations building in central Tehran. We knew they had accepted Islam as a condition of reprieve and that being taken to demonstrate their support for the regime was yet another condition to escape the execution. Inevitably ashamed, they were very obviously trying to hide their faces, and just as obviously, the guards encircled them and ordered them to show themselves to the camera. There were some women prisoners too, but as they were wearing chadors they were able to hide themselves from the cameras. I thought it was probably the first and only time these women had ever been happy to be in a chador.

Despite the visual evidence, the newscaster announced that although the demonstrators were prisoners, they loved the regime and had come willingly to the UN building to show their solidarity with Ayatollah Khomeini. It was such an incongruous absurdity lie, I wondered if anyone would possibly believe it.

With the wing normalising after the massacres, my friends and I started up our discussions again with some books Farkhondeh and some other prisoners had found in a storeroom in the 209 basement when they had been put there for punishment. They managed to take the books and hide them when the guards were not around. So we had books by Brecht, Pavlov and Hegel. There were Soviet novels too: The Gadfly, by Ethel Lilian Voynich; Twenty Years Hiding in Russia, Memories of a Kadrblshvyk; Felix means Lucky, by Karvlkvf, Yuri Mikhailovich; How the Steel was Tempered, by Nikolai Ostrovsky; and even Engels' Anti-Dühring in English, which only a few people could read.

We even found a copy of the Iranian Communist Party manifesto, which had been formed out of different groups, including mine, in 1983, a year after my arrest. The Islamic guards must have confiscated them when they carried out their house-raids.

Able to hold discussions again, we analysed our different political movements and their relationship with the struggle outside prison and how and why they could be related. We talked about why our struggle in prison was different from the people's struggle outside. We criticised the parties outside that had agreed to enter parliament.

Life went on like this for several months until February 1989, when a guard announced over the loudspeaker that everyone had to get ready for interrogation. The atmosphere in the wing changed to panic in an instant as we asked each other if the torture and killings were starting again.

We were taken to another building and into a large hall where the prison governor, Zamani, flanked by guards, was standing waiting for us. We were told to sit down on the floor, and Zamani began giving a speech:

'Imam Khomeini has issued an order for a prisoner amnesty. No matter how long your sentence or how much of it remains, anyone who recants and confesses now today will be freed immediately. You will not have to serve the rest of your sentence. You can go. The imam has forgiven you.'

This news was an enormous change of policy. Up till now, all prisoners, except trusties, had to complete their full sentences and then recant and confess before they were released, but now, if I had heard correctly, the governor Zamani was saying that prisoners with perhaps many years still to serve would be released right away if they recanted and confessed.

No one even reacted – we had trained our faces to be impassive – yet this news was genuinely interesting. It would not affect me, because I would never recant and confess, not even for immediate release, not even if it meant I would stay here in prison forever, but as I listened to the governor, I decided in my own mind this new policy was only the first of many and that even without recanting and confessing I might yet get out of prison.

I heard Zamani winding up his speech. 'Those of you who are willing to write their recantation and confession stay behind. The rest of you can go back to your wing.'

We all got up from the floor. As I walked towards the door, I looked back to see if anyone had taken up the governor's offer. There was one solitary woman among about a hundred of us who had gone up to the governor; the rest of us left.

I walked back with Raz and told her what I thought – that the killings were over and that the Islamic regime would release us sooner or later without us having to recant or confess.

There was certainly a real change in the air after the governor's amnesty speech, yet though I had new hope, the unpredictable life of the prison continued. At the end of March 1989, Fardeen's name was called. She was in the Tudeh Party, and had been given a death sentence years ago. For some reason, it hadn't been carried out, not even during the massacres of 1988 when many Tudeh men were killed, but now, out of nowhere, the regime just decided to end Fardeen's life. She was forty-one, and they had already executed her husband. I knew she had a daughter, who must have been at least a teenager by then.

CHAPTER 42
Assassination
Evin Prison, 1989

I liked Wing Three, not only because most of my friends were also there, but also because we were able to walk about in the corridor and the yard and go to toilet when we wanted. But again we were told to gather our belongings and go to Wing One, where the prisoners were kept on lockdown. As always, no reason was given. We hated being on lockdown – not being able to go to the toilet when needed was a terrible ordeal and even gruelling punishment, but we were also worried about being separated from each other.

Three of the rooms in Wing One housed prisoners whose sentences had been completed years ago, but as they had not recanted and confessed, they remained in prison. Three rooms were empty. Before the massacres they had been occupied by the Mujahidin, and now they were to be ours.

Raz, Huri and Sonia weren't put in my room, but Nazli, Maryam and I were put together along with about thirty other women, many of them Fedaian. The room was small and there was only one three-tiered bunk bed for all of us.

Whenever we were moved, we had to decide how to

organise our belongings and the rota of cleaning, but this time there was a big disagreement. The Fedaian wanted to use the top bunk as a store for our small personal bags, but I had an idea that would give us storage but leave bunk three free. After a lot of arguing, the Fedaian told me to go ahead with my idea, but they wouldn't help me as they didn't think my plan would work.

Nazli and another two prisoners with manual skills created rope out of old material and made a net which we fixed to the ceiling between the bunks and the wall. We put all our personal bags in it and so left the top bunk to be used on a rota basis as a bed by night and during the day as a little private space where we could get away to write and read.

The rota meant each of us slept on one of the bunks about every two weeks, so usually I slept on a blanket under the small window, where we all knew mice came in. No one else liked the spot because of this, but I did because I could sit leaning against the wall and read or write letters. Once, after finishing a letter to Raz and folding it so small that I could hide it in the hole in the toilet wall brickwork for her to pick up, I saw a small tarantula walking over my blanket. I tried to kill it with my hand because I didn't have anything else – but it bit me. The pain was unbelievable. Without thinking what I was doing, I rubbed the bite vigorously to lessen the pain. It was the wrong thing to do, and the pain became so excruciating I didn't know what to do with myself. Nazli was fast asleep next to me, and Maryam was sleeping next to her. They looked so peaceful. I didn't want to wake them up, and I didn't think they could help me anyway. It was almost the time for the door to be opened so we could go to the toilet when Maryam awoke. I was sitting up, as I had been all night, rubbing my hand. I told her about the tarantula.

Maryam led me out of the room so she could see my hand in a good light. It was red and swollen.

'You should have woken me. I could have sucked the poison out. Why didn't you wake me? You must go to the clinic.'

I showed my hand to the guard on duty, Hasani, who was new in our wing. Young, she was ordinary in looks and weight. But her eyes and manner were very cold. I told her about the tarantula and said that I had to see the doctor. Hasani said fine, but she didn't call me to go to the clinic.

My hand got visibly better after a few days, but I still did not feel well.

One morning I had no interest at all in eating breakfast. I felt sick, and it seemed ages until Hasani opened the door for the first of our three daily visits to the toilet. I literally ran and got to the toilet just in time to vomit. I was horrified to see that I'd brought up a lot of blood. I went to Maryam and told her.

'Tell the guard that you've vomited blood. You must go and see the doctor.'

I told Hasani again. She said 'All right' but again she didn't call me to take me to the clinic.

Despite the blood, I felt better after vomiting, and I went back to the toilet and collected my letters from Raz, which I found in our usual hiding place. The top bunk bed was empty. So I climbed up onto it and started reading. We'd had visits the day before and I knew Raz would have something to tell me; it was not what I'd expected.

'Something terrible has happened in Kurdistan. Sedigh Kamangar has been assassinated by his bodyguard.'

Sedigh Kamangar was a leading communist in Kurdistan. It was his little six-year-old daughter, Golaleh, whom the Islamic regime had held hostage along with one of Kamangar's adult sisters, who I had met almost at the beginning of my imprisonment.

The Islamic regime had held Golaleh and her aunt hostage, as they thought Sedigh Kamangar might exchange himself for them. That ruse had failed and so now another had been tried. The Islamic regime managed to get an undercover agent employed as one of Kamangar's bodyguards. Raz explained how it had been done. Three years before the assassination, the undercover agent infiltrated the party. For three whole years this mole had successfully played the part of a genuine communist and a great Kamangar supporter. No one had suspected him and, being trusted, he was made a bodyguard. He had shot Kamangar when they were alone together.

I wanted to write back to Raz – she would be expecting to find a letter from me in our secret hiding place – but my stomach had begun to hurt and I felt sick again and I suddenly felt incredibly sleepy. I forced myself to keep awake as I wanted to write a few short letters. By the middle of the day, though, I was feeling really sick. I wanted to retch and I felt the need to go to the toilet as well. I knocked on the cell door and Hasani came and opened it just enough so she could see me.

'I need to use the toilet.'

'It's not your turn yet,' she said, and slammed the door shut. I was desperate.

Maryam came up to me. 'Use the bucket in the room,' she said. 'It's there for those who really need it. Don't wait until toilet time. Use the bucket.'

'No, I couldn't bear that. It's humiliating and not fair to the others.'

I don't know how I endured until the door was finally opened, but I managed to get to the toilet in time. Though I felt sick, I didn't throw up, but there was blood in my diarrhoea. I told Hasani that I had to see the doctor, and she said 'OK' yet again and did nothing.

My sickness and bleeding had now been going on for five days, and I still hadn't been called to see a doctor. I couldn't eat anything, and I was sleeping most of the time. When they brought the food into the room, the smell of the camphor the guards always put in the tea to take away our sexual feelings made me vomit. I brought up stomach acid that was bitter like poison; it burnt my throat and mouth and tasted vile.

Hasani had gone off duty, and Maryam told her replacement that I was in a critical condition and needed a doctor. The new guard also said 'OK', but she too did not call me to go to the clinic.

I became worse. The room was warm, but I was on fire. I longed to put ice on my stomach and in my mouth – but of course we had none. Nazli tried to cool me down with a wet cloth, but it was a losing battle. I was weak. I could no longer shower on my own. I could only go to the toilet with the help of my friends, and I was constantly sleeping.

On visitors' day, Nazli told me that I must tell my family that I needed a doctor and medicine.

'They won't listen to my family. They do whatever they wish.'

My family were horrified when they saw me, as I could barely walk into the room holding onto the wall. I told them about the bleeding and that I hadn't been taken to see the doctor. My father became extremely angry and cursed the regime. He said, 'If they want to kill you, why don't they just put you out of your misery with a bullet, like the others? Why do they torture you like this?'

I was sorry to see my family so anguished. They left the booth with tear-filled eyes. I knew my father would run from pillar to post contacting and pleading with as many organisations and people he could find willing to speak to him, all in a desperate attempt to get me taken to hospital.

I felt even hotter, but I slept again. Nazli took care of me; Maryam told her what to do. I now couldn't walk at all without support.

One morning, totally unexpectedly, a guard came and took me to the prison clinic. A doctor came in and asked me some questions and examined me. He ordered some tests and hooked me up to a drip to rehydrate me. The doctor prescribed an injection of painkiller twice a day: morning and night.

The all-male nurses worked in two shifts. The dayshift nurse was hostile to me; he sometimes changed the drip and sometimes did not bother. He clearly didn't want to touch me, and he went to ask a female guard to inject me with the painkiller. Sometimes he claimed he couldn't find one; other times that he had found one but she was busy and unable to come. The night shift nurse was different. He was young, aged just about nineteen. He changed my drip carefully and was happy to inject me with the painkiller. I was surprised by his kindness and I asked him, 'Why are you working in the prison clinic?'

'It's part of my military service. I finish next month. How long have you been in prison?'

'Around seven years.'

His face changed as he asked me sadly, 'Why?'

'Because I wanted food for everyone, not only the rich. I wanted freedom and equality for the people: for women, men and children. Is that wrong?'

He left the room without responding. Somehow this young man woke up my memories of revolution in my mind.

Days passed. I slept almost continuously, still hooked up to the drip. A guard used to come to bring me clean clothes and to take away the soiled ones to be washed by my friends.

One day, no one was in the room, and I needed to go to the toilet. I unhooked myself and managed to get myself there, but I saw blood from my arm was spilling onto the floor and my clothes. I became agitated, holding my arm up to stop the bleeding. I came out of the toilet; the guards were sitting in the corridor. They hooked me up again to the drip. I managed to change my clothes and place them in a plastic bag for the guard to remove. I was worried about how my friends would feel when they washed my clothes and the water ran with blood. They would imagine the worst.

One evening when the day shift nurse had refused to inject my painkiller again and no female guard was found willing to do it, an old man working at the clinic as the receptionist came and said, 'If you want, I can give you the injection.'

I said, 'You?'

'Don't tell anyone I did it. I'm here to answer the phones. Anyway, I wanted to tell you that a few days ago they connected your father to the clinic, and I was able to tell him you're here receiving treatment. The line is monitored so I couldn't tell him that the treatment is a farce and that they've really left you here to die. If you give me your home phone number, I will call your father from outside and tell him.'

I looked at him closely for the first time. He was the same age as my father and he was clearly upset for me. I said, 'It may be difficult to believe, but I have been in prison so long I don't even remember my parents' phone number. I wish I did, but I don't.'

'If you remember later, tell me. From now on, I'll give you the injection during the daytime shift.'

I remember the day clearly. On 3 June 1989, one of the guards came in with her eyes red from weeping. Later a male guard appeared, and I saw he'd been crying, too. That whole day, all the guards, male and female, had red eyes from crying; they were also angry and particularly spiteful, all of them unwilling to inject me with the painkiller, and some of them swore at me.

In the evening, one of the red-eyed guards told me to collect my clothes as I was going back to my room. My friends were surprised to see me, as I was obviously not better, and then they told me why all the guards had been crying. Khomeini was dead and they were all broken-hearted.

CHAPTER 43
Meeting Death
Evin Prison, 1989

I was lying on the bunk bed, still feeling weak and every so often throwing up into a bowl. It was visitors' day. My visitors' slot was usually midday. One by one, everyone else went out to see their families, but I wasn't called.

When Nazli came back from seeing her family, she came up to me and said, 'I told my family to tell yours that the regime has left you here to die. I asked my mother to do something.'

Some of the other prisoners had also told their families I was near death. One of them said, 'The guards told your family you shan't be receiving visitors today. And your family said they won't leave the prison without seeing you or they'll set themselves on fire.'

It was evening when the guard finally called me to see my family. I was taken to the visitors' booths in a chair because I couldn't stand up. When my family saw me, they were filled with horror and disbelief. They asked why I wasn't being treated. I told them it was the regime's policy to kill prisoners one way or another. My parents cried; my sister tried not to. I told them all not to worry; I'd get better. I knew as well as they did that I was lying. But what else could I say or do? My father swore at the regime and said he'd gone back and forth to all the government offices and they'd all promised that I'd be treated.

I shall never forget the look on their faces when they left. A mix of their sorrow at losing me and the pain of their total powerlessness.

Although I couldn't eat, I was still throwing up and I had diarrhoea, but when I knocked on the door in desperation to ask Hasani or any of the other guards on duty to let me out so I could go to the toilet, they'd say, 'It's not your turn yet.'

My condition became ever more critical, and Maryam told the other prisoners not to talk to me as I had to conserve my energy. Whenever a guard opened the door for any reasons, my friends asked her why I wasn't being taken to hospital. She'd shrug and say it wasn't up to her.

I now had severe pain in my stomach as well. I became used to it and could sleep fitfully. Once I heard Nazli talking to Maryam. 'I don't understand. Nasrin doesn't eat anything, but she still vomits and has diarrhoea.' I didn't hear what Maryam said back to her. My mind was blurred and I just couldn't follow their conversation; my mouth was so dry I couldn't speak. I just slept.

For two days, the guards kept opening the door to our room to look at me, but they'd just close the door without speaking and go away. They must have been reporting back to the prison governor. It appeared as if they were all just waiting for me to die.

Once I awoke and saw Nazli sitting by me. She was caressing my hair; it was lovely. Generally we avoided touching each other, as during our first days in prison, women who touched each other had been branded lesbians and were flogged in front of the other prisoners. So we had no habit of hugging each other, or brushing each other's hair. Now, with Nazli gently caressing my head and hair, I foggily thought of the past and the future, but they were meaningless. I knew I was near death. I said, 'I'm so tired.'

'Tired of what?' Nazli asked with surprise.

'Of a lifeless life. I can't do anything. I'm tired of all this sleeping – I wish it would end.'

In all my years in prison I had used my imagination, but now I no longer had the energy to dream. I was unable to move, to talk, even to listen, yet I had a bitter acid taste coming up from my stomach, burning my throat and mouth. It had the smell of death, and I longed to smell something sweet and good: an orange or a hyacinth. I also felt death was coming to bring me the peace that comes after all battles. I wondered why people were so scared of death. I thought of all those who'd died in prison, suffering in pain, and of all those who'd been executed.

Out of nowhere, a guard opened the door and told me to go with her. I couldn't walk unaided and she helped me along the corridor, took me to the office and sat me on a chair. Rahimi, the head of the women's section at the prison, was sitting behind her large desk. She told the guard to leave, and then said, 'I know why you have internal bleeding. The other prisoners put pressure on you because you are different from them.'

She was talking nonsense. Nazli and my other friends all had different political ideas from most of the other prisoners too, but they were not sick. I thought of what to say in reply, and then I said something I knew she would hate.

'I have internal bleeding because of the Ramadan fast, that's when my stomach started bleeding.'

As weak and energy-less as I felt, I still enjoyed looking at her face become angry. She controlled herself and moved on.

'Well, never mind that, you can help yourself now. If you write a letter of recantation and repudiate your socialist group, and confess everything, we'll treat your illness right away. Governor Zamani himself has told me personally that if you do this, he'll send you to a hospital outside the prison tomorrow morning. And after that, you'll be freed.'

I said, 'It's my right to have medical treatment. You kill prisoners either with a bullet or with lack of treatment. How you kill me isn't important – but I shan't recant or confess just to receive treatment.'

'Very well, but go away and think about it.'

'I don't need to.'

The guard returned me to the room, and I told everyone about Rahimi's offer. Later, I heard Nazli telling Maryam, 'You are a doctor, you must tell the guard that Nasrin must be hooked up to a drip or she'll die.'

'It's too late for that.'

Nazli cried.

The following day, Maryam came and sat by me. She didn't directly tell me to accept the regime's offer, but I felt that's what she meant. I told her I'd rather die than recant and confess. She said, 'Then you should know you'll be conscious for another two days at most. You'll then be unconscious for a few days before dying.'

I said nothing and Maryam went off and sat alone. I could see she was crying, though she had no tears and made no sound.

I thought about what she'd said – that I wouldn't be alive in a week, that in just another two days of pain I would be finished as if I never existed; the space I was using in the room would be empty and used by another prisoner. Just two more days and I would know nothing of all this. My heart rebelled, and I managed to turn my head towards Maryam. I could see her distressed face clearly. I tried to ask her to come to me, but at first she didn't move. Again, I tried to ask her to come to me. This time she saw and she came. In a voice that seemed to come out from deep within the earth, I said, 'I don't want to die. Help me to eat and to drink water. I've decided to live.'

She looked at me as if I was insane. She put her hand on my stomach and examined me. She said, 'You can't control life and death by will power, you need treatment, medicine! The moment you drink water you'll throw it up. Your only hope is to go to hospital. You need proper medical treatment.'

Although speaking made me nauseous, I managed to say, 'Let's try it. I won't move at all, I'll just lie here. Perhaps that will help keep water down.'

'All right, I'll spoon water into you so that you don't have to move.'

Maryam dissolved honey into a glass of water. She got Nazli and my other friends to very gently raise my head just a little. Then she poured one tiny teaspoonful of the honeyed water into my mouth. It tasted delicious. My friends lowered my head very gently so that the water in my stomach didn't move; I felt nauseous immediately, yet I stopped myself from throwing up. Using all my powers of will and concentration, I shut my eyes and let my thoughts carry me away from the feeling of wanting to vomit. I focused back on something simple, pleasant and relaxing – the beautiful jasmine that grew in our garden. I tried to remember the smell of it, which used to greet me when I first woke up in the morning. Then I slept.

About once every two hours or so, my friends would raise my head, and Maryam would place a spoonful of honeyed water in my mouth. I'd then concentrate hard on something simple and innocuous, willing myself not to retch and vomit. My mind would wander and I'd fall asleep until the next spoonful was due. The entire room watched intently to see if I could win this battle against death or whether the regime would defeat me.

Three days passed with me sipping honeyed water, and I felt I was coming back to life. I'd only thrown up twice, and Maryam decided to try me with little bits of food.

I ate just a mouthful every hour, with larger sips of honeyed water. I kept it all down, and they told me that Nazli had left a note in the toilet for a friend in the next room saying, 'Nasrin's coming back to life. She needs honey if you have any.'

The next time the door opened for the toilet break, there were several small jars of honey outside the door. The guards knew they were for me, but they had left them there untouched and said nothing.

I began to be awake more, and my friends now talked to me again and read me the newspaper.

Nazanin, one of the prisoners I'd never talked to, came to me and told me that she had put aside her cheese for me. Nazanin was with Fedaian and one of those who had fought for the coloured chador. I told her that I had enough cheese and didn't need any more. She said, 'If you don't eat it, I will think it is because of our political differences.'

I remembered what I had heard about Nazanin – that when prisoners were under lockdown in the basement of Wing 209, a few of them had made a ball with their socks and played with it. Nazanin had told them that their behaviour was not political and that they should not play and laugh. A few days later, the prison warden visited the room and told the prisoners that the sounds of their laughter were heard and that they should not laugh. At this time, Nazanin, who was sitting near where the ball was hidden, kicked it and the ball rolled to the middle of the room. The warden took the ball with him as he left their room. Another time, a few prisoners were tortured in front of other prisoners and one of them, who was younger, moaned as she was flogged. Nazanin had told the poor girl that she was no longer a fighter and that she could not hold her head up with pride because she had shown weakness under torture.

I said to her, 'Then I'll eat it.'

I thanked her. I didn't know the reaction she'd receive from her friends because of what she had done. She was of medium height and had greyish hair, and she was older than most of the other prisoners. She had spent time in prison during the Shah's time. She was bossy and didn't have any relationship with those who were not in her line of politics, and I was surprised that she wanted me to take her cheese. She seemed to believe that socialism meant living in poverty rather than struggling for a better life for everyone. I had a feeling that she enjoyed struggle for the sake of struggle rather than achieving something or improving any situation, but she had done me this kindness.

Less than a week after I began eating, we had visits. I wanted to see my family. They arrived early that day. I slowly left the cell unaided but was still very gaunt and weak. My family looked at me in amazement. They thought I'd been receiving treatment as my father had gone to see all kinds of officials, who had promised him that they would see to it. I told my father I was sorry he'd gone to so much trouble but I hadn't had any treatment and I had been told they'd only take me to hospital if I recanted and confessed – and of course I'd refused. My father said he'd go and see the officials who'd promised to get me to hospital and tell them they were liars; I told him he shouldn't bother. There was no point; I was getting well, and I was fortunate to be with good friends as if I'd been in solitary, I'd certainly have died.

I continued to get stronger, but it was summer and hotter than normal. Soon the weather reached forty-two degrees Celsius, and our small overcrowded cell was like an oven. The ventilator wasn't working and everyone was lethargic. My stomach still burnt, and I felt we would all suffocate on top of each other if we didn't get the ventilator fixed. I didn't know anything about electricity – none of us did – but I took out our hidden screwdriver and tried to take the back off to see if anything was so obviously wrong that I could easily fix it. Maryam came over to me and said, 'You mustn't tire yourself out doing things like this. You must save your energy – you're still very weak. You need to lie down and rest.'

'I have to try, I'm boiling.'

Maryam was right: I didn't have the strength. I just had no energy. I couldn't do it, but then Tahere came up to help. I knew her a little. She had a science degree. Her husband, who had been a prisoner in the Shah's time as well as under the Islamic regime, had been executed in the massacre.

Tahere didn't say anything but took the screwdriver from my hand and removed the screws and the cover. We looked inside the ventilator together. I asked her, 'Do you know how this works?'

'No,' she said.

We disconnected the electricity and began to talk about how the ventilator might work. We played around with it a bit and we had beginner's luck, as when we reconnected the electricity, the ventilator worked. I sat as near as I could to it without blocking it for others.

One day Nazli showed me a beautiful gold ring that one of her friends in another room had made for her out of five-toman coin. It was very pretty, and exactly the right size for her finger. I couldn't believe she had made it by hand; it must have taken her months. Around this time, Raz also sent me a beautiful black pendant necklace she'd carved for me from stone; it was an unusual lopsided triangle shape, and I loved it.

I was still not completely better, and I couldn't stand the taste of many ordinary things. Even water nauseated me. Nazli suggested buying fruit juice from the store to mix with water so that I could drink it. Some of the prisoners, like Nazanin, still viewed such purchases as bourgeois, but we ignored them. Their numbers were depleted anyway as by now several leftist women with the same hard-line views about what was bourgeois food and what was proletarian had recanted and confessed and been freed.

As I got better day by day, I began to take my turn washing the dishes and carrying out other light duties. I also wrote to my friends, telling them they could write to me again but not very long letters because I still had difficulty concentrating for any length of time.

Slowly, I was resuming my normal life, when totally unexpectedly a guard told me to get ready for the clinic. I wanted to tell her I didn't need the clinic any more, but I bit my tongue, as I thought the internal bleeding might begin again. Maryam urged me, 'Tell the doctor to prescribe special food for you. You can't eat honey and cheese forever – your body needs nourishment. Tell the doctor you can't eat prison food.'

I went to the doctor's room along with the guard. The doctor was a specialist, and I realised my father's efforts had been rewarded. The doctor examined me and questioned me about my bleeding and the treatment I'd received. When I said I'd not been treated because I'd refused to recant and confess, he said, 'You must have an endoscopic examination so I can see the current state of your stomach. Until the next time I see you, after the examination, eat only your special foods. Be sure to take your vitamins too.'

'What vitamins? What special foods? I'm only eating cheese and honey.'

He was very surprised and said, 'Don't they give you special foods?'

'No.'

'When you go to the canteen for your meal, aren't the vitamins placed by your plate on the table for you to take?'

I thought at first the doctor was making fun of me, but from the look on his face I saw he was completely serious.

'We have neither a canteen nor a table nor vitamins. We eat on the floor.'

He was visibly shocked. 'Don't they give you yogurt every day?'

'No.'

The guard said, 'She's lying. We give them yogurt every week.'

'She's right, every week they give us two spoonful of yogurt. But now I need ice more than anything else because my stomach is really hot, and if I have ice I can cool my stomach by chewing on it. Can you prescribe ice for me?'

'Definitely, but you must have meat as well. It's essential.'

'It makes my diarrhoea worse and I can't tolerate the pain I have already because we only go to the toilet three times a day.'

He was bewildered. 'Why don't you go to the toilet more than three times a day?'

'Because the door of our room is locked, and the guard only opens it for half an hour three times a day so that we can use the toilet and shower.'

The doctor was staggered. He went to say something and changed his mind.

'Waiting for the toilet is very painful.'

He asked, 'How long have you been in this situation behind locked doors?'

'On this occasion, for eight continuous months.'

The doctor shook his head; he was so clearly horror-struck, but he was also equally inhibited from saying anything in the presence of the guard. For a moment it was as if the doctor realised he was also in prison with me.

He wrote out instructions for my treatment. He included ice, writing that it would prevent my stomach from beginning to bleed again. He also underlined that I had to be allowed to use the toilet whenever I needed it. He read his list out to me and I laughed.

He asked, 'Why are you laughing?'

'Because they won't give me most of those things.'

The guard looked at me with hatred and said, 'Liar. Come,' and pulled at my chador. I thanked the doctor as I got up.

He said, 'Your stomach could start bleeding again, you must take care.' And then he added, 'Good luck.'

I smiled at him as I followed the guard.

When she got me back to the room, she opened the door and literally threw me in.

However, I was now given special food: rice with chicken or red meat, though it was not always fit to eat.

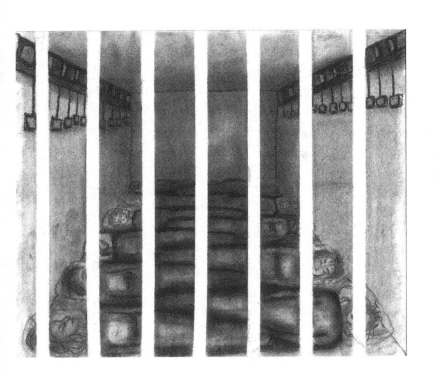

CHAPTER 44
The Magic of the Outside World
Evin Prison, 1989

When my family next visited, my father said he'd gone to see all kinds of officials to get a specialist to see me. I realised how much he must have begged and humiliated himself, and I asked him to stop and do no more. My father said that he'd do whatever he could to make things better for me in prison and to get me out. He told me that a UN human rights group was going to visit the prison. I told him not to expect anything. I was sure the regime wouldn't let the UN inspectors see us; they'd only be allowed to talk to the trusties, who, in their desperation to get out, would tell them anything the regime wanted them to. My sister was more trusting, and she contradicted me. She knew the UN had our names and she was sure they'd ask specifically to see us.

Nazli came up to me with news after her visit and said, 'Zahra has been freed because of her psychological problems. My mother said Zahra has been to see her a few times. It seems Zahra is coping most of the time and works full time in a factory, but every so often she gets violent – not with anyone else, just herself. She starts breaking windows and tries to hurt herself. Her family take her to hospital when that happens and she stays in for a while. She sends us all greetings.'

The news was disturbing as I had thought that once out of prison, Zahra would recover. She had survived the Shah's prison before, so I'd just imagined that she would overcome the damage done to her in the Islamic regime's prison too. But it seems I was wrong. I suppose each of us have a threshold or tipping point. Maybe Zahra's had been when they'd taken her to a small solitary cell and left her for weeks on end with her hands fastened to the toilet pipe and made her eat from a bowl on the floor like a dog.

A few days later, a guard came and told me to go with her. She took me to a car; an unarmed female guard and two armed male guards were already in it. They didn't tell me where I was being taken. As the car moved out of the prison grounds, they told me to remove my blindfold. From Evin, the car turned into what had been Pahlavi Avenue, and the Islamic regime had changed it to Valiasr.

The avenue was about twenty metres wide with tall trees on each side. On my left, I saw the old Meli University. On my right I could see part of Luna Park where our families had to assemble on visiting days. I also saw the Hilton Hotel. I saw a sign for the mountains of Velenjak and I thought of the times I had taken that road with my friends and my family. My memories became sweeter seeing the big Ladan confectionary and ice cream shop, where we always stopped and bought ice creams after returning from a mountain trek.

We reached Tajrish Square and as the car stopped in the traffic, I saw that Shemiran Avenue was now called Shariati. I knew a bit further on there was the Zahiroldoleh

Cemetery, where famous artists such as Forugh Farrokhzad were buried, and then I saw Tajrish Hospital. There were a few shops and an old alley that I knew led a maze of other old alleyways and a bazaar full of stalls and small shops. I could see fruit stalls, and I longed to buy some fresh fruit to take them back to Evin for us all to eat together. I remembered how, years ago during the Shah's time, my married sister and her husband sometimes took me and my younger sisters to eat something at one of the street food stalls in Tajrish Square. There were even a few shops selling alcohol, which is haram now.

Even though I didn't know where I was being taken, I really enjoyed this unexpected drive through the Tehran streets. It was such a strange experience after being locked up for so long. It was like watching a film, although close up; everything seemed distant and the outside world was all totally new to me. The smallest most ordinary things were interesting: people buying fruit, their clothes, the expressions of faces, the different colours of the shop doors. It was as if I was an alien from another planet.

It was still unreal when we parked at Tajrish Hospital, and I realised my father had ignored me when I'd told him not to go around begging officials to help me any more. Holding my wrist so tightly under her chador that it hurt, the female guard told me to come with her into the clinic. The two armed male guards got out of the car and followed us closely. We all made our way through the crowded corridors. I looked at people as we passed; they looked at me too, but no one seemed to realise I was a prisoner. I wanted to scream out and tell everyone I'd been brought from a slaughterhouse of human beings, but I said nothing.

We finally reached a consulting room and one of the guards knocked on the door. A beautiful nurse opened it. Behind her, sitting at a desk, there was an equally handsome doctor. One of the armed male guards spoke to the nurse, and she spoke to the doctor. It all seemed to be taking place in slow motion.

The nurse asked me to enter politely; the female guard wanted to come in too, but the nurse said, 'No, that is not possible. The doctor will not examine the patient in the presence of a guard.'

One of the armed male guards stuck his foot in the door. 'Her guard must come in. We'll stand outside here, but the female guard must accompany the prisoner at all times. We can't let her out of our sight, even for a minute. She's very dangerous.'

I burst into laughter.

The nurse looked at me briefly and said to the guard that she has to ask the doctor; she soon returned and said the same thing. 'I'm sorry. If you come in, the doctor won't examine the patient.'

There was an impasse, but after some discussion among themselves, the guards backed down and I went in to see the doctor alone, though the door was left slightly ajar. It was a victory over the guards, which made me feel happy.

The nurse took my hand, told me I had been sent to have an endoscopic examination, and she explained what the doctor was going to do. I was mesmerised by her friendliness. She asked how long I had been in prison.

'Seven years.'

Tears welled up in her eyes and she asked me about the massacres. 'How many did they kill?'

'About five thousand.'

The doctor also looked at me with kindness, and I felt so comfortable with them, I hardly noticed the endoscopy. What was the discomfort of a tube down my throat compared to what I had endured?

When the doctor had finished, the nurse explained that my throat would hurt for a while, but that it was normal and the pain was temporary. They both wished me luck and told me to take care of myself. I thanked them both. After such a long time, to find myself being treated like a human being was balm on my wounds. The whole experience had given me hope.

A few days later I was taken to the prison clinic, where two men who called each other doctor asked me about my stomach pains. They said they had the hospital results and told me I had a duodenal stomach ulcer and that they needed to do another test. I didn't understand the need for this if they had my results, but I did as they told me. They gave me a thick, whitish liquid to drink, which made me nauseous immediately. They then told me to stand behind some kind of X-ray machine while they looked at a screen, which they said would tell them more than the endoscopy. There was something very odd about their behaviour; they somehow didn't seem like doctors, yet I thought they must be, but then they did something very peculiar.

Looking at the screen, they burst into laughter. No normal doctor would do that. By then I felt more than just nauseous and I opened my mouth and vomited up all the thick whitish liquid into the bowl placed beside me. I retched as if my body wanted to bring up my guts. The doctors were not laughing now and asked me to drink some more of the thick whitish liquid so they could continue with the examination, but I refused. I was now convinced that they wanted to make me vomit so that my stomach would start bleeding again.

Through all my years in prison, I'd longed to have contact with my comrades on the outside to get hold of new political material for us to discuss, but they must have thought contacting us would be too dangerous for them and I had never received as much as a postcard from anyone in the party.

I asked Nazli, 'Have you asked your comrades outside to send anything to you?'

'Yes, I asked, but my handler told them not to as it was just too dangerous – not for them, but for me, because I'd be flogged again.'

Nazli's handler, Sayeh, had escaped to Europe, and was in touch with Nazli's mother and often sent her greetings. I asked her if we could get a coded message somehow through her mother for her to send on to Sayeh and he could contact the party and get some political material to us.

'In theory it was possible, but if it fell into the regime's hands, what would happen to my mother? I don't want her imprisoned too.'

'We can send a message in our own version of Morse, and after we know Sayeh has got it, we can send him the key to the code.'

Nazli said, 'We can use a poem as the key. When the coded letter reaches Sayeh, I need only send him the name of the poem.'

I was delighted. Nazli asked, 'But how can I give the

message to my mother? We can't write it on paper.'

'Embroidery. We'll send the message in some embroidery. We can give it to your mother as a present for her birthday.'

We set about stitching a picture based on what we could remember of Van Gogh's Boatman and put the coded message in it. It took us ages, but it was a pleasure to do.

Every once in a while, some prisoners were permitted face-to-face visits, and we planned to hand the completed work over to a friend who was to be allowed one such visit. This friend would then ask her family to give it to Nazli's mother, who would get it to Sayeh. We felt sure that no one apart from Sayeh would realise that the colours of the sea, the sky and the boats spoke of our conditions and conveyed our need for intellectual nourishment and news of party's current thinking.

The plan went well. We got the finished piece to Nazli's mother, who sent it to Sayeh, and in a separate letter she sent him the name of the poem. She made it as clear as she could, but nothing came from Sayeh. Years later, I learnt Sayeh had not understood any of our clues and had just thought Nazli and I had just sent him a present; he had framed the embroidered Boatman and put it on his wall.

Sometimes I think I preferred writing letters to talking. Writing things down clarifies thought, and even though we were living in the same room, Nazli and I sometimes wrote to each other about any serious issue we wanted to discuss. One day in February 1990, still under lockdown, Nazli and I were sitting beside the long curtain that covered the shelves. It was quiet time; everyone was reading. Nazli said she needed our list of Marx's quotes, which we kept hidden behind the shelves. She held the curtain in such a way that no one could see what I was doing. I lay down behind the curtain so that one of my hands reached behind the back of the cabinet. It was difficult, but I eventually managed to bring out the sponge where I'd hidden the list of Marx's quotes. Sponges were good for hiding small rolled-up pieces of paper. Once I had it, I stretched my hand out towards Nazli. She just screamed and ran over to the other side of the room. I was amazed and was very aware that other women were glaring at us as though we'd done something terrible. Nazli came back to me and said, 'I'm sorry, it looked like a cockroach!'

I looked at it; the package measured about three centimetres by one centimetre and had been wrapped in black plastic and tied with black string. The four pieces of string did make it resemble a cockroach – I couldn't stop myself from laughing, and neither could Nazli.

Once again we were transferred to a wing in Building 216, where we had stayed before the massacre took place, but still we were in lockdown. When we arrived I had quickly hidden my illegal writings in the space under the heater. Just a few days later I was surprised when I went to retrieve it and felt a small package. Opening it, I saw it was an article written by a male prisoner who had been in the room sometime before us. I wondered if he was still alive or if he had been killed in the massacres.

News reached us that Roozhin, who had been put in solitary confinement a few months before for refusing to recant and confess, had become depressed and no longer able to endure solitary. She had agreed to write a recantation and confession so she would be released from prison. Some condemned her when they heard for no longer being a revolutionary; but I couldn't. I hoped Roozhin would not blame herself, and once she was outside prison that she would be able to live with her decision.

It was spring 1990 and we opened the top window for air. It made a sort of shelf and soon we saw a wonderful sight of two white doves building a nest of dry branches. We were fascinated and were careful not to scare them away. When they'd finished, the hen dove sat and laid her eggs. We watched as her mate brought her food. Seeing their love and care for each other was wondrous.

A week passed and in the peace of night I was suddenly woken by an awful screeching noise. Everyone else was woken too, and we all stared up, horrified, at the window, where the noise was coming from. The two doves were jumping about squawking while a massive tomcat tried to catch them; blood dripped from the doves smearing the glass, and there were feathers stuck on the window. We were all frozen helplessly. The scene was desperate as the white doves, our symbols of freedom and hope, were cornered and killed. The great victorious tomcat disappeared along the guttering, clasping between its teeth the bloodied lifeless bodies of our two doves. I lay down and pulled the blanket over my face, and in the quietness of night, I let go of my tears which I had suppressed for so long through torture and massacre.

CHAPTER 45
The Un Human Rights Inspection
Evin Prison, 1990

We were expecting the UN Human Rights Inspection at any time. One morning we went to fetch our tea urn as normal and discovered a wall had been built right across corridor 216.

We realised immediately why the wall had been built. Even though we knew our parents had given the UN our individual names, we understood that the inspectors were not going to be allowed to meet us as our two wings were full of prisoners who refused to recant and confess. Farkhondeh's wing (Four) housed prisoners who had completed their sentences but who were denied their freedom as they still refused to recant and confess. While my wing (Three) had many prisoners still serving their sentences, who had made it very clear that they would never recant and confess.

Instead of meeting the 'Irreconcilables', the UN inspectors would be guided towards Wing One and Two where they would find the broken and trusty prisoners, all of them too defeated and too frightened to say anything against the Islamic regime for fear it would jeopardise their release.

We had always suspected that, somehow or other,

the UN inspectors would be prevented from meeting us, 'Irreconcilables', but we had never imagined that the Islamic regime would do something quite as simple and effective as building a wall overnight. We still wondered what the regime would do if the inspectors asked to see us by name.

We were so cut off by the newly built wall that we only learnt from our families at the next visitors' day that the inspection of Evin by the United Nations Commission on Human Rights, headed by Professor Reynaldo Galindo Pohl, had already taken place. Our families all wanted to know what we had said to the inspectors and what they had said back to us. They could not quite believe us when we explained that we had not met the inspectors and that a new wall had been built to conceal us from them, and if the inspectors had asked for us by name, they must have been fobbed off.

Years later, I discovered that despite having a list of our names, the UN inspectors had not even asked about us, let alone asked to see us. The inspection had been a piece of political theatre.

Our families were furious. Unlike us, they had a naive faith in the UN as an arbitrator between powers, and they said they would go back to the UN and demand a new inspection. We tried to tell them that the UN was really just another propaganda arm of the Western powers and whatever the UN said in public, it had its own agenda which obviously did not entail offending the Islamic regime by talking to us.

Another day, a guard came into our room to take our shopping order, and for the first time ever since I had been in prison said that we could order strawberries. They were in season and cheap, so my group of friends decided to order a kilo to share between us.

The group, which worried about bourgeois and proletarian food, felt they needed to debate the 'issue of strawberries', as irrespective of the price, they were traditionally seen by the working class as a luxury item, and so these leftist women were unsure if it was politically right to order them. They took a vote. Two of them said they wanted strawberries, not because they were delicious, as that would be self-indulgent, but because they were cheap and nutritious. The other women voted against buying strawberries because indulging in such a luxury would inevitably lead to wholesale bourgeois decadence. I stopped myself from calling out to them that as strawberries were red they could be seen as revolutionary, as I knew they would not see the joke. I felt sorry for the two women who had been outvoted on the strawberries; I thought they should have been allowed to have some for themselves, even if the majority were against, but their particular political group did not allow any individual choice at all. Everything was collective. The strawberries might seem a comic 'issue' to argue about politically, but it set me wondering about the balance between the individual and the collective. To me, strawberries were too petty to debate, but where and how is the line drawn?

On a following visitors' day, we all received very interesting news. The full-term 'irreconcilable' women prisoners, like Farkhondeh, were being offered a three-week furlough. No conditions were attached. If, at the end of the three weeks they agreed to recant and confess, they would be freed permanently; otherwise they had to come back to prison as before and stay indefinitely.

Obviously the regime knew that during these three weeks of freedom, the women would come under intense pressure from their families to recant and confess, and that some of the women would enjoy their furlough so much they would be willing to even without much pressure. Yet though I saw it as a trick, I also saw the offer of the furlough as further evidence of a change in the regime's thinking and tactics. It seemed a real shifting of the sands, and again it gave me hope of more changes of policy to come.

Just a few weeks later, a guard came and told us all to put on our chadors. This meant a man was coming to see us, and sure enough Nasserian, one of the most macho and sadistic of floggers and mass executioners of 1988, soon swaggered into the room. He paused for effect at the door before telling us, 'We have decided to temporarily release all prisoners. All you have to do to obtain three weeks of freedom outside is to make a formal request for leave.'

He said nothing about recantation and confession, but we all understood that we didn't have to recant and confess to get this furlough, but if we wanted to remain free when the three weeks were up, we would then have to recant and confess.

Nasserian asked who among us wanted to make a formal request for leave.

One member of the Tudeh Party raised her hand.

The rest of us were solid. We didn't want to ask the regime for anything, not even for a temporary release.

Nasserian left abruptly, but a guard soon came to fetch the Tudeh Party woman. We were sure we would not see her again.

Although only one Tudeh woman had accepted the regime's offer, more and more I sensed that the regime was searching for a way to release us all without losing too much face.

But I was still determined (and so were my closest prison friends) that we would make the regime release us unconditionally, and now I was beginning to think that this would happen soon. Others disagreed with my new optimism and argued that whatever new tricks the regime thought up, they all still included recantation and confession, and that we would never be released unless we bowed to their will, or unless there was an uprising against the regime, as there had been in 1978 against the Shah.

I listened, but to me the regime showed other signs of loosening its grip. On one of the next visitors' days, instead of only being allowed to talk to our families via telephone, we were allowed to sit with them and even touch them. That was a happy day; I kissed my parents for the first time in seven-and-a-half long years. My father tried so hard not to cry that he was unable to speak. He just looked at me. Although the guards were walking about watching us, I managed to put the pendant Raz had made for me around my mother's neck as I hugged her. I told her about Raz making it and that it was precious and asked her to look after it.

Then we talked about the outside world and the future. My parents told me that my sisters wanted them to go and see them in Europe, but they felt they couldn't leave me while I was still in prison and that I had to be free before they went visiting any of my sisters.

'Don't worry about that. I'm fine, and I'd love you to

go and bring news from my sisters – and my friends too. Please go.'

My father refused. 'No, I've told them I'll go the minute you're released. How can I go and leave you when they still might kill you?'

'Things are changing, the killing is over. Go to Germany, my sisters need to see you too.'

When the guard came and told us the visit had to end, I just didn't want to part from my parents, and they didn't want to part from me.

The guard insisted, so finally I kissed my parents goodbye; as my father left, he gave me some chocolate. It was the first time he'd been allowed to bring me any, and I laughed joyfully that he'd remembered how much I liked it.

CHAPTER 46
Minster's brothel
Evin Prison, 1990

I t was early afternoon, quiet time and we were all reading, when we heard the sound of new prisoners being moved into Room Four. We wondered immediately who they were, what had happened outside and what organisations they belonged to, and if any of them were our comrades. Less than an hour later, we heard their voices in the yard. We went over to the windows, looked out and saw about ten really beautiful young girls. None of them could have been more than sixteen; one of them looked about twelve. They were all wearing short colourful low-cut dresses, and were showing their legs and breasts. They were all chattering away, unconcerned, as if they were on a day out. They looked well fed and healthy and they most definitely had not been tortured and were clearly not political prisoners; who on earth were they?

Curious, Nazanin climbed up to reach one of the two small windows. She attracted the new prisoners' attention and beckoned them over. Once they were in earshot, she asked them who they were and why they'd been arrested. One of them, about thirteen, danced up to the window wriggling her hips and told us, 'We don't know. We've never had any problems before – the guards just raided the house and arrested us all. We thought we were protected because all the clients are high-ups, one of them is a minister.'

She didn't need to say anymore. We understood. The 'house' was a brothel. Their clients were members of the government, but there were different factions in the regime and sometimes one section of the governing elite attacked another. Arresting all the girls in a minister's favourite brothel would be part of some internal battle between different members of the regime. Maybe the girls from some opposing minster's brothel would arrive next.

Nazanin asked the girl how old she was.

In a pantomime of provocation, the girl said she was fifteen. She shrugged off our other questions about where her parents were and how she had come to be in the 'house'. The past clearly didn't interest her, not even her own.

She and the others thought a mistake had been made and that they wouldn't be kept in prison for very long, and they just refused to be intimidated by the bleak environment. They were happy and joked and laughed, certain that the ministers and 'high-ups' would miss them and pay whoever needed to be paid to have them released quickly.

The special treatment they received confirmed this. While we continued to be cooped up on the lockdown system, unable to go to the toilet when we wanted, let alone walk in the yard, they were allowed to spend the whole day outside. They soon noticed that the guards on the rooftops were men and they began to play up to them, wriggling their hips and lifting up their short skirts. Brought to live and 'work' in a brothel at such a young age and all kept together, isolated from the outside world, they must have thought their behaviour was normal.

They were right, though, about their immediate situation. They were released after a few days and sent back to their brothel, which they clearly didn't even realise was another form of prison.

One day, a guard opened the door and read out a list of names. Nazli and Maryam were on it; all the named women had to go with the guard as they were being transferred. As always, they were not told where. Nazli and I kissed and told each other we hoped we'd meet again outside prison. Separation from Nazli was difficult; all the time I'd been sick she'd stayed beside me, and she had done everything she could for me. I knew I'd miss her, but what could I do?

I kissed Maryam goodbye too and thanked her for all her help when I'd been ill. Nazli and Maryam left with the other women, and although I had been feeling confident that none of us would be in prison much longer, I was now really saddened. Just a few hours later the door of our room opened again, and the guard told the rest of us, myself included, to gather our belongings as we were going to Room One. The day was a rollercoaster of emotions. Unless Raz and Sonia had been moved (which was possible) they were in Room One, and so though I'd lost Nazli and Maryam, it looked like I was going to gain Raz and Sonia.

When we got to Room One, I saw Raz and Sonia immediately, and I could see they were just as happy to see me as I was happy to see them. The guard said nothing, but she left without shutting the door. The effect of this was enormous. By the simple act of not closing the door, the guard told us Room One was no longer on lockdown and we could all go to the toilet when we wanted and walk about the corridor. We could hardly believe the sudden change in our fortune, but such unpredictability was intrinsic to Evin.

Just a few days later, when we were all getting ready to go to sleep, we heard noises coming from the hall next to our wing. We went into the corridor to see what it was. Through the barred gate we could see about two hundred women milling about in the hall. They looked terrible, dressed far worse than us in old haphazard clothes. They looked haggard, even the young ones. They didn't look like political prisoners, but they certainly didn't look like the young well-fed prostitutes of the month before either.

Finally a guard came and opened the barred gate to the wing; they all rushed forward, pushing each other in their hurry to find somewhere to sit down and sleep. It seemed they knew they were to occupy the five empty rooms on our wing, though their sheer numbers meant about forty women would have to fit into a room originally intended for five. One of the women, about forty-five years old, thin and, like the others, poor and haggard-looking, pointed to us and asked the woman next to her if we were drug smugglers too.

It turned out they were a mix of drug smugglers, thieves, prostitutes and one murderer.

There was more noise as they settled down for the night, but in the end we all slept. In the morning, Manijeh went to tell the new women about our cleaning rota system. They were walking or standing in the corridor; none of them stopped talking to listen to her. A factory worker before her arrest, Manijeh was used to making herself heard above machinery, but she just couldn't get their attention, until finally one of the women among the newcomers just bawled out, 'Shut up, everyone. The lady wants to talk to us.' This woman had real power as the entire corridor went quiet in an instant. The scene was comic and made me laugh.

Manijeh swallowed her own laugh as she said politely, 'We need to sit down with each other and discuss the cleaning rota.'

There was no problem; they all readily agreed to send one woman from each room to talk to us, and then the noise in the corridor returned to its previous volume. It all seemed friendly and co-operative, but later one of the new women came to us and warned us to 'watch our things', as there were many thieves among the new prisoners.

In the middle of the night, when everyone was sleeping, I used to walk in the corridor. After the long period under lockdown, I just needed to move about. Sometimes I paced so much that I felt that my legs were as tired as if I'd walked for hours on the mountains. One night when I had worn myself out walking the corridor, I went to the washroom before going to bed and I sensed the shadow of a child behind me. I glanced back and saw a pale young girl. I thought I must have been dreaming for surely there were no children in the wing, yet she looked so real. I asked her 'What are you doing here? What's your name?'

'I'm a prisoner too. My name's Mina.'

'You're a child! You should be at home.'

She stared at the floor.

'What are you accused of?'

She whispered, 'Prostitution.'

I asked her how old she was

333

'Twelve.'

She was so small and so sad-looking, poor, thin and downcast, I was horrified. I took her in my arms and hugged her, and said, 'Mina, you are not a prostitute. How can a twelve-year-old child be a prostitute of their own volition?'

She just stared at the floor.

'The men who used you are criminals, not you. You are a rape victim. You have nothing to be ashamed of. This sick society needs to be ashamed, not you.'

'The others want me moved. They don't want to share a room with a prostitute.'

'What others? The thieves, the murderers and the smugglers?'

'Yes,' she said quietly.

I felt for the girl like she was my own child.

'How long is your sentence?' I asked.

'Five years and a hundred lashes.'

She was really being punished for being poor and 'unprotected'. My blood boiled at the cruelty of it.

'How did it begin?' I asked. 'Where were your parents?'

'My parents are dead. My brother looked after me. About two years ago, he started taking me to his boss's house every Friday. It happened there. My brother got money for it. I didn't want to go, but if I resisted, my brother beat me. So I went every Friday. Then, six months ago, Islamic guards came to our house and arrested me.'

'Did they arrest your brother and his boss too?'

'I don't know about the boss, but my brother wasn't home, and I know he isn't in prison.'

'Did your brother send you to school ever?'

'No, I've never been to school. I can't read or write. I've

334

always worked. Except on the Fridays when I went to the boss's house, I washed clothes and cleaned houses.'

I told her that I would teach her to read and write. 'Come to me in Room One tomorrow afternoon and we'll begin.'

In the morning at breakfast I told the others about Mina. They were as horrified as I was, but some others told me that I could not teach a prostitute in the room. Mina came early and I took her into the corridor for her first lesson. After we had worked for half an hour or so, and I had given her some homework to do, I asked her about the other women in her room. Did all of them want her to be moved?

'No, not all of them'. Mina pointed out a large woman, 'That's Mrs Firouzeh. She doesn't want me moved. She is very strong. One of the guards insulted her and she turned on her and beat her up. For this, Mrs Firouzeh was flogged terribly in the hall in front of everyone. Five male guards took turns flogging her with a really thick cable. They were all sweating with the effort. She didn't make a sound, but the noises of the lashes was horrifying. The guard she'd beaten up was watching Mrs Firouzeh being flogged with glee, and you could see she was longing to hear her scream. Even when they finished the flogging, though Mrs Firouzeh must have been in agony with every move, she still didn't utter a cry – she got up, slowly shook her chador and just went and sat down in front of the guard and stared at her. It was extraordinary. I saw Mrs Firouzeh's back afterwards – it was red and black, and you could see the imprints of the whip. How she endured it is beyond me. All prisoners respected such courage and endurance under a terrible whipping.'

What Mina told me about Mrs Firouzeh reminded me of Nazli's ordeal a few years earlier, when I was still in Ghezel Hesar prison. Nazli, who had been in the Graves, whose brother had been executed and who had nursed me back to life, also had that courage and endurance. She had been in solitary when a guard had come and told us to put on our chadors. A man was coming onto the wing. We waited in our cells. Eventually a big male guard arrived, carrying a whip in one hand and some kind of large pallet in the other. Four women trusties followed. We could see them all clearly through the bars of our cells. We also saw that Nazli was with them. We were told to come out into the corridor and to sit down and watch Nazli being flogged. No one had moved. The male guard put the pallet on the floor. He told Nazli to lie down on it. She lay down on her stomach and the four trusties went to hold her hands and feet. Nazli said, 'Don't touch me. I don't want anyone to hold me.'

The male guard said, 'But you'll move and get up.'

Nazli said, 'I won't move.'

He took her at her word and began the flogging, but Nazli made no struggle or sound. We too were silent. It was a deep silence only broken by the swish of the whip. I placed my head on my knees, trying to create a small refuge for myself. I didn't want to hear the lashes or think of them. I felt such sorrow for Nazli. She received a hundred lashes, the exact same number Mina would be made to endure.

When the flogging finally stopped. Nazli stood up and I heard her say, 'You have beaten my body, but you can't touch my mind or my soul.'

The male guard said nothing, just picked up the pallet and left the wing with the four women trusties. Nazli was taken back into solitary confinement.

Later on, I saw Mrs Firouzeh was walking about alone. I went up to her and started walking alongside her. I told her that I'd heard about her being tortured in front of the other prisoners and how she had endured it very bravely.

She smiled at me, and I could see traces of her lost beauty.

'Why did you beat the guard?' I asked.

'We were in the yard. The guard came out, and some of the prisoners began telling her that we didn't have enough food, cleaning materials, etc. She just started insulting us, calling us prostitutes – who should be killed like vermin, that we shouldn't be fed at all. I just became angry, and I went up to her and, not realising what I was doing, I just grabbed her by the neck, raised her up and slammed her down. The other prisoners pulled me away, but it was too late. I had acted on impulse and I paid a high price. It's not wise to be impulsive in prison.'

'And why you are in prison?'

'I killed my husband's murderer.'

That came as a surprise, and I asked her who had killed her husband and why.

'My husband was killed over money.'

'You must have loved your husband?'

'Yes. I'd chosen him; we wanted each other. When I told my mother that a man would be coming to our house to eat on Friday, my mother thought she'd misheard. She asked me, "Who?" I told her, "The man I want to marry." She went crazy. She wanted to arrange my marriage, but I'd never have submitted to that– I'd seen the outcome of arranged marriages in the lives of my parents and friends.

I wanted to marry for love and I did just that. We lived together for fifteen years. We didn't have children and we remained everything to each other. He never once uttered an unkind word to me, raised his voice or laid his hand on me. When he was killed, I didn't hesitate. I found a gun and killed his murderer. I don't regret what I did – I haven't had one sleepless night because of it. I knew what I was doing was right. I meted out justice.'

'Why didn't you just take his murderer to court?'

'I did. It took a year, but he bribed the judge.'

We walked about for a bit and then she asked me, 'Have you ever killed anyone?'

'No.'

'Haven't any of the political activists in your room killed anyone?'

'No.'

'So why did they arrest you?'

'They arrested us for our opinions.'

CHAPTER 47
Hunger Strike
Evin Prison, 1990

I soon felt Mina and Firouzeh were friends. I enjoyed talking to them and they seemed to like talking with me. There was a big problem with our new friendship, though. Some of the other political prisoners were furious that we had been mixed with 'common criminals' and were planning to go on hunger strike in protest. I knew Mina and Firouzeh would be very upset when they heard.

The day after the hunger strike began, Firouzeh joined me in the yard. She looked troubled and gloomy.

'I was so happy when I met you. Getting to know you made me feel I could endure prison until the end of my life if I could just have you as my friend. But now you are on hunger strike. I never realised you felt humiliated by being forced to be with us ordinary prisoners.'

'What on earth are you talking about? I'm not on hunger strike. I don't feel humiliated by knowing you. Why should I? If this society was not so sick, you wouldn't be in prison. From the bottom of my heart I tell you I'm opposed to this hunger strike.'

Firouzeh's gloomy face changed into smiles in an instant. 'When I heard that the prisoners in Room One were on hunger strike, I thought it was all of you. I should have realised you wouldn't be. I just presumed you were.'

'Look, I know "criminals" are often decent people just fallen foul of the law because of unemployment, poverty and misery, or as in your case because of our culture of bribery and corruption. If your husband's murderer had been arrested and charged as he should have been, you wouldn't have killed him, would you? You wouldn't be here now. You must not think we political prisoners are different from you. If there was justice, none of us would be here – not me, and not you.'

'The hunger strikers obviously don't think like you.'

I shrugged. 'We have different political ideas about some things. The hunger strikers fear being put together with "criminals" will blur their political identity. They see being recognised as political prisoners as a right, as a badge of honour.'

We walked in silence for a short while and then she asked me, 'But why don't you also think like that?'

'As I have said, I see you as fellow victims of the regime. That's my politics. And as for these hunger strikers, they never suggested going on hunger strike when we had to share with the trusties. Because they were political prisoners. Yet many women were executed or tortured because of the trusties' reports on them.'

'Well,' Firouzeh said, 'I'm glad you're not starving yourself, that you are not part of this hunger strike. You know, when I heard about it, I felt bereft, as I thought you had abandoned our friendship. For the first time, I truly wished I was dead. But now I think I'd like to be one of you. Tell me about politics. I don't know anything about politics.'

'The way you spoke to me about your husband and how you had chosen him for yourself and that you wanted the equality of women and men tells me that you are one of us already, even though you didn't know it. If you want what we want, then you are one of us.'

Firouzeh embraced me and kissed my cheeks and said, 'You give me the hope and strength to believe life is worth living.'

The guards had told the 'criminal' prisoners not to mix with us, but Firouzeh regularly came and talked to me right in front of them. She got into the habit of telling me stories about her life and the people she knew outside prison. Once she told me, 'Last year, armed guards came to the wing and made us get onto a bus. We didn't know where they were taking us and it was intimidating. Eventually the bus stopped at a graveyard and the armed guards ushered us out. We were sent over to join some men and women already standing around a large pile of stones. I couldn't make out what was going on and asked one of the armed guards why they had brought us here. "Wait, you'll see," I was told. After a while a mullah appeared and preached to us about the unforgiveable crime of adultery and how the Koran says an adulteress must be stoned to death. I looked about as the mullah droned on, and realised that a hole had been dug in the earth about twenty-five metres away from us. The mullah finally finished talking, and some guards came in sight, dragging a struggling woman towards the hole. She was still struggling when they pushed her into it. She was made to stand up in the hole. The soil was banked up all around her until only her head and shoulders were outside it. Chadored, only her terrified face was visible.

341

It was obvious by now that she was going to be stoned to death, that she was standing in her own grave. I was consumed with anger at the woman's fate and by my own powerlessness to help her, I wanted to go to the woman, haul her out of her grave, but how could I? We were surrounded by armed guards who would kill us if we made any move to help the woman.'

Firouzeh paused and became silent in her sadness.

'The mullah was the first to throw a stone. Others soon joined in. The woman was soon bleeding profusely. Although her plight was hopeless, instinct made the woman try to pull herself out of the hole. And though we were surrounded by armed guards, we prisoners could not stop ourselves and began shouting encouragements to her, telling her to use all her strength and pull herself out. The armed guards started threatening us, but we wanted the woman to escape so much that we barely heard the threats. Some women fainted with emotion, and I was crying, but I kept on shouting to the woman to get out, to escape. And would you believe it? She did. She somehow had the strength to throw off the banked-up soil and get out of the hole. We all clapped and clapped her. I wanted to go and hug her. Her injuries were already mortal and she soon just dropped to the ground and didn't move.'

'Was she dead?'

'Yes. She was dead. They told us afterwards her skull was broken.'

For some time we walked in silence. I had never talked to anyone who had witnessed a stoning. It was barbarism, a return to barbarism.

Stoning to death had been brought back by the Islamic

regime and it was now Article 104 in the new legal code.

I continued to teach Mina to read and write. I gave her homework; she always did more than I had set. I felt myself becoming very fond of her. It was a really good feeling. Like mother and daughter, I felt pride as she progressed. She was so quick and clever. I knew that learning to read and write would give her self-confidence and would help her when she was free.

One afternoon, when I went as usual to teach Mina, she wasn't in our normal meeting place. I was worried at once as she was always the first to arrive. I looked into her room. Some women seemed to be sleeping under their blankets; I didn't know if Mina was one of them, as they were just shapeless bundles, but I didn't want to disturb any of them to ask, so I continued looking for Mina, I went to the washroom and showers, but I just couldn't find her. Then I saw Aseman, another 'criminal' prisoner. She told me, 'Mina is one of the shapeless bundles in bed; she's huddled up under a blanket crying. A guard told her she'd be given a hundred lashes if she talks to you just one more time. She's heart-broken that she can't see you any more and we can't stop her from crying.'

'I have to talk to her,' I said.

'OK, you go to the second washroom and put out the cleaning sign and shut the door. I'll bring Mina to you.'

I did what Aseman told me and waited for Mina; I didn't know why Aseman was in prison, but I knew she was always kind and often helped other prisoners, even at the risk of being flogged for it. She seemed to have a sixth sense about where the guards were at any one time, and I felt sure she would be able to bring Mina to me safely.

When Mina came, her eyes were swollen from crying, and she looked gaunt like the dying. I hugged her and tried to console her as I struggled to stop my own tears. She sobbed and sobbed. I caressed her hair, and said, 'Prison means separation. It means being next to each other but not having the permission to speak and feel.'

She wiped her tears and listened.

'Try to be strong. Don't let them see you as weak. Don't let them think they've crushed you with their rules and their power. Try to stay alive and get out of prison. You'll have a long future – try to enjoy it. Don't let them destroy it.'

'But I really want to learn to read and write. I hate being illiterate.'

'I'm glad to hear that. If you hate illiteracy you'll struggle against it. You can still learn to read and write. Ask one of the women in your room to teach you. One of them will, I am sure. I'll get you all the notebooks, pens and pencils you need. Go and find yourself a teacher.'

'I wish I could still learn with you.'

'No, you can't be flogged. I don't want them to torture you.'

Mina asked me, 'Did they torture you?'

'Yes.'

'Was it very painful?'

'Of course it was, that's the idea of torture: pain, suffering, humiliation. It's intended to break the soul, but as you see, I didn't die and I am not defeated.'

I didn't tell her that so many others had died in lonely agony and despair.

I hugged her; she squeezed me and said, 'In my dreams, I imagine you're my mother. I wish you were my mother.'

'I feel the same way– it's like you're my daughter, even if we can't speak to each other. We have this feeling in our hearts – they can't take that away, can they?'

'No, they can't.'

We said these words in front of Aseman. Though she pretended she was cleaning the washroom, I felt all her attention was on us.

I finally kissed Mina goodbye on both cheeks and thanked Aseman, who took Mina back with her safely.

Aseman worked in the kitchen and, unlike us, she was allowed in and out of all the wings as one of her jobs was to collect the big food pots and take them to the kitchen. Even though it was a risk, she used to take messages and sometimes she would even pass letters. Through Aseman I was able to communicate with Farkhondeh and Huri on Wing Four. Once late at night, when the others were sleeping and I was pacing about the corridor, Aseman came up to me and slipped something into my hand as she passed silently by. I waited a short while and then I went to the toilet to look at it. It was a tightly wrapped-up letter from Huri.

Huri described how one of the women in her room had suddenly accused the rest of the women of being bourgeois and, refusing to talk to anyone else in the room, she had isolated herself. It was like there was an invisible wall between herself and the others. One of the women she had previously been friendly with had become angry at being told she was 'bourgeois', and the whole madness had degenerated into a melee with the two women throwing plates at each other while the 'criminal' prisoners out in the yard looked up at them through the window in bafflement.

This behaviour was absurd, but so familiar. The sheer, continual stress of being in prison indefinitely turned some of us against each other over nothing. It was the regime that had a good laugh.

CHAPTER 48
Dialectics of Nature by Friedrich Engels
Evin Prison, 1990

In the summer of 1990, a guard came to our room and told us that if we wanted books, we could order them. It was the first time we'd been able to do this. The store supervisor asked each of us to give her the name of just one book. Sonia, Manijeh, and Raz said we should each order a book we thought we'd all find interesting and share them between us. But I said, 'I'd like to order something banned to tell them that despite everything I'm still a socialist. I want to order Engels' Dialectics of Nature.'

'But they won't let you have it.'

'I know, but it will annoy them.'

After a few days, the books arrived. As I expected, Dialectics of Nature wasn't among them.

Although my father had not wanted to go and visit my sisters in Germany, he had given in to my pleas and he had gone with my mother. They were away for over a month. On the first visitors' day after they returned, I was looking forwards to hearing their news, but my mother did not come; my father came in alone. He looked miserable and I asked him where my mother was, thinking she must be ill.

He said she was fine but he was vague about why she had not come. I changed the subject and asked him what sort of trip they'd had. He didn't answer my question, but just said, 'How could we enjoy a trip abroad, knowing you were still here in prison?' Then he said something that startled me. 'You know they're freeing prisoners today, right now, if they recant and confess?'

It was the first time my father had ever even implied I should recant, and I was horrified,

'If I wanted to recant and confess, I'd have done so years ago.'

My father began to shake with emotion. He cried out, 'I saw some of your old friends in Germany, and they're all happy. They're living normal lives, studying, working, marrying, having children, going dancing! While you're in here behind bars. Think about yourself for once, just as they thought about themselves.'

I was so infuriated – not really at my father, but at the bastards, whoever they were, who had got him thinking like this, condemning me for refusing to recant and confess instead of condemning the regime for demanding that I did.

'I am happy they are all living happily in Europe, but it's not in me to recant and confess. You don't want me to come home defeated and miserable, do you? I could not live with myself. You must understand that.'

'Even if it means you stay rotting in prison for ever?'

'Yes, even if it means I stay here forever.'

My father cried out again. 'I'm sick and tired of coming and seeing you behind bars. You are young, you should be living, and you are not safe here. The massacres could happen again. One day I might come here and instead of seeing you, they will give me your belongings in a bag. And tell me that after all these long years, they've killed you too. I can't endure it any longer. I am at the end of my tether.'

'I'm sorry, but if you think I should recant and confess, then don't come and see me any more.'

The visit was terrible. My father calmed down after a while, and I tried to tell him that this was just the regime putting more pressure on him and that I was sure that things were changing and they would release me without my having to recant and confess. That would be a great victory, I said and asked him to endure a little longer. I promised him I would be out by New Year, in six months.

The phone was disconnected as I said it but that meant nothing in particular; visitors' time was over. My father left. Despite all my words he looked dejected and despairing, and it hurt me to see him leave like that. He shuffled out like an old man.

CHAPTER 49
Freedom
Evin Prison, 1990

There was a moment
when we were waiting for the bus
and you were talking to me happily
yet still watching the streets at the same time
to make sure the Islamic guards were not around
I suddenly felt desire for you
I lost the thread of what you were saying.
I wanted so much to stretch my body up to you
and kiss your mouth forever.

This was eight years ago and the very last time I saw Sorkh. I have no idea what happened to him and perhaps I never will.

It was early autumn 1990 when a guard came to our room and told us all to collect our belongings and follow her. I quickly gathered my clothes, as I wanted to try to see Mina and Firouzeh before I left the wing.

I managed to see Firouzeh. We talked for a little while. I told her that although the guard had said nothing, I felt sure I was going to be released.

'I hope so for your sake, though I will miss you. Strange, Evin is a fearful place, notorious in the outside world, yet inside it has some wonderful people. Getting to know you has been wonderful, and even if I never see you again, I'll never forget our friendship.'

'I'll never forget our friendship either. Let's meet one day outside prison.'

We embraced and kissed, and I asked her to watch over Mina. I also saw Aseman, who took me to say goodbye to Mina, who was in the washroom sobbing. Aseman shut the door and stood watch outside. I hugged Mina tightly and told her to look after herself and continue to learn to read and write. She promised she would do so and then handed me a piece of paper. 'I did this for you.'

It was a drawing of a bird in flight. Under it she had written in her childlike beginner's scrawl 'To my only friend.'

'But I'm not your only friend, Mina, believe me. Firouzeh and Aseman are your friends too. Try to be happy, and be proud of yourself. You're a good person and you will be freed. This horror will end.'

Even though I hadn't been able to do anything for her for a while, I felt terrible at leaving her. We embraced and kissed again, and then I left; I knew Mina would go back to sobbing her eyes out, but there was nothing I could do. Aseman was still standing watch in front of the toilet door, and I thanked her again; she hugged me and wished me freedom. I wished her freedom, too.

Although I was somehow sure the transfer meant we were going to be released, there really was no real sign of it. The guard still said nothing as we were each put in a solitary cell. But this time we were allowed to keep all our things, and I had paper, pen, pencil, and books. To me this was all additional evidence that this time we had not been put in solitary as a torture but as a preliminary to freedom. Yet I also had a worry at the back of my mind, as I knew when my parents learnt I was in solitary they would believe the very worst.

The wing was fairly new. It had actually been built while I was in prison, yet here and there on the walls there was prisoners' graffiti. I remembered when I was in England, I had visited a museum which had once been a prison. I wondered if one day Evin would be turned into a museum. The main part of Evin had been constructed in 1972 under the reign of Mohammad Reza Pahlavi. In those days the foothills of the Alborz Mountains had been outside Tehran, but now the city was growing, and I imagined the regime would want a new prison further away, in a more hidden place, where secrets could be better kept. If at some future date the regime turned Evin into a museum, would people come to see the graffiti walls, which had witnessed the very last hours of their children before they'd been executed? Would I come and see it? Unblindfolded.

I remembered my life in England and how different things would have been if I had stayed there and studied at university. Would I have learnt more than what I had learnt in prison? There in England, the media would have given me its political take on Iran; now I had lived its real politics. Was I sorry to lose that safe life and future? No, I thought. I would not change my experiences.

In solitary my cell was too far away from my own friends for me to Morse them. I tried at first, but each time the guard had realised I was Morsing and had told me to stop, but two prisoners in the cells next to me tapped to each other every afternoon. They used the Morse standard code, so I could understand everything. I sometimes heard another prisoner, further away from me, Morsing to someone even further away still; through them, I learnt of Saddam's invasion of Kuwait.

I also found out that Nazanin (also in solitary) had been on a hunger strike for two weeks in support of the workers of Iraq and the Middle East. Nobody would know of her hunger strike, and it seemed such a futile gesture, though I suppose you had to admire her ideological tenacity.

I found I had known Yosefi, one of the guards, when I had been in solitary before in 1985 and 1987. When she came round to take my order for fruit and the other things we were allowed, she squatted down by my cell door and talked to me about the prisoner massacres. I was surprised, but I listened. She said she had guarded some of the women Mujahidin in solitary before they were executed. She had obviously been very disturbed by the slaughter and seemed genuinely sorry for them. I imagined Yosefi was a devout Muslim, a follower of Khomeini, and that she could accept prison as a suitable punishment for people who had broken the regime's laws. She might see it as a way of redeeming them, but her heart just revolted over the mass killings. I wondered why she had to work in Evin. I presumed it was the need to earn a living; she was older than the other guards and everything about her was faded and broken down.

Yosefi would do favours for prisoners she trusted and, quite against the rules, she brought me a package from

Sonia. Unwrapping it, I found it was a book, The Gadfly, but I had already read it, so I asked Yosefi to give it to Raz and she did.

On the first visitors' day after we had been moved to solitary the guards didn't call me. In the afternoon, I asked one of them why. She told me that I was being punished for having tried to contact my friends by Morse.

I was really upset – not for me so much as for my family, as I knew they would be worried already by my move to solitary and now they might be thinking the worst. That evening, a guard opened the door angrily and told me to come with her; she took me to the visitors' hall. My sister was there with my father. They had just refused to leave without seeing me. My sister began to tell me that Farkhondeh and some others had been released without any conditions being imposed on them. Farkhondeh had gone to see my family and, through them, she had sent me good wishes.

I was overjoyed. I felt I'd never been so happy. I said, 'See, I told you we would be released unconditionally. I am sure I will be released too. Please endure just a little longer and have hope!'

My father still seemed depressed, but perhaps he was just a little more hopeful than last time. Anyway, he didn't ask me to recant and confess again – if Farkhondeh could get out without, so could I.

When my sister and father had gone I waited outside the visitors' hall for a guard to come to take me back to my cell. There were some wild blue flowers growing and I picked some and hid them under my chador, thinking ironically that the chador could be useful sometimes. Back in my solitary cell, I put the flowers in a jar and placed them at the window. I fed them a bit of sugar every day, and even after a week they still looked fresh. They didn't have a fragrance, but they were beautiful and carried a promise of the outside world and freedom.

I started thinking about Farkhondeh and her life outside prison. I also thought about Huri, waiting for freedom like me. I thought of her son and how it would be between them when they saw each other again after so long. He would be eight now, and he would surely know nothing of how, after Huri had been tortured, we had all been amazed that she had not miscarried, or how, after the torture, she had barely moved during her pregnancy for fear of losing her precious baby. I thought of when they had taken him away from her. Huri had only seen him on visitors' days. How even that had stopped when he was three as he had gone to live with his father in Europe. Huri would not be given legal permission to join them, but I knew, if ever she was let out of prison, she planned to escape from Iran and join her son and husband. I hoped against hope she would succeed.

I also thought of my own life outside prison and wondered how I would be.

Before prison, I had been sociable and I'd had lots of friends – but now, apart from the very few who asked my mother about me in prison, I couldn't remember any of their names. My memory was blank about them. My mind was even blank about my family. What had we talked about? What had we done together? Where did we go together? Except for our holidays by the Caspian Sea, I could not remember anything.

I tried to think about my sisters and brothers, the ones

who had not been able to visit me in prison, but found it difficult to remember them. Who was I close to and what did we talk about together? Where had we gone, what had we done? The past was not even a blur. It was a void. It seemed that my life had been sliced in two by my arrest, and now I could not join the parts together. Other memories were also elusive. I could remember some of the titles of books I'd read and sometimes the names of the writers, but not the contents.

I felt the person I had once been had disappeared and that during my eight years in prison a new person had emerged, inhabiting the same body but only some of the same mind.

Lots of the memories I had from before prison had been erased from my mind, but I was not frightened by that; a human being is not just memory bank. We are not just what we have done but what we are going to do. I did not want to live in the past and I felt the future was mine.

Eight years ago, my hair had been black; now, at the age of thirty-two, parts of my hair had turned white. Yet in contrast, while my hair looked old, my face was unchanged, there were no lines on it at all. I knew why. When my friends had been taken to execution or torture and my heart had been bleeding, I had kept my face so impassive that now it stared back at me in the mirror as young as when I had entered prison. It was strange and unsettling; the white-streaked hair and the too-young face.

It seemed as if I had not laughed, not cried, not bore pain in prison. The contrast between my hair and face – the contrast between aging and not aging – said a lot. Like many prisoners, I wore a strong face. When I was frightened inside, I wouldn't let it show, and the brave face had helped me. Now if I was released and no longer needed to act bravely, would I let go of the face I'd worn for so long? Or did I have two faces, one hiding behind the other? Or perhaps the new face had replaced the original one in the long road of struggle? Is it possible to become the person one is acting?

All those years when I was trying to maintain a brave face, in reality I was struggling with my limits. I didn't know why I had a kind of pain in my forehead, which was mistaken for sinus infection for which I was given antibiotics in prison; I didn't know why abruptly in the middle of a conversation with a friend I had to tell her that I could not continue our talk and we had to leave it until the next day; I didn't know why I became tired suddenly and it caused a disorientation and dizziness; I didn't know why after every transfer or when I was stressed, the 'headache' returned and didn't leave me for a few days – a few days during which my head felt full of clouds and I had to sit alone and look at the void, sometimes thinking of nothing, just resting.

All these symptoms were pieces of a puzzle that would be completed in 2012 when I was diagnosed with epilepsy. That blow to my head a month after my arrest had given birth to a meningioma tumour under the frontal lobe of my brain, located right between my eyebrows. How I have been able to live with the tumour until now and that I have been able to write the story of my imprisonment is a different story beyond this book, but all those years in prison, while the tumour used to beat into my brain, I held on to the brave mask in order to endure the twin pressures from inside and outside my body. The brave mask was one of my best companions, an invisible comrade that has helped me to act the way I wanted to despite the fact that I was in the hands of killers.

One night, as I was getting ready for bed, there were unexpected sounds in the corridor. I spread out my bedding on the floor, sat down and listened, trying to work out exactly what was going on. Then my cell door was opened abruptly, and the female guard said, 'Put your chador on and gather your bedding. Haji is here.'

'At bedtime?'

A man's cough came from behind the open cell door. I put the chador on, but I didn't gather my bedding. The prison governor, Pishva, appeared with some other younger bearded men. They looked around my cell as if they'd never seen one before. My underwear was hanging out to dry on a line above my head and they stared at it; they also took in the pretty blue wildflowers I'd put in the jam jar.

No one said anything for two or three minutes and then Pishva started talking, 'Your mother is sick. I saw your father today, and he asked me to release you. I promised him I'd free you if you recant and confess. Are you willing?'

'No.' I heard my own voice full of hatred.

'Isn't your mother important to you?'

'That's my business.'

One of the bearded young men sneered, 'She's still a socialist. She wants to remain loyal to her infidel group.'

With a sharp glance, Pishva told him to shut up; he looked back at me again. 'Although you don't care about your mother, I still feel sorry for your family. If you just ask for leave, I'll be magnanimous and let you go.'

'I won't ask you for anything, not even for my freedom.'

'So, will I have to throw you out of prison by force?'

'If you ever leave the doors open, I'll go. But I shan't ask you for anything. And I will not accept any conditions for my release.'

Pishva looked straight into my eyes. I looked straight back into his. After a long pause he said, 'I'll let you go home tomorrow.'

I felt I could burst with happiness, but I knew my face was still impassive. Pishva left the cell and the door slammed shut behind him. I couldn't believe it. I wanted to scream with joy and tell the world, my friends, everyone, that this was my last night in prison.

Suddenly the cell seemed different from the one I had slept in the night before. I thought about the next prisoner and the one after her and wondered for how much longer prisons and execution would be used to silence people.

The following day, Thursday 15 November, 1990, Raz and I were freed. Huri, Nazli and Sonia were released a couple of months later. No conditions were placed on us. We wrote no letter of repentance, made no recantation nor confession.

Prisoners would be searched before leaving the prison to make sure they would not take a note or a pebble with them. So I held the stone I'd carved in the palm of my hand when the guard searched me. Van Gogh's Peasants Digging was freed with me when I walked out of Evin and into what would prove to be a much bigger prison – the world.

EPILOGUE
London, 2002

I was in Tesco's in Colney Hatch Lane when I saw Hasani. The guard Hasani. She was not even one of the worst, but she was the one who, when my insides were bleeding and I was close to death and desperate, had so mercilessly refused to let me use the toilet.

What was she doing here in London? Was she working for the Iranian embassy? For those who work for the regime, it's easy to travel to any country. It's only those people who escape death and torture who are not welcome.

I stared at her now, close up enough to feel her fear.

She was trying to hide her face in a copy of Hello!. The little boy she had with her, about five years old, must have been her son. He looked up at me wide-eyed, clutching at his mother's long skirts.

But what could I say or do to her at this moment that would ever equal the eight years of suffering I had endured at her hands, my parents' grief and the friends I had lost to execution? How could I humiliate a woman in front of her little boy?

I abruptly turned away from her and walked out of store.

I wanted to be out in the spring sun. I breathed deeply

as I walked with the sounds of the life and bustle of the street in my ears. It was all light years away from Evin and Ghezel Hesar, and yet in some respects it was no distance at all.

Author's Notes

Farkhondeh, Huri, Nazli, Raz, and Sonia are living outside Iran as refugees. As am I.

Zahra committed suicide in 1998 in Iran.

*The anonymous poem 'Dear Fahimeh' was translated from Farsi by Hubert Moore and Nasrin Parvaz and was first published in English in 2005 in Modern Poetry in Translation, Series 3 No. 4, Between the Languages, edited by David Constantine and Helen Constantine.

Acknowledgements
(in alphabetical order):

Gillian Balance, Emma Cleave, Hame Fatahi, writer Leslie Forbes, Deborah Lavin, playwright and founding artistic director of Ice and Fire Theatre Sonja Linden, poet Hubert Moore, editor and journalist David Morgan, Claire O'Kell, writer John Petherbridge.

The Joint Committee Interrogation Centre was closed down in 2000. It opened again in 2003 with a new identity: the Ebrat Museum of Iran, exhibiting displays of torture that supporters of the Islamic Republic maintain were committed only under the Shah's regime and never under their own. 'Ebrat' means 'warning'. Children are frequently taken there on school trips.

The conversion of the Joint Committee Interrogation Centre is the setting of a novel The Secret Letters from X to A by Nasrin Parvaz.

About the Author

Writing is my way to fight back

Photograph: Copyright © Milan Svanderlik, London, UK

Nasrin Parvaz, acclaimed author of *The Secret Letters from X to A* published by Victorina Press, became a civil rights activist when the Islamic regime took power in Iran. She was arrested, tortured and sentenced to death in 1982. Her sentence was commuted to ten years' imprisonment and she was released after eight years, in 1990. After her release, Nasrin resumed her activities and once again she found herself being followed by Islamic guards. She realised she could no longer stay in Iran and fled to England, where she claimed asylum in 1993. She was granted refugee status a year later and has since lived in London.

She has published a novel in Farsi and her poems and short stories are published in several anthologies, such as: *Write to be Counted, Resistance Anthology,* 2017; *Over Land, Over Sea, Poems for those Seeking Refuge,* published by Five Leaves, in 2015. Her poems are published in *Live Encounters Magazine.*

Since 2005, together with poet Hubert Moore, Nasrin has translated some poems, prohibited in Iran, from Farsi into English. They appear in the *Modern Poetry in Translation* series.

Nasrin was the guest artist of *Our Lives,* May 1st – 8th 2018 Exhibition of Art by Foreign National Prisoners. Her paintings were accepted for inclusion in the exhibition's Calendar and for postcards.

She was guest speaker of Brighton SEAS – Socially Engaged Art Salon, Brighton; and her prison paintings were exhibited in the Other House exhibition – Brighton, from 6th to 27th May 2018.

The artwork inside this book are all paintings by Nasrin Parvaz.

To know more about the writer go to
http://nasrinparvaz.org/